D1158309

WHITE SETTLERS AND NATIVE PEOPLES

WHITE SETTLERS
AND
NATIVE PEOPLES

An Historical Study of Racial Contacts between
English-speaking Whites and Aboriginal Peoples in the
United States, Canada, Australia and New Zealand

By

A. GRENFELL PRICE, C.M.G., D.LITT., F.R.G.S.
Master, St. Mark's College
University of Adelaide

GREENWOOD PRESS, PUBLISHERS
WESTPORT, CONNECTICUT

The Library of Congress has catalogued this publication as follows:

Library of Congress Cataloging in Publication Data

Price, Sir Archibald Grenfell, 1892–
   White settlers and native peoples.

   Reprint of the 1950 ed.
   Bibliography: p.
   1. Indians of North America. 2. Australia--Native
races. 3. Maoris. 4. Race problems. I. Title.
[HT1523.P73 1972]   301.2   71-142320
ISBN 0-8371-5923-7

Originally published in 1950
by Georgian House, Melbourne

Reprinted with the permission
of Georgian House Pty. Ltd.

First Greenwood Reprinting 1972

Library of Congress Catalogue Card Number 71-142320

ISBN 0-8371-5923-7

Printed in the United States of America

CONTENTS

ILLUSTRATIONS

PAGE

MAPS

Introduction

The following book compares the impact of English-speaking whites on the American Indians, the New Zealand Maoris, and the Australian aborigines, primarily from the historical aspect. The author has been encouraged in his task by the reception given to "White Settlers in the Tropics". That book, which applied similar methods to a study of the North European invasions of the tropics, was published in 1939 by the American Geographical Society as a result of the author's work as a Travelling Fellow of the Rockefeller Foundation.

Leading anthropologists in several countries have rendered great help, but some have pointed out the danger of comparing the contacts between English-speaking invaders and aboriginal peoples when such contacts frequently occurred at different historical periods, in different geographical environments, and amongst peoples in different stages of development, and with different cultural potentialities. Such scientists would postpone generalisation until anthropologists have made many more local and tribal studies of culture contacts. Warning against dangerous and ill-founded generalisations is wise, but the author believes that the material already available reveals many remarkable similarities in the various invasions and in their results, and may assist those who are conducting native policy and administration. Use of the comparative method seems particularly important, for, although students have conducted considerable research on white-native impacts in the United States, and some research on white-native impacts in Canada, Australia and New Zealand, they have done very little comparative work—for example in comparing white-native contacts in Canada and the United States.

The thesis which follows indicates that in the majority of regions considered white-native relations fell broadly into three stages. During an opening period of pioneer invasion on moving frontiers the whites decimated the natives with their diseases;

1

WHITE SETTLERS AND NATIVE PEOPLES

occupied their lands by seizure or by pseudo-purchase; slaughtered those who resisted; intensified tribal warfare by supplying white weapons; ridiculed and disrupted native religions, society and culture, and generally reduced the unhappy peoples to a state of despondency under which they neither desired to live, nor to have children to undergo similar conditions. In a second stage, which largely resulted from the great British philanthropic movements about the beginning of the nineteenth century, the whites attempted to remedy their mistakes by gathering some of the survivors on small and often unsuitable reservations, where Government agents and missionaries laboured worthily but ineffectively to impart Christianity, an academic education, and a training in industries such as agriculture which were distasteful to nations of hunters. As a result almost all the aboriginal peoples became the decadent and disappearing recipients of their conquerors' bounty.

In a third stage, which opened slightly before the nineteen thirties, certain white governments began to realise the importance of scientific policy and administration; of adequate reservations; of practical education; and of industries suited to the native temperament and traditions. On their part many native peoples adjusted themselves to the impact of white civilisation and entered on a period of recovery and numerical increase, although this growth was, in many cases, primarily due to an increase of aboriginal-white mixed bloods. It now appears that, although in most cases the white majority peoples will absorb the native minorities, this absorption may never occur in regions such as New Zealand and the South-West of the United States, while in other areas it lies many generations ahead.

In the meantime grave problems exist. Aboriginal peoples, deprived of their lands and traditional modes of life, are rapidly increasing and form islands of malnutrition, disease, and social, educational and cultural weakness amongst the surrounding whites. On the environmental side white greed and native ignorance have often destroyed the historic and delicate balance between the aboriginal peoples and their land, its flora and fauna, with results, such as the creation of soil erosion or the destruction of indigenous game that have proved very serious to both the natives and the whites.

INTRODUCTION

In all the countries considered, with the possible exception of the United States, the problems arising from white-native contacts require more scientific examination, more competent administration and more generous government finance. The achievement of the Roosevelt-Collier "New Day for American Indians", which is examined below, is a glowing example to other English-speaking peoples of what an enlightened and generous policy can accomplish.

Much of the material presented was collected in the English-speaking countries visited in the years immediately before the Second World War, which long retarded the completion of the work. Hence, in general, the comparative study concludes in 1939, although some later material has been secured by correspondence.

It is impossible to thank all those who assisted the author in various countries and on many native reservations. Particular gratitude is, however, due to Mr. John Collier, United States Commissioner of Indian Affairs; to Mr. Harold W. McGill, Canadian Deputy Superintendent-General of Indian Affairs; and to Dr. Diamond Jenness, of the National Museum of Canada. Professor I. L. G. Sutherland, whose writings on Maori affairs are outstanding, provided most valuable comments upon the New Zealand section, and the Australian Ethnologists, Mr C. P. Mountford and Mr. N. B. Tindale, read the whole work in manuscript. The author also acknowledges with gratitude the photographs supplied by the United States Department of the Interior, the Governments of New Zealand, New South Wales, and South Australia, and by Mr. C. P. Mountford.

A. GRENFELL PRICE

St. Mark's College

University of Adelaide

August, 1949

CHAPTER I

The Moving Frontier in the United States

The Indians of the territory, which is now the United States, had developed varied, and, in certain cases, fairly advanced cultures prior to the European conquests. The white invasions, therefore, frequently produced on tribes, and even on individuals, a variety of results. The picture had, however, another and more important aspect.

The dominating factors were not the differing cultures of the Indian peoples but the greater material development of the whites. These latter possessed ships, horses, wheeled vehicles, firearms and manufactured goods. Their languages were comparatively few in number. They could communicate by writing, while their advanced political institutions enabled scattered European colonies to unite.

As the invaders could add to these advantages a certain tolerance to their own diseases, and to alcohol, they devastated the Indians in a process, which, despite the minor differences stressed by some ethnologists, was remarkably similar, notwithstanding variations in Indian tribes and culture, or in time and place.

In an opening period the whites of several nations destroyed the Indians by such factors as disease, slaughter, and land robbery, along a vast and moving frontier. In a middle period they applied to their victims such palliatives as small reservations, removals and missionary efforts. In very recent times, they attempted to salvage some of the human wreckage by philanthropic endeavour directed along scientific lines.

INDIAN ORIGIN AND NUMBERS

The American Indians were apparently of Mongoloid origin, their ancestors having crossed the waters or ice of the narrow Bering Strait at various times and in different stages of cultural development. The Viking settlements in Greenland (990-1409 A.D.), and the Viking explorations in continental America, south of the St. Lawrence (1000 A.D.) had no effect on the Indians, and, if the Polynesians made comparatively recent contacts with South America, as seems possible, such contacts had little influence.

The duration of Indian occupation is unknown. It may perhaps date from Pleistocene times, some 15,000 to 20,000 years ago. Then, with the retreat of the ice sheets, groups of Asiatics possibly followed to North America mammals, now in many cases extinct. The diversity of Indian physical types, languages and cultures at least suggests that the penetration began in times long distant.

Numerically the Indian peoples to the North of the Rio Grande were, and still remain, insignificant. Estimates vary considerably but leading authorities believe that, when the white invasions opened, there were rather less than 850,000 Indians in the present United States. But although their numbers were small, the Indians occupied a vast region of some 3,000,000 square miles. blessed in many areas with a temperate climate and resources of immense richness[1].

INDIAN CIVILISATION

Enthusiastic writers have paid glowing tributes to Indian civilisation, and have claimed that the natives surpassed their conquerors in aesthetic, ethnic, and social culture, and were inferior to them only in material development and powers of destruction. Certainly, before they degenerated at the hands of selfish white peoples, who usually failed to understand their mentality, religions or social systems, many tribes had reached a fairly advanced state. Jenness, for example, classes the more progressive groups with the Egyptian, Hittite, Assyrian and Babylonian civilisations of about 1500 B.C. and so places these Indian tribes some 3000 years behind the whites.

Physically many Indians were fine people, free from scourges of the Old World such as smallpox, measles, tuberculosis. syphilis, leprosy, scrofula and nervous prostration. The race held well toward the end of the human life cycle and there were many centenarians.

Walpi Pueblo, Arizona

Photo: Author

Walpi Pueblo, Interior.

Photo: Author

Indian Housing, Mescalero Apache Agency, New Mexico
Photo: Author

Paiute Indian Housing of poor type, Nevada
Photo: Author

THE MOVING FRONTIER IN THE UNITED STATES

Contemporary white accounts, like those of the Jesuit Fathers, paint, however, a somewhat different picture. Descriptions of comparatively advanced peoples, such as the Hurons, portray a society whose culture was marred by constant warfare, cannibalism, slavery, torture and other revolting practices. Broiling the tongues of living victims, including Jesuit Fathers, was by no means the most disgusting of these barbarities. Nor did customs, such as the digging up of corpses for the "Feast of the Dead", afford a pleasant savour to white nostrils[2].

That the Indians were less advanced than their white conquerors can be attributed to several factors. First, the Indian brain was possibly of slightly smaller average size than the European, although authorities such as Huntington admit that the data for this assumption is inadequate. Secondly, the Indians were isolated from Old World progress, and in many cases from progress in their own continents. A difficult terrain made the Isthmus of Panama a barrier rather than a connection, whilst throughout the length of both the Americas huge mountain ranges impeded communications East and West. Furthermore, the Indians possessed no cereal excepting maize; no milk producing animal like the cow, and no effective transport animal such as the horse. The buffalo was too fierce and stupid to tame, and, although dogs were used to pull sledges, and the llama to carry light loads in its limited habitat, these means of transport were of comparatively slight importance.

Some features of Indian life—the agriculture of the East and South—the architecture of the Pueblos—the political systems of tribes such as the Iroquois and Natchez and the woodwork of the North-West coastal groups had reached fairly advanced standards. In general, however, the Indians of the United States had failed to develop the great civilisations evolved by their fellows in Mexico, Peru and Guatemala, and in certain cultural aspects were far behind the whites.

They remained for the most part nomadic food gatherers or semi-nomadic agriculturists, grouped in some thousands of small tribes or communities which spoke some 600 different dialects. Such a people, primitive, sparse, and disunited, were utterly unable to resist the weight of European attack.

Examining Indian civilisation in detail we find local differences which produced minor variations of response under white impacts, although, as noted above, the general pattern was remarkable for its similarities rather than its contrasts. The detailed story is extremely complicated. To take only one aspect the percentage of Indian survival depended upon many factors—some of which were not recorded in the early stages of the conquest. We can see, however, that amongst these factors were the protection afforded by isolation, and the numbers and cultural status of the Indian groups, together with the attitudes of these groups to white attack.

Thus in the Eastern areas the English-speaking whites largely decimated the native tribes, although some of these were numerous, warlike and culturally advanced. In the South-West, however, isolation, the arid territory and Spanish policy in its later and more tolerant phases fostered a survival which was later followed by an increase. The recent researches by Kroeber and other authorities have explained the importance of isolation in protecting certain groups of Californian Indians, and have also shown that survival was regulated by the numerical strength of both Indians and whites.

South of the English conquest zone, where the Indians were numerous and advanced, and the later policies of the Spanish conquerors moderate, the native peoples not only survived but greatly increased. Leading authorities consider that pre-Columbian numbers for the Hemisphere South of the Rio Grande were from six to nine millions. By 1930, some four and a half centuries later, these numbers had increased to over 20 million Indian full bloods and 30 million mestizos.

Recent times have witnessed one of the most interesting counter invasions in history—a Spanish-Indian (Mexican) penetration of the English-speaking United States[3].

CULTURE REGIONS

Clark Wissler and others have divided the Pre-Columbian culture of the United States Indians into six main regions. These are the Eastern Woodlands, the Central Plains, the South-West, the Central Plateau, California and the North-West Pacific Coast. The last of these lies mainly in Canada, and will be discussed in the Canadian section of this book[4].

THE MOVING FRONTIER IN THE UNITED STATES

Differences in these regions were partly due to race and history but were also determined by food supply and other factors of the environment. The South-West of the United States is largely arid country—a fascinating land of red mesas and red deserts, now teeming with important archaeological remains such as cliff dwellings. Here lived the Pueblo Indians, whose culture, largely derived from the great civilisations to the South, was strongly religious in character, and fairly advanced. These Indians, who practised agriculture in valleys watered by low and uncertain summer rains, were the only builders of stone villages north of the Rio Grande. Archaeological evidence indicates that they were much more numerous in prehistoric times, but declined, possibly because the climate became more arid.

North-East of this region lay the East Coast areas, which largely consisted of warm or cold forest lands. In the south of this division tribes such as the Muskhogean family (the Creeks, Chickasaws and so on) occupied the country along the Gulf of Mexico, east of the Mississippi. These people were hunters and agriculturists. They lived in strongly palisaded villages and possessed some local political organisation, but they lacked the ability to create extensive States. The people of the colder northern woodlands were also food gatherers and agriculturists. Some groups, which had probably moved northwards, were culturally advanced. Amongst these were the Mound Builders of the Ohio Valley and the Iroquoian tribes who, about 1570, formed the famous league of Five Nations—a confederacy of warlike and progressive type. Kroeber believes that warfare, with its attendant confusion and destruction, was the chief cause of population remaining low in the east.

West of the forests lay the great plains. There the Indians did not practise agriculture, and wild animals such as the buffalo and antelope largely determined the cultural and economic life. Very sparse nomadic populations lived by the chase, camping in tepis (tents made of buffalo hide) and using dogs to drag transport frames. Some of the northern groups, such as the Dakotas—the main branch of the Sioux family—showed considerable moral and physical strength. Southern groups like the Yguases of Texas were of poorer type.

West of the plains lay the great mountain plateaux and the

WHITE SETTLERS AND NATIVE PEOPLES

Pacific coast. Over much of this area the Indians were amongst the most backward in the Americas. Maize, beans, and pumpkins, the great staples of pre-Columbian agriculture, are summer crops, which require much water in July and August. California has little rain at this season. Hence many of the groups were nomadic food gatherers, who lived in the poorest of shelters and had little political strength.

There were, however, some exceptions. The Mohave, who practised agriculture on the Colorado river, were people of fine physique with some knowledge of pottery and other arts.

The Kutenai tribes of the northern mountains were skilful hunters and fishers, with high standards of morality, hospitality, and kindness. The northern coastal tribes, such as the Chinook of the lower Columbia, were also more advanced, and their culture approached the higher civilisation of the British Columbian coast.

Authorities differ as to the permanent value of Indian civilisation to the whites, but it undoubtedly was of great importance in the early stages of the invasions. The whites learnt from the natives the cultivation of corn, beans, pumpkins and tobacco. They utilised the Indians as guides and hunters. They adopted canoes, snow shoes and articles of clothing such as fur mittens, caps and moccasins. Indeed it is fair to say that without the aid of the Indians and their culture many of the early settlers would have starved through inexperience or failed through lack of staples for trade[5].

THE SWEEP OF BRITISH CONQUEST

The British objects in invading North America were trade and the flag, accompanied, as in the case of the Puritans, by some religious motives. Henry VII, who ended the Wars of the Roses and founded a strong government, listened to his merchants and supported the explorations of John Cabot. Cabot in 1497 discovered the North-East American coast, and also reported an abundance of cod on the Newfoundland Banks. European fishermen were quickly on the scene and there are indications that these people, landing on the American coast to secure bait and dry fish, traded with the Indians and doubtless produced the same results as did the later whalers and sealers in Australia and

New Zealand. It is certainly significant that the plague which decimated the New England Indians, prior to the arrival of the Pilgrim Fathers, very possibly spread southwards from the coastal regions of the North[6].

Under the Tudor and Stuart sovereigns British national expansion took the form of the trading and colonisation typical of a Western European island power which possessed great geographical and economic advantages. From 1607, when a companv with a "Royal Charter" founded a "London Colony" in South Virginia, and from 1620 when English businessmen sent the "Pilgrims" to New England, the English-speaking frontier rolled steadily westwards to the Pacific.

The British peoples first established a compact group of colonies down the East Coast, largely eliminating the Indians in the process. Then, after about a century and a half, they broke through the barrier of the Appalachian Highlands and Eastern Forests, liquidating powerful Indian tribes in their advance.

When the British began their conquests in 1607 they were only just emerging from the later Middle Ages—a period of turmoil, barbarity, and discomfort. For some centuries they had conducted long and fierce wars with the French and Spanish, and these three white peoples now transplanted their rivalry and warfare to the American continent. The English and Lowland Scots were particularly experienced in subduing unruly peoples, for before and during their American invasions they practised against the Scottish Highlanders, the Irish, and their own rebels the massacres, enslavements, transportations and reservation policies which they perpetrated across the Atlantic

The British sovereigns in general lacked those religious ideals and motives which, despite all failings and weaknesses, were genuine attributes of the Spanish monarchs. Their officials and subjects followed their example, and, until the Humanitarian Revolution at the end of the eighteenth century, showed to the colonial natives a harsh attitude which British Parliamentary Committees later admitted freely[7].

At the outset the British Governments ignored any Indian rights to sovereignty or land. By right of discovery they claimed complete supremacy against both their European rivals and the aborigines. They conducted colonisation by means of companies

11

or proprietors, and, although they frequently supplied colonial governors, they could or would not control the relations between the colonists and the natives. The local authorities in turn were usually too weak to control, even if they wished to do so, the frontier settlers, who generally represented both the best and the worst elements of contemporary British society. Some colonists, such as the town dwellers of Quaker Pennsylvania, attempted to protect the Indians. Others, like the uncontrollable slaughterers and slavers of Georgia, openly perpetrated their injustices. The murder, in 1675, of Indian ambassadors by Colonel John Washington—the great-grandfather of the President—and the failure to bring the murderer to justice, was only one of many instances in which white criminals escaped punishment. Even the Puritans followed the example of their contemporaries in Britain, and frequently modelled their behaviour on that of the Hebrew exterminators of the Old Testament. They enslaved Indian women, kidnapped Indian children, and burnt and slaughtered, sometimes under clerical inspiration and leadership. Only too often the Puritan attitude was that of Johnson, who wrote in his account of Puritan settlement a chapter on the plague of 1616-20 entitled "The Wonderful Preparation the Lord Christ by His Providence Wrought for His People's Abode in this Western World". This "Wonderful Preparation" was a plague which decimated the Indians in Massachusetts and left their wigwams "full of corpses". "By this means", said Johnson, "Christ, whose great and glorious works throughout the earth are all for the benefit of His churches and chosen, not only made room for His people to plant, but also tamed the breasts of these barbarous Indians⁸".

Later Massachusetts followed Dutch precedent in paying scalp bounties, and even the British General Braddock offered these, not only for Indian scalps, but for the scalp of a Jesuit Missionary. Fortunately white attitudes were by no means consistently savage, and seem to have varied greatly under the influence of fear and wars. In 1676, for example, Massachusetts hanged two white men for the wanton killing of Indian men, women and children. Yet, in the following year, the women of Marblehead, returning from church, encountered and massacred some captured Indians, after which "the rough element" went off to kill the women and children of a neighbouring Indian village⁹.

The truth was that the frontier attracted both oppressors and oppressed from a Europe and Britain which were wracked by religious and political dissensions. The Home Government was apathetic or ineffective. The local governments were land hungry and weak. The frontiersmen were greedy and primitive. Fear played its usual part, with the result that the frontier frequently presented a picture of bloody atrocities and reprisals.

Some American authorities claim that the Colonial Governments were "reasonably solicitous regarding the moral and legal rights of the aboriginal inhabitants¹⁰". The majority paint a sorry picture of a regime which enabled the whites to perpetrate invasions, land robbery, enslavement, slaughter, burnings, disease, drunkenness and social economic destruction. Not unnaturally the Indians retaliated with the brutality of untamed savages, and their fiendish tortures, and their massacres of innocent women and children aroused the permanent hatred of the whites. The invaders, moreover, began to possess an overwhelming superiority in numbers and equipment which permitted them virtually to exterminate many Indian groups".

Towards the middle of the eighteenth century the British Home Governments showed far greater appreciation of their imperial obligations, and in 1756, at the instigation of the Board of Trade, the Motherland appointed Indian superintendents for the northern and southern colonial districts. In 1761 she attempted to prevent the colonists from occupying the lands beyond the Alleghanies, pending a settlement of Indian problems, and withdrew the power of purchasing Indian lands from the Colonial Governments. Confronted, however, by new and great difficulties British policy proved uncertain and vacillating, and British good intentions, as noted, merely helped to goad the Colonists into the War of Independence¹².

INDIAN ATTITUDES TO THE BRITISH

Had the Indians united they could have overwhelmed the initial British settlements. Even at a later date an abandonment of neutrality by the Iroquois, who commanded the Hudson River gap and other inland routes, would have exposed the British colonies to very grave danger from the French. Far from being hostile, however, leaders of the coastal tribes, such as Powhatan in Virginia, welcomed the whites both as traders and as potential allies against Indian rivals. Nor did these leaders grudge the comparatively small amount of land required, particularly as some of the colonists resorted to purchasing land in order to avoid difficulties of title—a policy which certain colonial governments sought to restrict by legislative enactment. Very soon, however, a growing flood of colonists, white aggression, and white participation in native wars, opened the eyes of the Indian leaders and led to bloody and costly conflicts. As the Emperor Powhatan pathetically asked the Virginian settlers, "Why should you destroy us who have provided you with food?" "Why should you take by force from us that which you can obtain by love?" A twelve years war in the Virginia area virtually exterminated tribe after tribe. Again, in 1675-6, King Phillip's War practically destroyed the Indian race and influence in New England. In this war half the hostile Indians together with one eleventh of the adult white males and an unrecorded number of white women and children perished. From 1649 onwards the Iroquois, frequently armed with white weapons, destroyed or conquered the Hurons, Susquehannocks, Delawares, the Moundbuilders of the Ohio valley and other native peoples. This aggression depopulated a large part of North America and left the Iroquois themselves exhausted and depleted in numbers even before they completed their ruin by participating in the Anglo-French wars.

Two centuries of European invasion saw the initial friendly relations (including frequent marriages between white traders and Indian women) pass into a period of hatred and race prejudice. The Indians learnt to despise the traders for their cheating, rum selling, sexual irregularities, kidnapping and slave raiding, and to detest the frontiersman who invaded, occupied and despoiled their hunting territories. From the white viewpoint the Indian men and women were of value to the trader. To the frontier settler, however, Indian males proved of little use as labourers, while Indian women proved inferior to European women experienced in domestic or farm life. For these and other reasons the settlers frequently attempted to exterminate the Indians. Some groups

THE MOVING FRONTIER IN THE UNITED STATES

retreated westwards to the territories of other groups. with resulting disturbances, and colonial governments established small reservations as havens of refuge for the dispossessed survivors and even began to consider moving all the Indians westwards in the hope of placing them beyond the reach of "the Indian slaying frontiersman[13]".

AMERICAN AND INDIAN CONTACTS

During the century which followed the War of Independence the American frontier rolled across the continent. The process was marked by American policies and atrocities possibly even less excusable than those of the Colonial-British, for philanthropic ideas had advanced, and the centre of Government was now seated within the United States. The young Republic gained the right to regulate commerce with the Indian tribes and this power gave Congress "almost unlimited control over Indian affairs" excepting in certain of the original Thirteen States[14]. As early as 1775 the Continental Congress appointed Northern, Middle and Southern Departments to replace the British organisations, and in 1789 the first Congress gave the War Department all duties "relative to Indian affairs[15]".

The years 1789-1871 have been called the "Treaty Making Period", because the Federal Government made treaties with the tribes as the white wave foamed across their territories. The Government attempted by treaty and legislation to prevent the whites trespassing on Indian country; to monopolise land purchases; to prohibit the sale of liquor and to prevent outrages by either side. Nevertheless from Washington's presidency onwards the Federal failure to control white delinquencies resulted in constant wars and a steady decline of Indian population. As an American historian has put it the uncontrollable frontiersmen constantly encroached on Indian lands in defiance of treaty; they destroyed the game on which the Indians depended for food and clothing, and in many cases were ready to slay any redskin on sight. Of course the savages were often the aggressors, but the inexorable westward thrust of the whites was the principal cause of conflict[16].

Soon after the American Revolution General Wayne invaded the Ohio Great Lakes region and subdued it for white settlement by the devastating campaign of 1794. In the following years

WHITE SETTLERS AND NATIVE PEOPLES

the whites descended on the great Indian Confederations of the South-East—the Chickasaws, Choctaws, Creeks and Cherokees, and the demand grew that these peoples should be transplanted west of the Mississippi. Devastated by smallpox most of the surviving Chickasaws, Choctaws and Creeks emigrated voluntarily, but the Federal Government and the State of Georgia were forced to exercise great pressure to move the Cherokees. The story ranks amongst the worst in English-speaking history. The Americans dragged from their homes a largely civilised people; drove them to concentration camps at the point of the bayonet, and abandoned their dwellings and possession to white plunderers and thieves. From the white viewpoint the deportation was "a complete success". Of twelve thousand Indians "probably four thousand slept in unmarked graves around concentration camps or along the line of march" to the west". A Georgian volunteer summed up this atrocity of 1838 in one biting sentence, "I fought through the Civil War, and have seen men shot to pieces and slaughtered by thousands, but the Cherokee removal was the cruellest work I ever-knew¹⁸⁷".

The mass of surviving Indians was now across the Mississippi and for a passing moment the Americans played with the idea that they could segregate the natives in a consolidated Indian territory between the frontier farms along the Mississippi and the mountains and deserts of the West. As a Senate Committee on Indian affairs smugly reported in 1836, "With this uninhabitable region on the west of the Indian territory, they cannot be surrounded by white population. They are on the outside of us, and in a place which will ever remain on the outside¹⁹'".

Even in 1836 such hopes were mere folly. The Americans were already establishing communications by road, canal and river steamer. They were founding States and Territories west of the Mississippi, and they were penetrating the Indian country by the Santa Fe and Oregon trails to the Pacific, where, since 1811, they had been extending their trading posts.

In 1846-7 the Mormons made their heroic trek and proved that Utah was suitable for white settlement, and when gold was discovered in California in 1848, thousands of miners traversed the Indian country by the Oregon trail.

Owing largely to the gold discoveries the whites disrupted the

THE MOVING FRONTIER IN THE UNITED STATES

Indians of the Pacific areas before they descended on those of the plains. In Oregon and California from the eighteen forties to the eighteen seventies miners and settlers displayed a brutality, and the United States Government a neglect, which were all the more scandalous because they extended into allegedly civilised times". In Oregon the legislature, politicians, subordinate Indian agents and even Methodist clergy participated in massacres which were embellished but not disguised by the title of Indian wars. In California the whites killed Indians as "a sport to enliven Sundays and holidays"". In 1871 the kindly Kingsley wrote that he had had to use his 38 calibre revolver to shoot children as his 56 calibre rifle "tore them up so bad"".

A recent student, A. G. Harper, paints a ghastly picture in an official report of 1939. The miners, he says, were followed by lumbermen, farmers and cattlemen, who were contemptuous of the peaceful Indians. No quarter was given. Those who escaped slaughter or enslavement were ruthlessly pushed up and down the country. Women were raped and enslaved in a sudden and brutal race-miscegenation that created many mixed bloods. In spite of such crimes the Government remained disgracefully passive. In 1852 no less than eighteen treaties were signed with Indian groups providing for the creation of reservations in return for the surrender of farm lands. Californian influences prevented their ratification lest the proposed reservations contained gold deposits. Later when the unfortunate Indians established small farms and orchards the Californians ruthlessly evicted the owners. From 1906-1927 the Government granted the dispossessed natives some minute reservations of worthless land on the public domain".

There remained the solid block of country between the Pacific region and the Mississippi States. From time to time proposals were made to create this an Indian State, but these did not eventuate and the whites broke the territory into fragments. The invasions were marked by treaties which were often forced upon the natives and were sometimes fraudulent. Land robbery and the destruction of resources, particularly the buffalo, reduced the tribes to destitution with consequent warfare and outrages on both sides. In 1864 a Methodist preacher-Colonel was responsible for a revolting liquidation of a Cheyenne village at Sand

WHITE SETTLERS AND NATIVE PEOPLES

Creek and as late as 1876 the Sioux annihilated Custer's army in a famous battle.

Clark Wissler has portrayed the terrible effects of the destruction of the buffalo on Indian tribal life. An agent wrote in 1884 that the natives were in a deplorable condition. Many were gradually dying of starvation; little children had suffered most, and many passed away. Owing to insufficient supplies of Government rations the Indians were stripping bark from the trees to appease their gnawing hunger[24].

The closing years of the nineteenth century saw the end of the moving frontier, for a vast white population had now spread over most of the country.

In 1823 Mr. Justice Marshall laid down that the Indians were domestic dependent nations with no rights of sovereignty or soil against those of the United States but had to be protected while in peaceful possession of their lands[25]. In 1871 Congress terminated all treaty-making with the surviving tribes. The once proud Indian natives now became wards of the United States, living on such reservations as Congress granted and subject to such enactments as Congress dictated[26].

INDIAN NUMERICAL DECREASE

By the end of the frontier period the whites had secured most of the Indians' lands. They had destroyed the natives' living resources, riddled them with disease and alcohol, slaughtered many directly, or indirectly by the sale of firearms, and wrecked their pride of life by ridiculing their religious and social customs.

At the beginning of the white conquests the Indians were probably increasing slowly in numbers. Indian population figures at any period are open to criticism but the decline from Mooney's pre-Columbian estimate of 846,000 to the Commissioner's estimates of 278,000 in 1870 and 244,000 in 1880 seems no exaggeration. Moreover, the later figures included many mixed bloods, including not a few in whom white blood predominated. Official estimates are variable and even contradictory, but the census of 1910 gave the proportion of full bloods as 56.51 of the total: the Indian office estimated them at 52% in 1938, and Clark Wissler, writing in the previous year, put them at about 50%. If we accept the census figures of 1910, which gave a full

18

blood Indian population of 150,053 the reduction from Mooney's figure of 840,000 is 82%. In January, 1938, the Office of Indian Affairs had 342,497 natives under its jurisdiction. Allowing that about half of these were full bloods the white invasions had by then reduced the full bloods from 840,000 to 171,000, a fall of 80%.

Much of the destruction is now shrouded by the mists of history, but the researches of Kroeber and Merriam on the Californian tragedy indicate the course of events in many regions. Kroeber considers that from 1770 to 1910 these Indians declined from 133,000 to 15,850, and Merriam that their numbers fell from 100,000 to 35,000 in the brief period, 1849-1860. Merriam states such decrease which "amounted to the complete annihilation of scores of tribes and the reduction to scattered remnants of scores of others, was wholly due to the coming of the white man". Kroeber notes that the survival of the Indian was in adverse ratio to the density of white population, which is a sad condemnation of the European".

DESTRUCTIVE FACTORS

At this period of time it is impossible to estimate the respective weight of the various destructive factors, but their nature is clear. Mooney placed their order as "smallpox and other epidemics, tuberculosis, social diseases, whisky and attendant dissipation, removals, starvation and subjection to unaccustomed conditions, low vitality due to depression, and wars". He believed that all these evils, with the exception of wars and tuberculosis, came from the whites, and that even here the increasing destruction of tuberculosis was largely due to conditions imposed by their advent".

Dr. J. G. Townsend, Director of Health, U.S. Office of Indian Affairs, has summed up the story. He quotes the opinion of Dr. Ales Hrdlicka, of the Smithsonian Institute, that before the white discovery America was one of the most healthful of continents, if not the most so. Skeletal remains, barring a few exceptions, are remarkably free from disease. Apparently there was no rachitis, no proved tuberculosis, no smallpox, measles or trachoma; cancer was rare and even fractures infrequent. Furthermore, there is not an instance thoroughly authenticated of pre-Columbian syphilis.

The white settlers sweeping across the continent brought diseases old in Europe but new and deadly to the Indians. Even before the Pilgrim Fathers landed smallpox reached New England from the French in the north or by coastal vessels. One reason that the Puritans were allowed to settle so peaceably was that the nearby Indian village had been abandoned owing to the epidemic. Back through the forest country the disease had made Indian forest sites "like a new Golgotha", littered with skulls and bones. The susceptible, unvaccinated Indians died off until the Massachusetts tribe was reduced from 3000 to 1000, and Delaware villages were abandoned, never to be revived.

Similar havoc accompanied and often preceded the whites in their westward advance. Smallpox, for example, repeatedly swept over wide areas, sometimes destroying half the natives in its path. There were historic outbreaks in 1781-2, 1801-2 and 1837-8, with results that read like a medieval chronicler's account of the Black Death. The same story comes from many parts of the country. In 1837, for example, smallpox, emanating from an employee on a river steamer, ravaged the Missouri valley. The Mandan tribe of 1600 persons was reduced to 31. The Minnetarees and Arickarees lost half their numbers. In a few weeks 10,000 Indians died and the land became a scene of desolation strewn with corpses[29]. Smallpox epidemics also swept the prairies, the Rockies and the far North-West. Other scourges were measles and tuberculosis. Tuberculosis possibly existed to some extent in pre-Columbian days, but the disease spread rapidly, particularly when the whites forced the Indians out on small reservations where they lived under conditions which differed greatly from their ancestral life. Although the Jesuit Fathers reported the existence of the disease as early as 1633, the Indians had little immunity and it spread with devastating results.

The recent researches of Meigs and Cook paint a vivid and important picture of the ravages of disease on the Pacific coast. Cook points out that there was little Indian-white or intertribal warfare in Baja California during the years 1697-1793. The Spanish missionaries prevented the ravages of alcohol and the white population was too small for extensive miscegenation. Neverthe-

THE MOVING FRONTIER IN THE UNITED STATES

less, during these eighty years, the Indians decreased from 41,000 to 4000 in nearly linear fashion; at least 20,000 persons perished from epidemic diseases while syphilis created further decline. Cook believes that from 30 to 40% of the diminution of population was due to the introduction of epidemic and venereal diseases. The balance of the shrinkage can be attributed to nutritional, social, and economic factors which cannot be evaluated quantitatively at the present time[30].

Meigs considers that the fundamental cause of the decline of the Spanish missions in Baja California was disease. Smallpox and other epidemics ravaged the Indians while syphilis attacked them ceaselessly[31].

Alcohol combined with poor hygiene to increase the incidence of disease. This curse of liquor preceded the main invasions as fur traders and others used alcohol for barter, while the French and English authorities, including even the Puritans, poured it out to weaken hostile tribes or to inflame Indian allies against white enemies. The natives possessed no alcoholic beverages and hence had no immunity. They evinced an insatiable craving for liquor, and comparatively small quantities produced insobriety, violence, and drunken slumber under exposed conditions which favoured the onset of disease. The chiefs of various tribes frequently begged the whites to forbid the sale of the "stinking water" which drove their young braves crazy. Some British colonies made efforts to curtail the traffic and prevention later became a feature of American legislation. Unfortunately the evil persisted. As late as the nineteen thirties Nash's account of the Seminole of Florida denounced the modern "bootlegger" as a twentieth century breed of vermin that has been systematically debauching the Indian since 1492[32]".

Other disruptive factors were firearms and horses. The British, French, Dutch and Swedes all armed native tribes for hunting or warfare with the tragic consequences that have been enumerated. Tribe after tribe invaded its neighbours' territories for war or the chase while the frontiersmen slaughtered the natives and the game on which they relied. Mooney gives warfare the last place in his list of disruptive factors, but it appears to deserve a higher place. Firearms certainly assisted the Iroquois in the invasions which exhausted these people and devastated their neighbours.

21

Mooney himself stated that the "enormous decrease" in the number of Californian Indians was chiefly due to the cruelties and wholesale massacres perpetrated by the miners and early settlers, and in these the rifle and revolver held a leading place[33].

The introduction of the horse provided a means of rapid communication and transport which increased tribal warfare, assisted to destroy Indian resources, and helped to disrupt tribal life. The Spaniards in the South imported horses at an early date and the Northern Europeans brought them to the East coast. The animals quickly revolutionised the lives of many tribes, particularly on the great plains. Wandering and slow-moving foot hunters, who had rarely met or clashed, now became ferocious mobile raiders equipped with white weapons and means of transport. Woodland tribes poured on to the prairies for battle and sport. No matter how varied were the human alliances and combats the peoples of all races successfully pursued one object. By the eighteen eighties they had destroyed almost completely the vast herds of buffalo which were the Indians' staff of life[34].

Destructive factors such as disease, alcohol, warfare, firearms, horses, the wrecking of native resources and land robbery are obvious. Important but far less easy to evaluate are aspects such as the disruption of native religion, culture, ambition and tribal life. Wissler believes that the early trading period brought to some groups a wider intellectual outlook, an enriched culture, economic prosperity and greater material equipment. Much of this progress was, however, deceptive. It rested on the destruction of capital such as hides and furs. It weakened social organisation, community life and co-operation, and it undermined the authority of the chiefs. The growing flood of land hungry settlers continued, and in most cases completed the disruptive process, with results which the following chapter will discuss[35].

Indian School—Mescalero Apache Reservation

Photo: Author

A Pueblo Village, New Mexico

Photo: Author

Paiute Food Grinders, Carson Indian Agency, Stewart, Nevada
Carson Indian Agency, Stewart, Nevada

Navajo Child, Window Rock, Arizona
Photo: Navajo Service, U.S. Dept. of Interior

CHAPTER II

The United States Administration

RESERVATIONS AND MISSIONS

The incompatibility of Ethnic groups has often resulted in segregation. It has long produced "foreign quarters" in towns and cities, "ethnic islands" of population, and reservations for aboriginal peoples. Sometimes the dominant races have segregated subject groups through fear or racial distastes; at other times because they have wished to preserve the dependent peoples. Frequently religious motives have played a part and the segregated areas have become centres of missionary zeal.

The history of the United States Indians provides examples of all these segregating processes. Before the end of the frontier period the surviving tribes had become ethnic islands of decline in the white ocean of population, or were moving west in what was usually a vain search for regions of geographical isolation.

The whites on their part helped the process by creating reservations in which they segregated the natives, often under the guidance of government agents and of missionaries. As we have seen in the case of the Cherokees, the Americans sometimes transplanted tribes to distant regions, which, for the time being, furnished safety from the invaders. Not until the end of the frontier period was there a reversal of the segregation policy. Then, from 1887 onwards, the United States attempted to merge the natives in the white population by granting the individual Indian his land together with citizenship of the United States.

Unfortunately reservations, missions, and allotment and citizenship all proved little more than palliatives. They failed to check the disintegration and degradation, and the natives continued to decrease despite the heroic labours of some faithful government agents and many devoted missionaries. The later policy of allot-

23

ment and citizenship served only to give greedy and land robbing whites a freer rein. Such persons fleeced the Indians of
much of their remaining land and greatly increased the burden
on the government. Nevertheless the twentieth century saw the
Americans evolve more humane, just and scientific methods. They
developed some of the remaining reservations in the genuine
interests of their native wards, and they advanced education,
health and other services in a process which laid some foundation
for President Franklin Roosevelt's "New Day for Indians".

THE SPANISH MISSION SYSTEM

The first European power to apply such palliatives as reservations and missions was Spain, and, although the Spanish story
lies outside the sphere of English-speaking settlements, the important experiments of this nation must be mentioned. The soc-
iologist, A. G. Keller, wrote:

"Alone amongst modern nations, Spain tried to put into practice in her relations with conquered peoples the principles of
humanity, justice and religion'" and this is certainly true as regards the Southern United States. Here the Spanish territories
formed the frontiers of "New Spain" and were occupied as mission regions, thus avoiding the ecomendero system—an alleged
trusteeship which, in its early stages, brought slavery or
death to thousands of unhappy Indians. The Spanish mission
system, as applied in Florida, the Pueblo region and California,
showed a humanity, a sincerity, and a transitory success which
contrast sharply both with the ecomendero system and with English-speaking brutality and indifference in the regions to the
North.

As the Spanish monarchs genuinely wished to Christianise their
natives they supported the "misioneros" and made them an official
section of the machinery of civilisation and conquest. On their
part the Fathers were in many cases high born and heroic men,
sufficiently wise to isolate their wards from the evils of white
contact; to treat them like children; to elevate them slowly and
tolerantly; to overlook for a time such barbarities as cannibalism
and to found Christian progress on a solid economic basis.

The Fathers realised that immediate and full contact with a

24

higher civilisation would harm their charges, and they therefore ran their missions on reservation principles. They controlled trade, and superintended travellers, usually permitting them at the most only one night's lodging.

The Spaniards intended that Florida should be forever a land of Christian Indians. The Bishop of Cuba was its de facto ruler and the authorities prohibited immigration and the entry of European settlers.

The Spaniards began their occupation in 1565, and, by 1617, their missions had charge of 16,000 Indians. Unfortunately the Fathers were unable to defeat the worst of the white scourges—disease—and in 1617 smallpox killed half the natives. In spite of this the work continued, and by 1655 missions in Florida and Georgia supervised 26,000 Indians. By this time, however, the English had established themselves in the Carolinas, and English slavers, supported by savage Creek auxiliaries, began raiding South. England and Spain now came to war and in 1704-6 English expeditions, one of which was commanded by Governor Moore, of Carolina, wiped out the prosperous Spanish settlements. The English killed or enslaved the Christian Indians and permitted their Creek auxiliaries to torture both Franciscan Fathers and their converts at the stake. By 1745 the Mission villages and their stone churches were woodland ruins; the Christians of Florida and Georgia had been enslaved or scattered, and pagan Creeks occupied their place[2].

The story of the Pueblo Missions, which the Spaniards established from 1598, was more fortunate, and by 1630 the region contained 60,000 Christian Indians in 90 pueblos which included 25 principal mission centres and churches. The missions survived the historic Pueblo revolt of 1680, which temporarily drove Spain from New Mexico, and the terrible smallpox epidemic of 1780-81. The territory gradually assumed a Spanish-Indian character. The missions became "Pueblos de Indios", and, later, villages of Spanish type, while the missionaries were supplanted by secular priests. Today the majority of these groups, excepting the Hopi and Zuni, are nominal Christians[3].

Most important from the viewpoint of this work were the Spanish missions in California, for here the comparatively recent researches of Kroeber, Meigs, Cook and others have revealed a most significant picture. From 1797 onwards the Spanish Fathers established their famous missions in Lower California, which is now part of Mexico. In 1769 they entered Upper California, now part of the United States, and by 1823 had founded 23 mission villages as far north as San Francisco. By means of these missions the Fathers transformed the low grade, food-gathering peoples into relatively prosperous farmers and pastoralists. Although from 1803 onwards they were mercilessly robbed by the Mexican government, the Missions as late as 1834 contained 15,000 Indians, possessed 424,000 cattle, 62,500 horses and mules, 321,900 sheep and hogs, and produced 122,500 bushels of corn and wheat.

In the eighteen forties the American miners made their onslaught, but the United States Government, then in control, did little or nothing to protect its Christian Indians. As noted above, it herded them into barren reservations on which the whites constantly encroached, until, by 1906, only a few degraded survivors remained of the once prosperous mission communities.

Earlier historians gave high praise to the achievements of the Spanish missions but the later researches of Kroeber and Meigs greatly modify the former conclusions. Kroeber considers that "the brute upshot of missionisation, in spite of its kindly flavour and humanitarian root, was only one thing—death!" "What the Franciscan commenced with his concentrations, the Americans finished by settlement'".

Meigs reached the important conclusion that each mission passed through a cycle of rise and decline which covered about fifty years[5]. He believed that the declines were due to disease, to alterations in diet, clothing and dwellings, and to white contacts. We shall see in the Australian section of this book that the Benedictine Fathers, who planted the New Norcia mission on the Victoria Plains in Western Australia, met with the same sad experience. The Californian Mission cycle apparently covered fifty years. The last aboriginal full blood of the Victoria Plains died sixty-seven years after the Benedictine work commenced[6].

A further criticism of the missions is that the patriarchal rule of the padres taught the Indians something of the white man's civilisation but did not teach them how to maintain that civilisation on the removal of supervision. The mission Indians were unable to retain their standards under the impact of the Mexican Revolution and republican tenets. Work almost stopped, and the Indians, no longer under compulsion, gave themselves over to laziness, gambling and drink[7].

On the whole it appears that, in spite of eulogistic and well deserved tributes, the Spanish missions approached far closer to the later general pattern of missionary enterprise and failure that was realised by the historians of the past. The fathers could not protect their charges from white diseases; nor did their paternal compulsion equip the natives to resist for themselves the evil influences of evil whites. Nevertheless, Spanish missionary enterprise smoothed the pillow of dying races with greater efficiency than any other early palliative, and for this reason, apart from all others, it deserves sincere respect.

COLONIAL RESERVATIONS

When the English and Scots began their invasion of America in 1607 they had already practised in the Scottish and Irish borderlands their policies of proprietary and company colonisation; of exterminating native groups, and of segregating tribes in reservations. James I adopted the last named expedient in his famous Plantation of Ulster in 1609, when he ordered the Irish to leave the six British counties and to gather on reservations. In Ireland again, at a slightly later date, the Puritan, Oliver Cromwell, provided examples of extermination, enslavement and removals which many American Puritans seemed only too ready to follow[8].

We have seen that the English Government, like the Spanish, claimed the sovereignty and ownership of all Indian lands. From about 1649, however, colonies such as Massachusetts, Connecticut and Virginia began to "assign" land to Indian groups which had become Christian or which they desired to protect[9]. At first the colonies utilised the Indian chiefs or sub-chiefs as Government agents, but in 1656 Massachusetts took a step towards creating an Indian Department when it appointed a white superintendent with magisterial powers to supervise all the Indians in the colony. Maryland, Pennsylvania and the Carolinas similarly established small reservations for remnants of the broken coastal peoples.

WHITE SETTLERS AND NATIVE PEOPLES

Some of these still survive in the Eastern United States, but they are islands of Indian population decay, for their inhabitants are nearly all mixed bloods or negroes[10].

COLONIAL MISSIONS

In addition to reservations the English colonists utilised the services of missions. The English missions were, however, far less effective than the Spanish as they never became an official part of the machinery of colonisation. The English monarchs, unlike the Spanish, left the conversion and civilising of their unhappy Indian subjects to different and differing religious denominations; or to philanthropic organisations and persons. Moreover, in the absence of any official or uniform policy of segregation and reservation, the Colonial missions were usually scattered about in little islands of Indian population which were surrounded by white settlers. Such conditions exposed the Christian Indians to the full force of European vice and disease and not infrequently to racial hatred and massacre[11].

Several churches — Episcopalian, Congregational, Roman Catholic, Lutheran and Moravian—conducted missions in the English colonies. It is impossible to trace their detailed history but the story in New England will afford an example.

French Jesuits began work in Maine in 1613 but an English fleet promptly destroyed their mission. During the next seventy years, however, the Jesuits did much work amongst the Abnaki Indians of the North, until attacks by the New Englanders forced them to withdraw to Canada. The Abnaki missions in Maine were restored after the Revolution, and, in recent times, the Jesuits were still conducting missions in this region[12].

Protestant missionary work was begun in New England in the sixteen thirties and forties by Roger Williams, Thomas Mayhew and the Rev. John Eliot, the last two being Congregationalists. Williams won such influence amongst the Wampanoags and Narragansets that he kept them friendly during the critical Pequot war, an action which probably saved the white settlements. Mayhew and Eliot were so successful that in 1644 the Massachusetts Government made provision for instructing the Indians in Christianity, and in 1649 a "Corporation for the Pro-

28

pagation of the Gospel to the Indians in New England" was established in Britain. During the next twenty-five years Massachusetts and Plymouth saw the growth of many villages of Christian or "Praying Indians", but these people belonged to broken or subject tribes and largely disappeared during King Phillip's war, which aroused intense racial hatred. Much of the same story comes from Connecticut, from other parts of New England, and indeed from most parts of the colonies. The missionaries learnt the native languages, compiled invaluable dictionaries, translated the gospels, made converts, who sometimes numbered several thousands, and pioneered some educational development. Their devoted and often heroic labours were worthy of greater results, but war and racial hatred dispersed the Indians; disease and drink reduced their numbers and miscegenation diluted their blood. By the end of the Colonial period the East Coast tribes had been reduced to scattered remnants[13], despite all missionary efforts.

IMPERIAL POLICY

As indicated previously the British sovereigns and governments did little for their Indian charges during the early stages of colonisation. In the eighteenth century, however, the swarming of the British hive, the consequent colonial expansion, and great and successful wars conjured up a new and splendid vision of Imperial destiny. In the seventeen fifties the British Board of Trade became interested in the westward surge of the American colonists and perceived the growing importance of centralising colonial administration and of evolving uniform policies in regard to the west.

Settlers were now pressing into this country, and official and uniform measures to control the sale of Indian lands and to regulate trades were becoming a necessity. In 1755 therefore, Britain appointed the famous Sir William Johnson agent to the Northern tribes such as the Iroquois, and Atkin agent for Southern tribes like the Cherokees.

During the following period the Motherland attempted to reserve the Indian territory pending a clarification and settlement of difficulties. As noted above, however, her policy proved vacillating when confronted with new and great difficulties, on some

29

occasions preventing the colonists pressing westwards and acquiring Indian lands; on others withdrawing the military forces which protected frontier districts and throwing the Indian problems on the colonies. This weak and contradictory policy was satisfactory neither to the colonists nor the Indians, and did much to stimulate the American Revolution. On the whole it can be said that, although the British Government made some effort to reserve Indian territory during its dying years in the United States, it was unable to do much for Indian welfare and failed to apply even such palliatives as reservations and missions[14]".

THE GROWTH OF THE RESERVATION SYSTEM

On its foundation in 1776 the United States took over much of the Indian policy of Britain and her former colonies. At the outset the young republic did not create reservations but it followed the British practices of securing white occupancy of Indian land by treaty, of promising to protect Indian occupancy; of conducting Indian relations through agents and of giving presents to the natives. As indicated above some colonies had created small reservations for the remnants of certain groups. This practice—the outstanding feature of reservation policy as practised in English-speaking countries—was not adopted by the Republic until 1853 when it began to segregate the Californian Indians by authorising the President to proclaim five reservations of not more than 25,000 acres each[15].

When the United States was formed the Indian tribes still occupied a huge and solid block of territory from the Appalachian highlands to the Pacific. As the white pioneers moved westwards the Republic purchased occupancy rights from group after group. splitting them from the mass; isolating them from their neighbours and reducing them to islands of ethnic decay like the survivors in the East. The Republic frequently guaranteed the Indians the possession of their remaining lands, but in the face of the encroaching frontiersmen such guarantees were often worthless. As Secretary of War McHenry wrote in 1798, "The arts and practices to obtain Indian land, in defiance of treaties and laws, and at the risk of involving the whole country in war, have become so daring, and received such countenance from

30

Community Housing Scheme for Paiute Indians
Photo: Author

Navajo Indian High School, Navajo Reservation
Photo: Author

Navajo Indians, Window Rock, Arizona
Photo: Navajo Service, U.S. Dept. of Interior

View of Window Rock through Arch, Arizona
Photo: Navajo Service, U.S. Dept. of Interior

persons of prominent influence, as to render it necessary that the means to counteract them should be augmented[16]". It may be noted that the "arts and practices" to rob the Indian of his lands continued until very recent times and that the "persons of prominent influence" included even members of State ministries[17].

Up to the abandonment of treaty-making the United States made 370 agreements with the Indians. Many of these were sincere attempts to protect them in the occupation of worthwhile country but some forced the natives into worthless territory whilst others were "manifestly fraudulent". In Minnesota, in 1866, an agent urged the Chippewas to sign a treaty for the surrender of all their valuable lands, and stated that although the winds of fifty-five winters had blown over his head and silvered it with grey he had never done wrong to a single human being. To this the chief of the Millehao replied, "The winds of fifty-five winters have blown over my head and silvered it with grey. But—they haven't blown my brains away[18]".

In spite of such opposition the Americans continued to dispossess the natives of lands which had been solemnly guaranteed to them by treaty with the result that by 1887 they owned under Government trust only 133,695,000 acres which the allotment system further reduced to 47,311,089 acres by 1930. Much of this remaining land was desert, semi-desert or other land of very little worth. It has been estimated that between 1887 and 1930 the natives lost in value four-fifths of their territory[19].

THE ALLOTMENT POLICY

From 1871 to 1930 the United States attempted to solve the Indian problem first by segregating the Indians and later by the directly opposite policy of merging them in the white community.

In 1871 it terminated the policy of treaty-making and from that year until 1887 concentrated on segregating the Indians in reservations, supplying them with rations and using Government agents to supervise and elevate them[20].

In 1887 the Republic empowered the President to allot reservation land to individual Indians and to create them citizens. The Government made some attempt to guard these allotted lands by placing them in temporary trusteeship. In spite of this provision

31

the whites secured Indian territory faster than ever, while administration was clogged by a fantastically complicated system of heirship.

It has been frequently said, with some truth, that the Dawes Allotment Act of 1887 was passed in order to facilitate the operations of greedy land grabbers, lumber exploiters and railway and mining profiteers, yet the allotment policy was supported by many Americans who genuinely desired to advance the welfare of the natives[21].

Neither the reservation policy nor that of allotment and citizenship proved in any degree effective. "In literally hundreds of cases, white land seekers persuaded Congress or the Indian Service to violate Indian treaties and to ignore Indian land titles". This immorality proved extremely expensive. It bred wars which cost the Government up to a million dollars for the slaughter of each Indian. It produced huge Indian claims for treaty violations or for the mismanagement of tribal funds—the claims outstanding in 1935 being estimated at $1,500,000,000. Worst of all it reduced the Indians to a dispossessed and poverty stricken people—charges upon the Government and plague spots in the white community[22].

In addition to land robbery two important factors contributed to the failure of these American palliatives. Firstly, under the Secretary of War until 1835, and thenceforth under the Secretary of the Interior and Board of Indian Commissioners, the personnel engaged in Indian supervision was frequently neglectful, inefficient or dishonest. Even in its later and better years the service suffered from low entrance standards and salaries, while in the earlier days it was the "dumping ground for the sweepings of the political party in power" and was rightly regarded as corrupt and incompetent. From the very outset good and honest men laboured to improve the Indians, but there were all too many agents who had no regard for their charges, and not a few robbed them of their annuities and goods. In the words of a shocking indictment penned by the Peace Commission of 1867, "The records are abundant to show that agents have pocketed the funds appropriated by the Government and driven the Indians to starvation. Indian wars have originated from this cause[23]". As late as 1901 the Indian agents were still largely political appointees

32

and even in President McKinley's first term only nine agents were allowed to serve out their term and only one was then re-appointed.

Another weakness in the American system of palliatives lay in the payment of annuities. The English, French and Americans all exchanged presents with the Indians, but as time went on the presents made by the Europeans became greater and greater and those made by the Indians less and less. This was partly because the whites began to realise that it was much less costly to bribe the Indians to keep the peace than to pay the cost of warring against them. As the Indian Commissioners reported from California in 1850, "it was cheaper to feed the whole flock for one year than to fight them for one week[24]".

The Indians received a further money income from selling or leasing their lands, and from annuities secured by treaty agreement. Payments of this type were demoralising as productive of degradation and laziness. Reporting on the annuities system the Commissioner of Indian Affairs stated in 1873, "Facts show that ordinarily the Indians, who have received most money in this form, are in the most unfavourable condition for civilisation. The bounty of the Government has pauperised them, and in some cases has tended more to brutalise than to civilise[25]".

In addition to those enumerated above other palliatives were attempted or suggested during the years of treaty-making, reservations, and allotment and citizenship. American Statesmen of the eighteen twenties and thirties had high hopes of segregating the surviving Indians of the East in the vast Indian territory to the west of the Missouri and Mississippi. Presidents Monroe and Adams attempted to secure this objective by inducing the Indians to emigrate voluntarily, but President Jackson used force, as has been related in the story of his brutal treatment of the Cherokees. During these years many of both the northern and southern tribes migrated, but some of the northern peoples of Michigan, Wisconsin and eastern Minnesota were loath to leave their old haunts, and, although they generally agreed to emigrate, they artfully avoided the fulfilment of treaties.

In the earlier years, and particularly before the whites began to stream across the continent, interesting suggestions were made for the creation of an Indian State which should have representation in Congress. A treaty with the Delawares made in 1778, and re-affirmed by Congress as late as 1805, provided for an Indian State, of which the Delaware nation should be head and send representatives to Congress. A treaty of 1785 gave a similar right to representation to the Cherokees. In Jefferson's administration, after the Louisiana Purchase, it was seriously thought that the Indians west of the Mississippi could be confederated into a Protectorate and used to extend the influence of the Republic to the Pacific[26].

Such ideas appear illusory in the light of later events—the flood of trans-Atlantic European emigration and the trans-American thrust of white settlement. The evolution of the American nation could not and should not have been arrested in the interests of a comparatively small number of natives. At the same time the Republic could have treated its Indian wards with greater justice. Congress could have reserved larger areas, protected the natives against land robbery and allotment, fostered tribal government and culture, and paid earlier and greater attention to economic resources, education and health. For several generations the Republic applied only palliatives to the festering sore of Indian problems and applied these palliatives incompetently and ungenerously. American writers have themselves christened these years, "The Treaty Breaking Period", or "The Century of Dishonour". It was not a credit to the United States.

MISSIONS

As in the early English colonies American missionary enterprise was unofficial in type. Nevertheless, in spite of governmental disinterest, Congressional log-rolling, wars, massacres, settler hostility and the enforced transplantation of Christian natives, the missions spread to most of the Indian Groups. Lindquist wrote after his survey of 1919-22 that of 340,000 Indians 80,000 were Protestant and 65,000 Catholic. The various denominations possessed 597 mission stations and 428 churches. Of the reservation Indians only about 46,000 lay outside the scope of religious influence. Unfortunately, however, spiritual vigour cannot be wholly judged from numerical statistics.

During the Republican period a number of denominations

added their weight to the pioneer churches of the colonial days in furthering Christian progress. In addition to the Episcopalians, Roman Catholics, Congregationalists, Lutherans and Moravians, the Presbyterians, Methodists, Baptists, Mormons and other bodies spread Christian missions throughout the United States. Even though the Government was frequently unenthusiastic, it generally gave some support to missionary effort. Thus it granted the denominations land on or near Indian reservations, gave the missioners entry to the reservations and to the government educational institutions, and for many decades afforded some funds for the upkeep of mission schools. President Grant went even further and permitted the denominations to nominate the reservation superintendents, an arrangement which lasted some twelve years. If at the outset the Republic had thus handed the problem to Christian institutions, divided the tribes between these institutions and genuinely supported their efforts the Indians might have been spared much misery as was to some extent the case with those who enjoyed the semi-religious management of Canada or Spain. Unfortunately, however, the innovation was too long delayed. Grant apparently handed the administration to the denominations, partly in the hope of checking their rivalries, but by 1870 these rivalries were unassailably entrenched. The contending and apathetic churches failed to support adequately Grant's unique effort to end "the long period of brutality and corruption". They failed to find sufficient honest and efficient men who would face in the Indian Service low salaries, isolated posts and the bureaucratic rule of the Indian Office, with the result that log-rolling politicians were able to restore their henchmen to office. The Government continued to assist the educational side of missionary effort but even this aroused denominational strife and in 1901 Congress withdrew most of the grants".

Missionary enterprise in the United States, therefore, presents both credits and debits. On the credit side the churches performed an invaluable task by constantly holding up before the American Governments and public the ideal of Christian and moral duties, an ideal which at long last was adopted by the Roosevelt administration with the approval of a large part of the American public. The missions also provided much of the pioneering service in Indian health and education. In the words of the Meriam

Report, "The finest work of the missionaries has unquestionably been the establishment of mission schools for Indian children[28]". In addition to this the early mission workers pioneered the study of Indian languages and customs, translated the scriptures and provided text books for the schools. Without doubt, but for their labours, much knowledge of Indian history, anthropology and ethnology would have been lost.

On the debit side the missions have had to face many criticisms, some of which are soundly based. Unfortunately the denominations cannot deny that their disharmony, rivalry and ceaseless bickerings confused the minds of the unfortunate Indians, brought grave political consequences, and impaired the effective utilisation of Indian funds. Very serious was the failure of many missionaries to study sympathetically and to utilise the religions, cultures and economic systems of the Indian peoples as the foundations of Christian progress. A vital lesson in this connection was the fact that the most successful missionaries—Eliot, Whipple, Hare and others—all based their work on Indian religion and ethics[29].

Serious as are these criticisms perhaps the most serious is the charge that the Christian missions disrupted native culture without substituting in its place any deep Christian spiritual life. The Meriam survey of 1926-28 gave high praise to the majority of missionaries as "earnest, devoted and self-sacrificing" but it considered the situation "somewhat depressing". Without white aid the Indians themselves supported very few churches, mainly through lack of interest. Furthermore, Christianity exercised very little influence on the Indian's family life or home, although it is only fair to quote the opinion of the surveyors that up to that time Governments efforts had had equally slight results[30].

Margaret Mead reached the same conclusion in her study of the Antler group in the Mississippi Valley in 1930. About 1850 these people were converted to Presbyterianism with "most deceptive swiftness", and by 1890 were all nominally Presbyterian. They easily adapted the old beliefs, revamped their prayers and picked up a certain amount of Christian patter, but the new faith had no deep root. Other sects came in "with little success". The Peyote cult flourished for a time as an Indian Church but failed to prove a permanent or absorbing interest. White civilisation destroyed the old institutions and culture and wrecked morality but left no illuminating self-consciousness in place of the old beliefs. The individual members of the primitive society found themselves "floundering in a heterogeneous welter of meaningless unco-ordinated and disintegrating institutions". The change had been too rapid and too great[31]. Once again it must be emphasised that the chief blame for this disintegration does not lie with the churches. In the words of the distinguished American ethnologist, Clark Wissler, "Many harsh charges have been hurled at the missionaries, blaming them for everything seemingly wrong on the reservation, but like most such statements this is going quite too far. Most of the blame should be laid to the drivers of the economic and administrative steam-rollers which crushed down everything before them in spite of the churches, and don't forget the bootlegger plying his trade in the wreckage. In the onward swing of these tragedies the few missteps of the missionary count for little[32]".

MESSIAH RELIGIONS

Down the avenues of history persecuted peoples, like the Jews, have looked for a Messianic Saviour. In this respect the Indians of the United States, the Indians of Canada and the Maoris have proved no exception. In the United States a Delaware Indian prophet appeared as early as 1762, and was followed by the Shawnee prophet, Tenkswatawa, 1795; Smohalla, an Indian of the Columbia plateaux, 1850; Tavibo, the Ute, about 1870; and Wovoka, the Paiute, 1886.

Many of the characteristics of Messiah religions are discernible in the lives of these Indians. Thus the rise of the prophets generally followed some particularly striking step in native decline—in one case a massacre of Christian Indians, in another the disappearance of the buffalo. Like Christ himself, the prophets usually opened their missions in early manhood, several being about thirty years of age. Some again practised "withdrawal and return" like Christ and John the Baptist. For example, Tavibo on several occasions retired into solitude and returned with a message more acceptable to the Utes[33].

The claims which the prophets made generally consisted of a revelation from the Great Spirit who, they said, was angry with the Indians for giving up their ancestral ways and adopting those of the whites. Hence the prophets demanded a return to native culture and a purer life, although Smohalla's ritual and organisation showed Roman Catholic and Mormon influences. Most of the prophets foretold the destruction of the whites in a great cataclysm. The Indians, however, would survive or rise in a resurrection to inhabit a paradise with their ancestors. One or two prophets proclaimed that their religions would protect their followers in war, but in general they advocated peaceful relations both between Indian and Indian and between Indian and white.

Tenkswatawa played an important part in the Indian war of 1811 where, at the battle of Tippecanoe, he stood like Joshua on a neighbouring hill and performed incantations for victory. The prophet's claims that he could protect his followers from American bullets proved false. The Indians were defeated and the prophet discredited. Smohalla, Tavibo and Wovoka later exercised considerable weight in the West with their "Dreamer" and "Ghost Dance" religions, but, although these beliefs greatly excited many of the tribes for a while, they died away after the defeat of Sioux in the rebellion of 1890.

About this time, and for some years later the cult of Peyote made substantial headway. Peyote, a cactus from the Rio Grande, produces when eaten, an effect like hasheesh and promotes visions. Although the local Indians had long known of this the use of Peyote did not spread until the natives had lost the excitemen of the chase, their culture and their tribal organisation. Crowded listlessly on small reservations, they widely accepted the new interest, adapting it to Christian ritual and even using it for Sacramental purposes like the wine in the Holy Communion. As late as 1932 the Meriam Survey stated that the Peyote Church was still flourishing in the south and east of the Indian country and that it was reported to be increasing[34].

DEVELOPMENT OF RESERVATION RESOURCES
AND WELFARE SERVICES

The nineteenth century was "The Century of Dishonour" in the Indian policy of the United States. The opening years of the twentieth century saw improvements. Although the allotment

Navajo Indians, Window Rock, Arizona
Photo: Navajo Service, U.S. Dept. of Interior

Navajo Indians, Window Rock, Arizona (showing locally woven dress)
Photo: Navajo Service, U.S. Dept. of Interior

Fort Defiance Hospital, near Window Rock, Arizona
Photo: Navajo Service, U.S. Dept. of Interior

Navajo Indians, Window Rock (hogan in background)
Photo: Navajo Service, U.S. Dept. of Interior

system continued to rob the Indians of their estate the feeling grew that reservation resources were trust property which the Government should administer for the natives and that the Government should also pay greater attention to welfare services. This change of viewpoint is illustrated by the legislation governing timber cutting, oil production and irrigation on reservation lands and by the growing expenditure on health and education.

In regard to the cutting of timber the Government passed no general Act until that of 1889 which permitted the sale from the reservations of dead and down timber only. In 1910, however, a further Act "heralded an entirely new day in the administration of forested lands on Indian reservations", as it gave the Secretary of the Interior authority to protect reservation timber or to authorise its sale for the benefit of the natives. In the words of J. P. Kinney, "At last Congress had reached the conclusion that the forests on Indian reservations could generally be made to contribute to the support and advancement of the Indians through the sale of the products of the forest instead of the sale of the land with the timber thereon[35]".

From 1909 to 1932 over 7,762,000,000 feet of timber to the value of $33,275,000 were cut from Indian lands, and over $30,500,000 were placed in the Treasury or in bonded banks for the benefit of the Indians from whose reservations the timber came[36].

The development of oil deposits on the reservations followed similar lines. An Act of 1891 permitted the Department of the Interior to lease oil on treaty reservations, and an Act of 1927 provided that the proceeds of oil and gas leases on executive order reservations should inure to the credit of the Indians. Up to 1932-33 the very large sum of $335,000,000 was realised from oil and gas leases for the benefit of the Osage Indians and the Five Civilised Tribes of Oklahoma[37].

Prior to 1910 the United States spent rather more than $5,000,000 on irrigation projects for Indian lands. The value of these irrigation lands and of power and reservoir sites upon them was then rapidly increasing, so that steps were taken to improve the value of these resources. For decades the Indians received over $2,000,000 per annum from farming and grazing leases[38].

Parallel with this twentieth century development and protection of Indian resources came a more liberal American attitude to the promotion of welfare services. The Republic began its care for native health in 1832 when it appropriated a small sum to provide "genuine vaccine matter" but as late as 1880 the whole Indian Service controlled only four hospitals and seventy-seven doctors. During the first decade of the twentieth century, however, health became a major activity and from 1911 onwards the number of hospitals, doctors, nurses and other medical necessities increased substantially[39].

The United States began its educational work for Indians on a small scale about 1819 and its boarding and day schools gradually surpassed those of the missions, which, after 1909, lost practically all government aid. From 1912 onwards the number of Indian children attending the Government schools rose considerably, and the rate of illiteracy in the Indian population over the age of ten declined in most States, although in general it still exceeded that of the rural whites[40].

This progress far from satisfied the American organisations and individuals seeking the welfare of the Indians. They vigorously attacked the allotment system, which continued to rob the natives of their lands, and they criticised with great bitterness other aspects of Indian policy and administration. The Meriam Report of 1926-28 justified many of these allegations, and the Quakers, Commissioner Rhoads and Assistant Commissioner Scattergood instituted important improvements during 1929-31[41]. In 1932 President Franklin D. Roosevelt gained office, and at long last a "New Day" dawned for the United States Indians.

CHAPTER III

THE UNITED STATES

The New Day for Indians

NUMERICAL INCREASE

By 1932 hard and pressing facts were forcing the American Congress and public to adopt a wiser and more generous outlook. It was now quite clear that, despite some doubtful features of the population figures, the persons described as Indians had weathered the shock of the white invasions and were rapidly increasing in numbers. In 1900 the Bureau of Indian Affairs reported a population of 270,544. By 1938 this had risen to 351,878, and by 1942 the growth had become consistently higher than that of the whites, and was greater than that of any other major population group in the country. The Navajos of the South-West, protected by an isolated and arid environment, increased from 10,000 in 1868 to 45,000 in 1938 and to 53,000 in 1943-44. A similar trend was discernible in other areas. Research by Clark Wissler, for example, indicated that a number of tribes had reached their low of population about 1904 and might become "conspicuous in American population". Wissler pointed out that the advances in health service would greatly accelerate the increase so that there soon might be more Indians in the United States and Canada than ever before.

It is impossible to weigh accurately the various causes of this growth. In part it was clearly due to recovery from the initial shock of impact. In part it was due to a more generous attitude by the whites towards Indian health. One suspects, however, that much of the advance was due to an infusion of white blood which produced heterosis or hybrid vigour. The Secretary of the Interior

41

reported in 1938 that from 1930 to 1937 the mixed bloods had increased by 22½% whereas the full bloods had advanced by only 3.5%. "If the present trend continues", said the report, "the day will come—except perhaps in certain reservations in the South-West—when there will be few full-blood American Indians left".

The United States census figures support those of the Indian office. These indicate that the full-blood ratio fell from 62% in 1920 to 52% in 1930, a decline occurring in all States which possessed a large Indian population. Although it has proved most difficult to differentiate accurately between full- and mixed-blood natives for census purposes there is little doubt that the general growth of Indian population is mainly due to an increase in mixed bloods, and this in turn provides strong reason to suspect that a prime factor in Indian recovery is hybrid vigour[1]. (See also Chapter X.)

VIEWS OF THE REFORMERS

As the previous chapter indicated the closing years of the nine-teenth century and the opening years of the twentieth century saw an American change of heart, a process which the Meriam Survey of 1926-28 greatly accelerated. John D. Rockefeller, Jr., proposed this famous survey and did much to finance it. The Government welcomed the proposal and the Institute of Government Research appointed Lewis Meriam to conduct it. The report, which was published in 1928 under the title of "The Problem of Indian Administration", was "comprehensive, factual, fearless and fundamental". It provided the basis for "the beginning of a new era in Indian administration"[2].

Meriam and his colleagues said much which justified the critics and showed conclusively that the policy of allotment and citizenship had proved disastrous. They stated that white civilisation had largely destroyed the primitive culture and living resources without adjusting the natives to the new social and economic environment. The allotment system had permitted the tribes to dispose of much of their land, and this together with rationing had produced pauperisation. The majority of Indians had become poor —even extremely poor—with the result that inadequate diet and shocking conditions of housing and sanitation had reduced their health considerably below that of the whites. The report also disclosed that, mainly through lack of government funds, the health and educational services were largely ineffective. Health work was insufficient. There was no broad or well-considered educational programme. The care of Indian children was "grossly inadequate" in the boarding schools, which were notable for their crowded dormitories, bad diet and neglect of the children's health. Both the Government service and the missions lacked trained personnel and had undermined instead of strengthened Indian morale and community life. The Indian Service had done some good work but it had failed to prevent white exploitation of Indian property. Finally in the opinion of the surveyors the Federal administration, State administrations and the missions were all lacking in co-operative spirit'.

As noted above this damning indictment led to the improved administration of Rhoads and Scattergood, who, realising the necessity of working with the Indians rather than for them, made cautious experiments in the right direction and began to repurchase for the Indians small amounts of land'. A complete programme of reform awaited, however, the election of President Roosevelt in 1932. Roosevelt was anxious to promote Indian welfare. This policy of liberal expenditure to counteract the depression provided the means, and in Harold L. Ickes, his Secretary of the Interior, and John Collier, whom he created Commissioner of Indian Affairs, the President found exceptionally capable agents. Collier had long been a caustic critic of certain aspects of Indian policy and administration and fully appreciated the weaknesses which the Meriam report had disclosed. Nevertheless, although he was bent on revolutionary changes, he was prepared to build on past progress where that progress had been sound. He realised that the Indians were no longer a vanishing race. He considered that they had undergone a temporary decline through the sweeping alteration of their society at the hands of the whites, and he was certain that they could be restored and would make a valuable contribution to American life. As Collier pointed out to Congress the historic Indian policy had systematically destroyed the Indian estate and self-support; it had wrecked the Indian way of life and thought; it had supplanted Indian customs and institutions by the rigid and bureaucratic discipline of the Indian office. The problem was, however, not insoluble.

WHITE SETTLERS AND NATIVE PEOPLES

Indian property must no longer pass to the whites; Indian organisation must be encouraged and assisted; Indian family life must be respected and reinforced; Indian culture must be appreciated, used, and brought into the stream of American culture as a whole. If this were done the Indian race would grow and live[5].

The reformers realised that as the vast majority of Indians were primary producers the key of their economic rehabilitation was the land. Here, from 1887 to 1933 the whites had used the allotment policy to deprive them of 90,000,000 acres and to create grave consequential problems such as erosion in the 50,000,000 acres remaining. In 1930, for example, the large Navajo reservation was stocked to double its capacity. Mountain slopes had been denuded to bedrock of their soil; great and rapidly growing gullies were devastating the best valleys. As the author himself saw, much of this country was being eroded into the Colorado river and was rapidly filling the Boulder dam. The new policy therefore was designed to restore, integrate and increase the shattered Indian estate and make it usable and used by the natives. It also attempted to prevent the further dissipation of Indian Trust funds by which the capital secured from land sales had been squandered in "coddling" such as rations and doles. Indian resources—augmented by a Government Trust fund and other assistance—were now to be used to foster irrigation, agriculture, pasturing, forestry and similar productive activities conducted by the Indians themselves.

The reformers linked to this land policy a scientific attempt to re-establish Indian social organisation and culture. The historic policy had wrecked and often deliberately wrecked the Indian religions, culture, and social organisation by compulsory Christianity and misdirected efforts in education. Consequently, as Margaret Mead had demonstrated in her researches on the Antlers, the Indians only too often suffered chronic ill-health, combined with the results of exposure, inadequate clothing and insufficient nourishment; while their social situation was "a caricature of any genuine educational adjustment to the demands made by white contact[6]".

In direct contradiction to this the new policy was designed to re-establish tribal government, organisation and self-respect; to permit religious freedom; to restore the native languages,

44

THE NEW DAY FOR INDIANS

philosophy, poetry, music, arts and crafts; and to re-orient education, particularly by concentrating on practical matters rather than academic questions. Above all it was to be the Indians themselves who were to conduct their New Day. Not only were they to restore voluntarily and to guide their tribal governments, they were to form, as soon as possible, a substantial part of the personnel of the Indian Office[7].

THE INDIAN REORGANISATION ACT

In June, 1934, the Reformers gained most of their way when Congress passed the Indian Reorganisation Act, frequently called the Wheeler-Howard Act. The basis of the new policy was generous finance. From 1930 to 1932 the annual Treasury expenditure on the Indians had increased from $18,879,935 to $27,030,046, and had then fallen in 1934 to $18,966,545. Under the new act it increased by 1939 to $33,519,762. Over the same period the expenditure from Indian Trust funds fell from $4,726,780 in 1930 to $1,851,109 in 1939. In 1939 the principal items of Government expenditure were: Education, $10,253,190; health, $5,432,000; general construction, $4,975,712; roads and bridges, $3,000,000; general purposes, $2,830,392; Indian support, $2,760,500; industrial assistance, $1,931,000; irrigation and water development, $1,317,196. This total of $33,000,000 represented an average expenditure of approximately $89 on each of the 372,497 Indians of the United States and Alaska. This expenditure far exceeded the contemporary outlay of Canada, New Zealand, and Australia on their natives per capita[8].

TRIBAL GOVERNMENT

The basis of the New Day policy was the effort to restore tribal organisation, community spirit and family life so that the Indians themselves would regain their former pride and self-sufficient life. What use asked the reformers were missions which destroyed the Indian religions while failing to Christianise, or boarding schools which wrecked the homes, or hospitals which treated disease but did not touch the underlying factors of poverty, squalor and psychosis[9]?

Under the Reorganisation and following acts, over 250,000

45

Indians, some 75% of the total in the United States and Alaska, adopted tribal constitutions and secured charters as corporations, which enabled them to promote economic enterprises and contract with States and counties for the enjoyment of local public welfare services. These arrangements gave them a legal basis for civil organisation comparable with that of the white communities. The response of the Indians to this opportunity for home rule "was enthusiastic, even overwhelming". As early as September, 1938, 85 tribes, with a population of 99,813, had held elections and adopted constitutions and 59 of these tribes had secured charters of incorporation. By the same year the Indian Service was employing 3627 natives—about half its total personnel. Of these more than 40% were full bloods and over 70% ranged from half breeds to full blood Indians.[10]

LAND POLICY

Such financial progress did not satisfy the reformers but it certainly made possible a "New Day for Indians". Where the tribes accepted the Reorganisation Act by vote its provisions debarred the further allotment of reservation lands; extended trust periods until Congress directed otherwise; provided that allotted and heirship lands could revert voluntarily to tribal ownership, and set up machinery for the purchase of land on behalf of landless Indians whose numbers were then estimated at one hundred thousand[11]. By the close of 1938 the Government had spent $2,207,145 in re-purchasing 159,770 acres, had restored to the reservations 392,487 acres which had been opened for sale or entry, and had plans in hand for the re-purchase or restoration of several million additional acres. In the year 1938 the Government leased for the use of the Navajos alone 499,523 acres[12].

The Department of Indian Affairs made all possible efforts to encourage the Indians to utilise their lands, and also attempted to extend and develop the irrigated and afforested areas. The Reorganisation and other acts provided a revolving credit of $12,000,000 for loans to Indian Co-operatives which made advances to individuals for the acquisition of livestock, equipment and machinery.

The office pressed on with irrigation projects so that irrigated lands owned or leased by Indians increased from 213,000 to

46

Poor Navajo sheep on poor, over-stocked land
Photo: Navajo Service, U.S. Dept. of Interior

Navajo Lumbering
Photo: Navajo Service, U.S. Dept. of Interior

Sewing on the day school sewing machine, Crystal, New Mexico
Photo: Navajo Service, U.S. Dept. of Interior

Soil Erosion—Navajo Reservation.
Photo: Navajo Service, U.S. Dept. of Interior

THE NEW DAY FOR INDIANS

303,000 acres. More timber lands were operated for native benefit under expert supervision, and the Indians themselves operated fourteen saw mills.

The Indian division of that splendid organisation, the Civilian Conservation Corps, employed 6,907 Indians on water supply, fencing, and the control of erosion and fire—a work which produced a better distribution of stock on the Indian range. These policies produced substantial increases in the acreage cultivated, the production of cereals, and the income from cattle, sheep and goats[13].

ARTS AND CRAFTS

As part of their policy of restoring Indian pride of life, and of raising Indian living standards, the reformers effected very important and interesting work in reviving native arts and crafts. The Indian office established an Arts and Crafts Board which worked to guide, stimulate and protect native manufactures and to increase the market for such manufactures. Much Indian handcraft was both beautiful and useful, for example, Navajo, Hopi and Pueblo silverware, Navajo textiles, Paiute basketware and Pueblo pottery—but these industries were suffering from exploitation and from Japanese imitation. Indian products were now stamped as genuine by the Government and sold at just prices through Government agencies, and many exhibitions such as the magnificent Indian section of the Golden Gate International Exposition of 1939 were arranged[14].

HEALTH AND EDUCATION

The New Day for Indians brought revolutionary progress in health and education, the health expenditure increasing from $3,281,800 in 1934 to $5,432,000 in 1939. By the latter year the Indian Office was supporting 81 general hospitals and 14 tuberculosis sanatoria. The personnel included over three hundred administrative, special and general doctors, nearly six hundred nurses and some 900 other employees. Dental treatment was supplied for over 27,000 Indians. The Service carried out a great deal of work in health education and a school was established to train Indian women as nurse aids. Progress was made with a vaccination programme to control tuberculosis, the greatest Indian scourge. Research was also conducted on trachoma, and immunisation programmes against contagious diseases such as chicken pox, measles and whooping cough made headway. Co-operation with State health services was strengthened[15].

In education the reformers made sweeping changes. In the past the Indian schools had very largely concentrated on the conventional white academic programme or on vocational training for urban industrialised labour. Moreover, great emphasis had been laid upon boarding schools which had broken down tribal and family tries by separating the community and parents from the children. The new policy diversified its efforts according to the various localities in which the natives lived. In areas where the Indians were assimilating rapidly the children attended the ordinary public schools. On the contrary for tribes such as the Navajos, where 90% of the population neither understood nor spoke English, the programme complied with the natives' economic needs. On the Navajo reservation, to take one example, 42 new day schools were founded and additions made to existing ones. The schools concentrated on health and home training; on the use of reservation resources; on preparation for participation in civic life and for the development of manual skill appropriate to reservation opportunities. In the first year of the new programme the attendance was increased by 1813 children. The American Indian is as devoted a parent as any other, and the boarding schools, which enforced the separation of parent and child, rapidly declined. The new policy also advanced adult education which it cleverly combined with the juvenile work of the schools. As the author saw in many of the fine new schools in the Indian West and South-West an Indian day school now contains classrooms and workshops for both adult and juvenile instruction, living quarters for the staff, a kitchen for preparing the daily lunch and for instructing both parents and children, a clinic for the use of the field nurse and travelling doctor, a laundry for community use in areas where water for domestic purposes is scarce and shower bath and toilet facilities for the use of both adults and pupils. In some instances the number of adults using these facilities exceeds the number of children.

Indian education still faces many difficulties, particularly amongst the nomadic peoples. In some cases progress has been ill-considered and hasty and large sums of money have been wasted. Nevertheless the Americans have made great advances. "The problems are very real but there is every confidence that sincere and effective efforts are being made to solve them[16]".

During 1939 the author visited a considerable number of hospitals and schools in Nevada, Arizona and New Mexico, and in many cases was greatly impressed with the fine modern buildings and equipment. It, was clear that the Americans were offering excellent educational facilities both for children and adults and that they were designing these facilities to meet the practical and varying needs of different types of tribal life. To take one instance, the authorities no longer pursued the ridiculous practice of training Indian girls for white housekeeping. They were being trained for domestic life in hogans and to cater for different numbers of people to meet future family needs.

In 1938 the United States Government spent $10,048,525 on education. The number of children enrolled was 65,166 so that the expenditure was $154 per child, although deduction should be made for the cost of adult and other services. Nearly all Indian children attended Federal institutions, the total attending State and Mission schools being only 7000.

SCIENTIFIC PROGRESS

In all this work — social or economic—the reformers sought scientific assistance by enlisting the help of the Bureau of American Ethnology, the Soil Conservation Service and other organisations. The Phelps-Stokes inquiry on the Navajo Indians gave a particularly clear account of the scientific motives and methods of the New Dealers. Until recently, said the report, the concern of anthropologists for the customs and culture of the Indians was "largely of antiquarian and museum interest. Gradually the scientific concern was leavened by a sense of altruistic responsibility for Indian heritage and Indian life". The Commissioner of Indian Affairs, vividly conscious of the renaissance in Indian life, proclaimed his devotion to the Indian heritage, and with characteristic energy and idealism issued orders, employed anthropologists, and almost passionately championed the new concern[17].

WHITE SETTLERS AND NATIVE PEOPLES

To take only one example the reformers faced in the problem of soil erosion a menace which was rapidly threatening the civilisation of the United States. On the one hand they contended with the indifference of the white public and on the other with the ignorance of a primitive people who opposed in the case of the Navajos, the reduction of stock on a range where 1,250,000 sheep units were wrecking country which could carry only 500.000. Nevertheless, in spite of the bitter resentment caused by essential reductions, the reformers were gaining by 1939 some better feeling and co-operation.

Amongst many minor but important scientific projects one can cite the sheep breeding laboratory at Fort Wingate. This laboratory was designed to develop for the Navajos a type of sheep which could compete in the commercial markets, provide a good feeder lamb, have a carcase with a maximum of meat for home consumption and provide a wool which was suitable for Navajo weavers. When the writer visited the station in 1939 it was thought that this splendid laboratory would secure the desired results by mating the native sheep with a breed such as the Romney or Corriedale.

THE MISSIONS

Prior to the New Day Indian children enrolled in the Government schools were forced to join a Christian sect; to receive instruction from that sect, and to attend its church. On many reservations native ceremonies were flatly forbidden, no matter how harmless their nature[18]. Collier, on the contrary, instructed Reservation Superintendents to insist on the fullest constitutional liberty for the Indians in all matters affecting religious observance or culture. Later regulations granted denominations and missionaries, including the representatives of Indian religions, the privilege of using rooms or other facilities in the boarding schools provided that the parents of the pupils requested the services of such missionaries. In the day schools Indian parents could obtain for their children excuse from religious instruction.

This change naturally produced some misunderstanding. There were strong differences of opinion as to whether or not certain Indian customs helped or hindered the adjustment of tribal life

50

to American standards, while some missionaries felt that their presence at Government schools was not welcomed. Also the missionaries varied greatly in type. Some were so evangelistic that they took no interest in welfare and confined their efforts to emotional appeals for conversion. On the other hand a growing majority became more and more aware of the intimate relationship of health, economics, housing and recreation to the well-being of the individual and community. Missionary training laid increasing weight upon a knowledge of rural life and agriculture, urban life and industry, anthropology, racial heritage and youth adjustment. Emphasis was also placed upon the necessity for working with the Indians rather than for them—an outlook corresponding with that of the New Dealers.

The Phelps-Stokes inquiry on the Navajos gave an important and impartial view of the missionary situation in that region. The report stated that American churches annually contributed the generous sum of $300,000 to the Navajos missions alone and employed 250 missionaries, including 64 Navajos, to assist in providing health and education services for thousands of Indians. In a more critical spirit the survey complained of the narrow evangelism of some of the missionaries and urged that an, onward and expanding conception of Christian service should be adopted for the sake of the Indians.

As in many cases over a long period of history the Roman Catholic missionaries created a particularly favourable impression. In the words of the report, "The services of the Franciscan Fathers, Sisters and Brothers to the Navajo Indians reflect the centuries of Catholic missionary experience and devotion in all the continents of the earth. Among the unique qualities of Catholic missions is that of the definiteness and persistence of their objectives and standards. Their historical church has transmitted to their missionaries the long time understanding of human affairs[19]".

On this matter the author was told an interesting story on one reservation. The authorities were unable to attract the Indians to a fine new hospital unless they secured the support of the tribal medicine men. They therefore arranged a dedication in which both various denominations and the medicine men would share.

WHITE SETTLERS AND NATIVE PEOPLES

The Roman Catholics alone had the wisdom and breadth of vision to agree to participate with the Indians.

In spite of various criticisms the conclusions of the Phelps-Stokes survey were hopeful. It was true that there had been friction in the past, but a remarkable progress had recently been made in the development of co-operation between the Government and the Missions[20].

A VISIT TO THE RESERVATIONS DURING THE "NEW DAY"

During 1939 the Secretary of the Interior, Mr. Harold L. Ickes and Mr. Commissioner Collier kindly made it possible for the author to travel extensively over the Paiute, Hopi, Navajo, Pueblo and Mescalero Apache Reservations, superintendents motoring him several thousand miles. The enthusiasm of the New Dealers and of service personnel and some of the results achieved were very impressive, particularly to an Australian who had witnessed in several regions the meanness and neglect exhibited by his own country to its aborigines.

The tour of inspection covered such matters as range conservation and control of erosion, irrigation, agricultural, pastoral, timber, community and housing projects, hospitals, schools and administrative centres, many of which were very recent and up-to-date, while all were being conducted on modern and scientific lines.

Amongst dozens of examples of recent scientific progress one can quote a Civilian Conservation Corps camp of over 400 young Indians whom the service was training in automobile mechanics, road-making, irrigation work and forest protection. The camp was completely motorised and mobile, and, in case of fire or flood, could move to any threatened point immediately. Another scientific development was the production of broadcasts by Navajos in Navajo to Navajos on such practical matters as sheep control. These broadcasts were given from the magnificent agency at Window Rock and were heard by Indians collected in groups all over the reservations.

One of the most remarkable achievements seen was the rehabilitation of the Mescalero Apaches whom F. W. Seymour, a

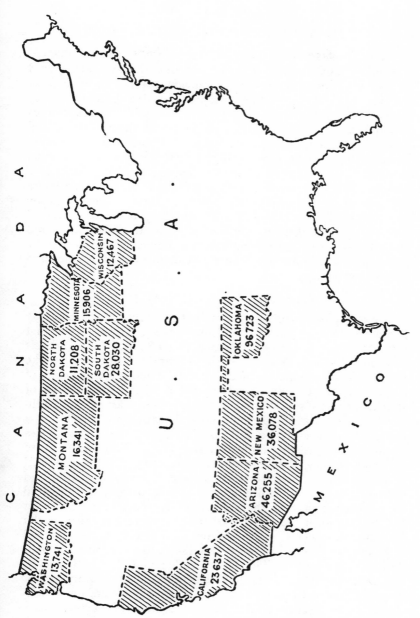

U.S. States containing more than 10,000 Indians in 1938. Statistics from official publications.

bitter critic of the New Day, had formerly described as demonstrating a combination of arrogance and importunity which should be met by a long-term policy of individualisation. In 1930 these Indians had failed as sheep people and had become agency hangers-on—"discouraged and broken in spirit". In 1936 they adopted a tribal constitution and charter of incorporation, and entered enthusiastically on a rehabilitation programme. Turning from sheep to cattle they borrowed $242,000 from the Government for cattle equipment and a housing scheme which gave each family a neat wooden cottage, a cattle barn, a chicken house and a privy. In 1935 the cattle income of these Indians was only $18,000; by 1937 it was $101,000, and they had already repaid $58,000 of their debt to the Government. In 1939 one found them to all appearances a contented, well-housed, and even prosperous group, utilising the resources of their beautiful wooded and mountainous reservation[21].

OPPOSITION TO THE NEW DAY

The sweeping changes wrought by the Collier policy naturally produced strong resentment and opposition[22]. It was alleged that the reformers acted too rapidly; that they offended Indian leaders and missions and that the young scientists introduced to the service had no experience of the natives. There were elements of truth in some of these allegations but a critical examination of attacks such as Flora Warren Seymour's "Thunder in the South-West" discloses much partisanship and biassed criticism[23].

Far more authoritative and convincing was the Phelps-Stokes report which gave the impression that those who came to curse remained to pray. While the inquiry condemned the enthusiasts' critical errors of haste, their impatience in experimentation and their intolerance of Indian apathy and ignorance, it supported almost every aspect of the Collier policy and administration in the dealings with the greatest of Indian reservations—that of the Navajos. Its concluding tribute should be read, learnt, marked and inwardly digested by other English-speaking peoples in their dealings with natives. The report ended as follows: "However, and most emphatically, the final conclusion of the inquiry cannot be justly limited to past errors and dangers. There are many difficulties to be overcome. But plans and trends of extraordinary

Navajo child Trachoma patients, Fort Defiance, Arizona
Photo: Navajo Service, U.S. Dept. of Interior

Paiute School Girls, Bishop, California
Photo: Phillips Studios, Bishop, California

*Roman Catholic
School, Vancouver,
British Columbia*

Photo: Author

*Indian Totem
Poles, British
Columbia*

Photo: Author

THE NEW DAY FOR INDIANS

value have been initiated. Results of continuing usefulness to the Navajos are being achieved. With seemingly almost reckless daring the soil conservationists are successfully combating the ruthless devastation of wind and water erosion, formerly believed to be subject only to divine providence or at any rate of an uncontrollable nature. Health and sanitation are limiting the ravages of diseases. Education in the simple essentials of daily life is being extended with marked effectiveness to children and adults in the lowly communities where they dwell. However pronounced the difference as to methods and expenditure, the inspiring fact remains that the United States of America is demonstrating an idealism in services for the Navajo Indians that may in time save the self-respect of the American people in their relationships to the uniquely important minority of our nation[24]". It appeared that this fine tribute applied with equal force to practically every reservation visited—Navajo, Hopi, Paiute, Apache or Pueblo.

INDIANS IN THE WORLD WAR

Although the subject lies beyond the scope of this book it may perhaps be suggested that an answer to the critics of the New Day possibly lies in the record of the Indians in the World War. By 1944 20,000 natives were serving in the armed forces of their country and their sacrifices were recorded in a heavy list of killed, wounded, missing and prisoners. The first American general to fall was an Indian—Clarence L. Tinker, lost at Midway. His nephew, Lieut. E. E. Tinker, an Osage, was reported missing over Bulgaria, and this Indian had three brothers serving.

Indian heroism was commemorated by a splendid list of decorations for gallant exploits on sea, land and in the air. These decorations included a Congressional Medal of Honour (the American Victoria Cross); 12 Distinguished Flying Crosses; 19 Air Medals (one with fourteen clusters); 17 Silver Stars; one Distinguished Service Cross; one Soldiers' Medal; and 58 Purple Hearts. Men and women from all parts of the Indian country shared these awards. The list included names from Alaska in the far north to Arizona and New Mexico in the far south, and east and west from Wisconsin, Oklahoma and the Dakotas to Oregon, Washington and California[25].

WHITE SETTLERS AND NATIVE PEOPLES

An analysis of the proportion of white blood in these heroic Indians would be of considerable value. The list certainly included many full bloods such as William Nelson—a full blood member of the once persecuted Paiutes. Nelson won the Silver Star "for conspicuous gallantry and intrepidity in action" while still under 20 years of age[26]. Lieut. Ernest Childers, who won the Congressional Medal of Honour for "supreme bravery in Italy" was a three-quarters Creek of Oklahoma.

Critics might assert that the Indian record was due to their alleged war-like nature. Such criticism might apply to peoples such as the Apaches and Navajos. Many tribes like the Paiutes and Pueblos, however, fought only when driven to desperation by white aggression and treaty-breaking. It may well be suspected that many educated Indians served so splendidly, not only in gratitude for recent American policies, but because they realised only too clearly that the Germans and Japanese were threatening to repeat the horrors which their ancestors had suffered at the hands of the English-speaking peoples[27].

On the home front the Indians showed that the New Day had progressed sufficiently for them to make a substantial contribution to the natives' needs. Large numbers of Indians left the reservations for the armed services and various war industries. Nevertheless, although the reservation population decreased from 230,238 in 1938 to 224,852 in 1942 the Indian population enrolled increased from 351,878 to 376,580, the Navajos alone reaching a total of 53,000 which included 2,500 in the services and 9,500 war workers. The Indians remaining on the reservations greatly increased their farm lands, irrigation areas, and sales of agricultural and pastoral products. Indeed the lands farmed increased by more than 100%, and the receipts from farm products by nearly the same figure. This was a remarkable achievement particularly as it was accomplished in wartime when progress was hampered by a reduction in Congressional appropriations and when Indian administration was divided between the centres of Washington and Chicago[28].

THE MINORITY PROBLEM

In January, 1945, John Collier resigned the office of Commissioner of Indian Affairs after eleven and a half years of strenuous and successful service, which gained a glowing tribute from President Roosevelt as an outstanding achievement in one of the most important and difficult offices of the Federal Government. Mr. Collier's chief object in resigning was to give his time to the chairmanship of a new and wider organisation—the Inter-American Institute of the Indian. This he helped to establish primarily for the benefit of the great Indian masses in Mexico and other republics of the Western hemisphere. Few will dispute his opinion that ethnic and other relationships between sovereign and dependent peoples in the Americas must be met on democratic lines if peace was to be maintained after the war. The work which Mr. Collier had successfully initiated and carried through for the comparatively small number of United States Indians had spread to a far wider sphere[29].

For good or for ill the American New Dealers effected a fundamental revolution in Indian policy. They swung the Republic from an avowed attempt to absorb the Indians as quickly as possible to a policy of rehabilitating them as vigorous minority groups. In spite of the New Deal policy many of these groups will almost certainly continue the process of assimilation, but others—such as the Apaches, the Pueblos and the rapidly increasing Navajos—may well expand like the Indian elements in some of the Latin American republics.

An examination of this process and its possible results would involve a discussion of many scientific problems: the differing qualities of human groups; the comparative qualities of the highly mixed white Americans as compared with the Indians; the value of Indian culture as a permanent feature of United States civilisation; and many ethnic political and other problems associated with minorities. The New Dealers did not, however, act from blind philanthropy. They deliberately sought to continue and even to increase an unabsorbed minority because they believed, almost fanatically, that the Indian was a worthwhile factor in American life.

Those who hold similar views as to the value of the Canadian Indian, the Maori and the Australian aborigine should know the magnificent words penned by Franklin D. Roosevelt almost at the close of his life, "During the last twelve years, more than ever before," wrote the President, "we have tried to impress upon the Indians that we are indeed Christian; that we not only avow but practice the qualities of freedom and liberty and opportunity that are explicit in our institutions. We have come to treat the Indian as a human being, as one who possesses the dignity and commands the respect of his fellow human beings. In encouraging him to pursue his own life and continue his own culture we have added to his worth and dignity. We have protected the Indian in his property rights while enlarging them. We have opened the window of his mind to the extent that we have had money with which to do it. We have improved his medical service, we have enlarged his intellectual programme. We have protected him in his religion and we have added to his stature[30]". Even those who see and fear the dangers of unassimilated minorities cannot challenge the fine objective and achievements of the New Day for the Indians of the United States.

CHAPTER IV

Canada - The Moving Frontier

The progress and results of the white invasions of Canada generally resemble those in the United States but there are some important contrasts. Canada and the United States are both vast regions comprising Eastern Highlands, Central Plains, Western Plateaux and Pacific coasts. The Republic possesses the gateways of the Hudson and Mississippi; Canada that of the St. Lawrence. The United States has hot deserts in the South-West. Canada has cold deserts in the North. In both countries the chief white incomers swept from east to west subduing and degrading the Indians to the shores of the Pacific. In both countries the deserts afforded some protection to the natives, but the standards of Indian culture and the strength of Indian revival were most striking in the deserts of the south.

The white invaders and their methods also showed both similarities and contrasts. The principal conquerors of Indian territory in the United States were the Spanish, British and French and the people of the young American Republic. The principal invaders of Canadian Indian territory were the French, the British and the citizens of the Dominion of Canada, together with the Russians who exercised a lengthy but comparatively slight influence on the North-West Pacific coast[1]. It seems fair to say that on the whole the British and French Home Governments and the Dominion of Canada treated the Indians of the North more justly and humanely than the British colonists and the earlier generations of American republicans treated the Indians further south, although no people achieved Spanish missionary standards until comparatively recent days. The main cause of this difference was undoubtedly the fur trade, which, while important in the United States, was for many decades the life blood of Canada and its colonists. The Indian, his squaw, and his methods of life and transport were vital to the traffic in the cold north, whereas in the agricultural and pastoral United States the natives were largely a hindrance and even a menace to white colonisation[2]. Moreover, the numbers both of invaders and invaded were comparatively small in the north; the shock of contact was less severe, and there was much racial mixture, particularly between the Indians and the French. For these reasons the white invasions reduced the number of Canadian Indians from a possible Pre-Columbian figure of 220,000 to 93,260 full bloods and 34,481 "half-breeds" in 1901—a total of 127,741, which represents a fall of 42%. In the United States the white invaders reduced the Indians from a Pre-Columbian figure of perhaps 840,000 to about 240,000, including mixed bloods in 1910—a fall of about 71%. Although much work has been done on Pre-Columbian population figures these are far from certain, while present day difficulties in defining an Indian, and other problems of census-taking, make it necessary to regard even recent figures with caution. Nevertheless statistics tend to support the thesis that geographical factors and white policies resulted in a higher percentage of Indian survival in Canada than in the United States[3].

PRIMITIVE INDIAN LIFE

Authorities divide Canada into four main geographical regions: the country to the east of the Great Lakes; the Prairies; the Pacific slope and the far north[4]. These regions can be further sub-divided into areas which exhibit local varieties of climate, fauna and flora. Hence the primitive Indians, living close to the land, differed to some extent in social organisation, religious beliefs and economic life.

At the beginning of the white invasions Eastern Canada was inhabited by two types of natives whose mode of living showed marked contrasts. In Southern Ontario and on the banks of the St. Lawrence were the Iroquois, who, about 1200 A.D., had penetrated northwards from Pennsylvania or the Ohio River, where they had learnt the cultivation of corn, beans, squash and tobacco from tribes still farther south. While they had not developed the comparatively advanced cultures of the Aztecs or Incas they lived a settled agricultural life in villages of shed-like houses. They also evinced considerable political genius which enabled them to subordinate their village communities to tribal units and to confederate these tribal units in nations "governed by representative councils and guided by truely democratic ideals⁵".

The second type of Indian in Eastern Canada was the Algonkians, who were scattered over the upland areas of Ontario and Quebec. These were hunting and fishing folk who moved about with canoes and toboggans and had little dealings with the Iroquois, save for some occasional exchange of furs for luxuries such as tobacco and corn. To the west of these peoples lay the Indians of the Great Plains whose primitive life is little known, for the only early visitor—the youth Kelsey, who journeyed amongst them about 1690—left but a slight account. Maize culture ascended the Red River to the boundaries of Manitoba, but was impossible on the prairies or western plateaux as the crop required a longer ripening season than was normal in these regions. Hence the prairie tribes, such as the Blackfoot and Gros Ventre, were wandering hunters who pursued the innumerable herds of buffalo and antelope with primitive weapons. The prairies were so vast and the game so plentiful that these wandering groups of foot hunters had little reason to fight, and in all probability rarely encountered one another.

The Canadian North and North-West, an area of cold temperate forest, also contained a hunting civilisation. The rigorous climate prohibited agriculture. Fishing was a strenuous occupation, and the mainstay of life was the caribou, which provided food, tents and clothing. Owing to its solitary habits Indians hunted this animal in small groups. Life was arduous. The chase brought plenty or starvation, and spiritual and material poverty characterised this hard region. Very different conditions prevailed on the Pacific coast where the groups, moving south from Asia and Alaska, drifted into a cul-de-sac, rich with timber, fish and fruits. There the Indians evolved an amazingly rich culture. They built immense plank houses and carved huge totem poles decorated with fantastic designs. They organised their society as nobles, commoners and slaves, while the comparatively easy life permitted elaborate religious and secular entertainments. These included great feasts called potlatches, which were marked by the

WHITE SETTLERS AND NATIVE PEOPLES

presentation of costly gifts. As, however, the recipients had to better these gifts at subsequent feasts the system was really a primitive form of banking. In woodwork, art and drama, these Pacific tribes such as the Haida and Tlinkit, far surpassed all other Canadian Indians⁶.

FRENCH AND ENGLISH

As in the United States the conquerors swept from east to west with many white evils proceeding the main invasions. The Norsemen were certainly in the North-East about 1000 A.D., and later European discoveries in this area may have narrowly pre-dated Columbus' voyage of 1492. At any rate John Cabot re-ported the abundance of cod on the Newfoundland banks as early as 1497, and English, French and Portugese fisherfolk, land-ing on American shores to dry fish or to collect bait, were soon in contact with the Indians. The fur trade, particularly in the im-portant beaver fur, began at any early date, and, when Jaques Cartier explored the St. Lawrence region for France in 1534, he found evidence of earlier fur trading. Cartier initiated a period of individual and company enterprise which lasted until the French Crown took control in 1663 under a regime which the British terminated in 1760.

Cartier landed at Carpe in New Brunswick and took possession of the country for Francis I. He later explored the St. Lawrence up to the Indian villages of Quebec and Montreal. From this time onwards French traders and missionaries roamed over an immense territory in an heroic period of romantic trade and ad-venture. In 1604 the French established the Port Royal Settle-ment in Acadia (Nova Scotia) and in 1608 Champlain founded Quebec. Colonisation followed, first under company manage-ment, and after 1663, when the Crown revoked the Charter of the French Canadian Fur Trading Company, by royal enter-prise. France sent out strong governors and many good colonists. Some of her immigrants were Norman peasant farmers, "habi-tants" who settled along the St. Lawrence in "seigneuries" under small overlords. These people, although comparatively few in numbers, possessed the essentials of nationhood—religion, ad-ministration, agriculture, craftsmanship and commerce. Mean-while French explorers—"voyageurs", missionaries and traders—

THE MOVING FRONTIER

penetrated far into the Indian territory. La Salle reached the upper Mississippi and descended the river to its mouth and lower basin which became the French territory of Louisiana at the end of the 17th century. By the middle of the 18th century the French had fought or traded their way up the St. Lawrence and Ottawa Rivers and had established a chain of forts around the Great Lakes. They had crossed the Red river and were trading on the Lake of Woods and Lake Winnipeg. They established settlements and forts along the Mississippi and Ohio, and began to push up the tributary rivers to the back doors of English colonies such as Pennsylvania, Virginia and the Carolinas, hemming the British in on the west and encouraging the Indians to attack their villages and farms.

By this time, however, the British had become far stronger than the French. Occupying the eastern coast from 1607 onwards they seized New York and the Hudson river gap from the Dutch in 1664, and consolidated their settlements, which were long protected from the French by the neutrality of the powerful Iroquois whose territories lay between the rival Europeans. Meanwhile Britain and France waged war along the coast and British seapower gained the day. By the Treaty of Utrecht, Nova Scotia and Newfoundland, the outworks of the French Canadian citadel, and Hudson Bay, the great fur trading region of the north-west were assured to Britain. By the middle of the eighteenth century the British had over a million settlers in their colonies as against only 80,000 people in the French possessions. When the inevitable struggle came on the Ohio and St. Lawrence the issue was never really in doubt. The peace of 1763 saw France no longer a power of any consequence in the North American continent'.

FRENCH-INDIAN CONTACTS

In the early trading stage of their invasion the French treated the Indian tribes as independent nations, and the Indians on their part usually agreed to alliances and permitted the French to establish trading posts. Later, when colonisation was more strongly marked, the French regarded the eastern natives as subject peoples, and organised their more closely settled territories as "seigneuries" where the Indians were christianised, educated, and granted titles to the land which they actually cultivated. This was a policy of peaceful penetration, largely effected by fur trading and mission establishments.

The French invaders were comparatively few in numbers and lived an extremely simple life. They freely borrowed Indian ideas; cultivated Indian crops, such as beans, pumpkins and tobacco, and adopted articles of Indian dress and methods of transport. Living close to the land, and with little education, the French pioneers differed only superficially from the Indians and mingled with them freely. Indian girls, trained in convents, made excellent wives for isolated farmers and traders. There was a shortage of white women in the colonies. The French had little of the racial prejudices so strongly embedded in the Northern European races and their American descendants so that neither the Indians nor the half breeds experienced disabilities. These conditions, which endured for a century and a half, blended the French and Indians as a new people, in certain regions.

It is impossible at this length of time to analyse the course of this absorption, but today a substantial population of French-Indian descent occupies the Indian reserves of Eastern Canada or roams over Northern Ontario and Quebec. Jenness considers that, although the eastern tribes of the maritime provinces and the St. Lawrence valley bore the first shock of invasion, they were in some respects the most fortunate. The figures which he gives for the migratory tribes of the East Canadian woodlands, for example the Ojibwa and Cree, and for agricultural peoples such as the Iroquois, show a far smaller decrease than tribes in other parts of Canada; for example, the Ojibwa declined only from 30,000 to 20,000, while the Crees and Iroquois showed no decrease and retained respectively populations of 20,000 and 16,000[8]. It must be remembered, however, that some groups were completely exterminated. English and French settlers united with the Micmac Indians to annihilate the unhappy Beothuks of Newfoundland. Even more important is the fact that a high proportion of the Indians of Canada now contain white blood. As official publications are silent on this vital question it is impossible to estimate the extent of the Indian decline in Eastern Canada.

THE MOVING FRONTIER

THE FRENCH MISSIONS

An outstanding feature of the French invasions was Catholic Missionary effort. The Recollects began work on the St. Lawrence in 1615, and the Jesuits joined them in 1626. Within about fifteen years they had won over the Hurons and had established what was virtually a mission State, but this was destroyed between 1641 and 1649 by New York Iroquois armed with firearms secured from the Dutch.

Nevertheless the good work went on. Canada received its first bishop in 1608 and the church fought valiantly against such evils as the Indian liquor traffic.

While all authorities recognise the heroic labours, the sufferings, and, in some cases, the martydoms of the French missionaries, it has been suggested that they achieved little of permanent value and that they did great harm by disrupting native life. For example W. C. Macleod, a warm admirer of the Spanish missions, states that in Canada and Louisiana the French fathers gained little but martyrdom. F. G. Speck, in his study of the Naskapi of Labrador makes a close and important examination of Christian influences. He believes that the missionaries had effects on the settled coastal tribes, but made little appeal to the nomadic hunting groups, who felt that Christianity neither controlled the spirits of wild animals or fish, nor saved human beings from freezing, drowning or starvation in a cold and barren wilderness. He wrote that during a prolonged siege by Roman influence these Indians were at first bewildered and later captivated by the unaccustomed splendour of Roman ritual, but relapsed quickly if away from the priests' influence. After prolonged effort there emerged only "a handful of miserable, unhappy and dwindling bands of errant hunters, galvanised with an ill-becoming sheen on feast days, but sick and corroded at heart". In support of this opinion a leading Roman Catholic missionary of great Canadian experience told the author that he would permit only the medical missionary to make contact with the Indians owing to the evils resulting from detribalising influences.

It will be argued of course that this criticism applies only to the most primitive and nomadic peoples, and that, as admitted by Speck, Christianity achieved, amongst the more settled Indians,

65

some useful results. This is possibly correct. It is certainly noteworthy that the French Catholic clergy made French Canada a
deeply religious country, and that the Indian numerical decline
was perhaps less sweeping in this region than in areas where the
Indians were in contact with English-speaking whites. The problem is, however, complicated by racial, environmental, economic
and other factors, and requires historical and scientific analysis
such as the Californian researches of Kroeber and Meigs⁹.

THE BRITISH

As previously noted the British long contended with the French
for the American North-East coast. Against the superior size,
population and military strength of France, Britain set decisive
advantages such as her sea power and colonising genius. Moreover, she possessed great manufacturing resources, which enabled
her, when dealing with the Indians, to supply better and cheaper
articles than the French. Where the French monarchs sought in
Europe military glory and territorial expansion, the British sought
sea expansion, commerce and settlement. Thus although the
British American colonies were small in area, and disunited in
comparison with the vast territories of France, they were more
compact, more populous and enjoyed safer communications
across the Atlantic. The War of the Spanish Succession illustrated these advantages, and the Treaty of Utrecht, in 1713, saw
France surrender her rights to the disputed territories of Newfoundland, Acadia and Hudson Bay. At that time the British
American colonies contained 300,000 settlers, while Canada, the
most populous French possession, contained only 20,000 French.
The British colonies now occupied the eastern shoreline from
Hudson Bay to Savannah, and, in spite of British military
blunders, the ultimate issue of the Seven Years War was never
seriously in doubt.

The disappearance of France, and the toleration which Britain
showed both to her new French Canadian subjects and to the
Indians, were major factors in the revolution which gave birth
to the United States. The proclamation of 1763 and the Quebec
Act of 1774 extended the boundaries of Quebec across the Great
Lakes to the Ohio river, and protected, as a temporary reserva-

tion, a vast territory to the west of the thirteen colonies—a territory which their frontiersmen had already penetrated. The thirteen colonies saw to their fury the motherland favouring the Papist religion, an alien people, and a few savages whom the colonists wished to push further west. For this and other reasons they flared into the revolt which gave them independence and ultimately the control of all the Indian peoples in what is now the United States.

At the close of the war the Mohawks and members of other tribes migrated to British territory, and the British gave the Iroquois £15,000 in compensation for their losses, together with a substantial reservation of fertile land on the Grand River.

The Treaty of Paris, which gained the United States their independence, neglected the Indians, who complained that the old treaties with Britain protected lands which the Americans were beginning to occupy. The Americans on their part complained that the British were secretly fomenting Indian resistance, and, as noted previously, Wayne and other American generals attacked the natives, slaughtering them and destroying their resources in the ravaging campaigns of 1791 and 1794. Under Jay's Treaty Britain retired, leaving the Republic to conduct Indian affairs in the old North-West as it was then called.

During the Anglo-American War of 1812, some of the Indian tribes materially assisted Britain, and the Treaty of Ghent restored all Indian possessions, privileges and rights as before 1811. After this war Britain and the United States were permanently at peace and could pursue their respective Indian policies without interruption.

From 1830 until 1841 the Provinces of Lower and Upper Canada had separate Indian Departments, but, after the Act of Union in 1841, the departments were united with an office at the seat of government. Up to 1860 the Imperial Government was responsible for the management and expense of Indian Affairs, but in that year the Province of Canada assumed charge. In 1867 the British North America Act established the Dominion of Canada with powers over "Indians and lands reserved for Indians", and in 1876 the Dominion passed the first Indian Act". It is therefore clear that for the greater part of the century 1763-

1860 the Imperial Government must carry the chief responsibility for Canadian-Indian relations.

BRITISH-INDIAN RELATIONS

British-Indian policy differed from that of the French, for Britain treated with the Indians as independent nations under the protection of the Crown. While Britain was prepared, however, to recognise Indian independence and land occupancy she showed her ultimate sovereignty by forbidding foreign nations or British subjects to purchase Indian lands. This gradually led to the Crown assuming direct control of Indian affairs, a policy which had been forecast as early as 1756 when Indian agents were appointed for the Northern and Southern parts of the colonies.

The Proclamation of 1763, the Canadian-Indian Magna Charta, protected Indian lands excepting where the tribes ceded them by treaty with the Crown, and, in spite of the rapidity with which the whites swept across Canada, successive British, Provincial and Dominion Governments, with the exception of British Columbia, honourably pursued this policy. After the French and American wars the outstanding problem was to liquidate Indian land titles with justice to both settlers and natives. Governor Sincoe began the process about 1791, and by 1841 the British had relieved a large part of Upper Canada from the Indian title, and had compensated the Indians by creating reservations, and by granting purchase money, annuities, and trust funds. Other provisions for Indian welfare regulated the fur trade and liquor traffic and exempted hunting Indians from the laws protecting game. F. H. Abbott, Secretary to the United States Board of Indian Commissioners, investigated the Canadian system in 1914. In his opinion the British-Canadian record in dealing with the Indians prior to 1867 was not without blemish, as the white settlers encroached on Indian lands; traders took advantage of the Indians, and officials were lax and dishonest in the management of Indian funds. Nevertheless the British-Canadian system of closed and unallotted reserves, the preservation of the native languages and cultures, and other wise policies had produced results which were infinitely superior to those achieved by the United States.

While the British-Canadian administration appears to have avoided a number of American errors it relied on much the same palliatives, for example, small reservations, appeasing gifts to the Indians, and missionary efforts. In its early stages the British administration was military in character and regarded the natives primarily as potential allies or foes. For this reason it sought to keep them quiet by presents which included firearms, ammunition and rum—a policy of appeasement which as usual spoilt the recipients and created anxiety for both the Colonial and Home Authorities.

By the eighteen thirties, however, the Philanthropic movement was strongly influencing the ministeries at Westminster, and Secretaries of State, such as Sir George Murray and Lord Glenelg, exhibited to the Canadian Indians the same philanthropic but ineffective goodwill as they displayed to the Australian aborigines. In 1830 Murray ended the military supervision and placed administration under the Provincial Governors. Henceforth Indian officials were to be no longer solely the purveyors of presents or almoners of Crown grants. They were to be "the executors of a humane and progressive plan for the civilisation of the aborigines."

The views of the local authorities on the best method of achieving this worthy object varied considerably and included such widely different panaceas as removals and reservations. One at least of the latter soon proved successful. At the close of the Revolutionary War, as noted above, Britain had granted the loyal Iroquois £15,000 in compensation for their losses and a fertile tract of land on the Grand River. Here, in the vicinity of Brantford, and under the able leadership of the Brants, the Iroquois staged a vigorous revival. The Six Nations still cultivate the 60,000 acres which remain of this grant.

Governor Kempt (1825) apparently believed that the Indians would make successful farmers. He wanted to collect them in agricultural villages; to provide them with houses, rations, seed and implements, and to give them religious instruction. Governor Head (1836-7) took the opposite view. He believed that attempts to make the Indians farmers had failed completely. The natives were disappearing before vice, rum and Christianity; which huddled them in hot houses to rot under tuberculosis. He made a fierce attack on white cruelty and said that the kindest policy would be to remove the Indians to islands in Lake Huron or to the far North-West.

Both local and home authorities fortunately perceived the extent to which presents such as drink were degrading the Indians, and in 1836 Lord Glenelg suggested that the gifts should be replaced by something of permanent benefit and use. After 1829 the Canadian officers no longer dispensed rum, and from 1845-6 they ceased .to supply firearms and gradually reduced the other gifts[11].

RELIGIOUS AND SOCIAL PROGRESS

Under the Imperial administration progress was very slow, for, as we shall see in the sections on Australia and New Zealand, the British Governments lacked the anthropological knowledge or financial resources to put their goodwill into effect. In Canada, the Lords of the Treasury limited the total expenditure of the Indian Department to £20,000 per annum, which met little save the cost of administration and of presents. Nor was British Missionary enterprise vigorous prior to the Humanitarian movements. Johnson wrote in 1763 that no such persons as the Jesuits could be found amongst the clergy. The English greed for land discredited their missionaries. The Mohawks thought that one reason they had no clergy amongst them as formerly was because they had no more land to spare[12]. Nevertheless, much of the little progress made up to the time of Confederation was due to the French and British missions. It was the success of the Wesleyan Methodists that first aroused some Government interest and efforts for the Indians.

It must be remembered that the age was one when not only native but even white culture received very little attention. Indeed, the first school established in Upper Canada (1784) was for Mohawk Indians, and the first church (Brantford, 1785) was for members of the Six Nations.

An official report of 1927 depicts the tardy advance of cultural facilities prior to confederation. The Government made grants to a few religious day and farm schools in Lower Canada, while in

Indian Housing, Brantford Reservation, Ontario, Canada
Photo: Author

Indian Housing, Vancouver, British Columbia
Photo: Author

The Historic Church, Brantford Reservation, Ontario, Canada

Photo: Author

Indian Children at Roman Catholic School, British Columbia
Photo: Author

Upper Canada it assisted only two of forty day schools and a few boarding establishments—the Mohawk Institute conducted by the New England Company, a Jesuit Boarding School, and two boarding schools organised by the Wesleyan Methodist Missionary Society. The Government of Upper Canada did, however, establish a community training centre, but this did not appeal to the Indian temperament and was abandoned in 1856 after twenty years of effort. A bright ray in this picture of neglect is the fact that in 1848 certain Indian bands of Upper Canada set apart for education one quarter of the money received in commutation of the annual payment for ammunition. This Indian school fund was largely used to support the Methodist boarding schools by per capita payments—so much per child per year. There can be seen at an early date the central characteristics of the later general system under which the churches co-operated in education and received per capita grants for the children in their residential establishments.

Prior to Confederation there was practically no organisation of Indian schools outside Upper and Lower Canada, and the Provincial governments largely left the missionaries to establish isolated classes wherever they saw opportunities of success. At the time of Confederation the missionary societies, religious orders and Indian bands were carrying the burden that the legislatures were shirking. In such circumstances salaries were low, attendances irregular, and the schools generally ineffective. In 1867 the Indian office recognised only one residential school and 49 day schools, with a combined total of 1716 pupils, while there were also in operation shortly after Confederation a few missionary schools which did not make returns to the Governments. The entire official expenditure on education was only $2600 per annum. Looking at the picture as a whole it is clear that while the British and Canadians treated the Indians tolerably well as regards their lands, the attention paid to social services such as education was far from adequate[13].

THE MOVING FRONTIER ON THE CANADIAN PLAINS

When young Kelsey traversed the great Canadian plains in 1690 the only important tribes were apparently the Blackfoot. Less than fifty years later white influences had already revolutionised Indian life. The Blackfoot had obtained firearms from the Hudson Bay Company and horses from a United States tribe to the South-West. Sarcee, Cree and Assiniboine Indians had pushed into the plains to share in hunting, which the new weapons and means of transport had made so profitable a sport. There followed, as usual, white diseases such as smallpox, human slaughter, and the permanent destruction of resources which were the native staff of life. The tribes organised themselves on a semi-military basis and "the plains became one guerrilla zone in which men hunted and were hunted without cease". "So largely through European influences, though before any Europeans had actually settled west of Ontario, the once peaceful prairies had become a bloody battle ground and did not regain tranquillity until the buffalo herds were exterminated and the starving Indians confined to narrow reserves".

The horse, the primary cause of this revolution, gave new standards of value and a new medium of exchange. With the horse the warrior purchased rank and wives. To secure horses the tribes conducted ever-increasing raids. In one of the most remarkable phenomena of history, isolated foot hunters became a people of daring warriors whose raids extended over thousands of miles.

Indians and whites shared in destroying the resources of the plains. "Last year", wrote De Smet in 1848, "110,000 buffalo robes, with skins of elk, gazelle, deer, otter, beaver, etc., and 25,000 salted tongues, were received in the warehouses of St. Louis". In the face of such destruction the buffalo diminished apace. About 1879 the herds failed to appear, and the starving Indians faced another revolution in native life. With reduced numbers and with insufficient food the tribes could no longer oppose the whites, who confined them to reservations. Here the Indians entered on a changed existence. A monotonous life of farming or ranching supplanted the excitement of warfare and the chase, and population figures steadily declined. Figures given by Jenness suggest that the plains Indians—the Blackfoot, Assiniboine, Cree and Sarcee decreased from about 22,000 to 8,000 between the early nineteenth and early twentieth centuries. Although authorities have attributed much of this decline to warfare, the destruction of the buffalo, and reservation life, great emphasis must be laid upon disease. In 1836, for example, a single epidemic of small-pox destroyed about half the Assiniboine Indians[14].

THE NORTH-WEST

As previously noted the Indians of the North-West were scattered through a bitter region as small groups of hunters. Life was strenuous and poor both in material wealth and culture. The only mercies were that it was healthy and fairly peaceful, but white diseases and white firearms destroyed even these blessings.

The Chipewyans and Crees early secured white weapons and conquered and enslaved their neighbours. Turmoil and strife prevailed until the terrible smallpox outbreak of 1781 killed nine-tenths of the Chipewyans and half the total Indian population. For a century peace then reigned. Scientific transport opened up the region for miners, tourists and other whites. The Indians made little progress, possibly through undernourishment and disease, and their numbers steadily declined. Useful as canoemen and carriers, they remained a valuable economic asset to the whites, and, even for this sordid motive, more might have been done for their welfare and progress. Jenness has estimated that the tribes of the Mackenzie and Yukon basins—the Kutchin, Hare, Dogrib, Chipewyan and others declined from about 14,000 to 6,000 between Pre-Columbian and modern times[15].

THE WESTERN PLATEAUX AND COAST

On the west of the Continent lay the tribes of the Cordillera and Pacific coast, some of which were amongst the most numerous and advanced in English-speaking America. In these regions the Indian decline reached tragic proportions in spite of the fact that the main white invasions came comparatively late. First in the field were the Russians, who established a number of trading settlements in Alaska from 1784 to 1867 when they sold that territory to the United States. The Russians occupied Fort Ross in California from 1812 to 1841, but they had little direct influence on the Indians south of Alaska, although their invasion of that region may have had indirect effects. European diseases and reports of the despotism, atrocities and slavery conducted by the Russian-American Company, which monopolised the colonisation, no doubt affected Indian-white relations further south. In its early stages the Russian penetration assumed the usual characteristics of a white moving frontier. The incomers slaughtered the natives, carried off their women, decimated the fur-bearing creatures, and contended with white competitors such as the Hudson Bay Company. In the later stages of the colonisation the Russians brought in a number of their own women; attempted some conservation of fur resources, and, in the smallpox epidemic of 1862, saved many of the natives under their control by the use of vaccination. The Russian Orthodox Church made fruitless attempts to convert the natives who killed Father Juvenal, at Lake Ikiamna, when he attempted to suppress polygamy, and vowed perpetual hatred of the Russian priesthood. Writing more particularly of the Russian-Eskimo contacts Anderson and Eells point out that the Russians failed to influence native religious expression, but introduced European tools, firearms, diet and dress to a limited extent. Where whalers came ashore they taught the women prostitution for gain, and spread venereal disease by such relationships[16]. In addition to the Russians other Europeans sailed to the North-West coasts in the closing years of the eighteenth century. These visitors began to introduce white diseases. In 1795, for example, Spanish navigators brought smallpox to the Tlinkit tribes of British Columbia, and the Haida were also afflicted by this disease. European colonisation began in the first quarter of the nineteenth century and at first confined itself to a small region around Victoria. By the middle of the century, however, the tide was running at full strength, and was disrupting the Indian social and economic life throughout British Columbia. The Europeans disregarded all grades of Indian rank. They abolished slavery; introduced new standards of wealth, and established fish canneries which interfered with the native food supply. Steamers traded up and down the coast and lumbermen invaded the forest country. Indians of stone age culture were thus caught in the maelstrom of modern industry and commerce without any preparation.

The first result was an acceleration of native life. Indians of low estate acquired sufficient wealth to hold potlatches; to build large and elaborately carved houses and to assume high rank.

The ancient custom of giving presents at the potlatches degenerated into reckless squandering and the destruction of property
threatened widespread destitution. When the Government inter-
vened and prohibited potlatches, including under this term all
secular and religious ceremonies, the natives lost their morale and
ambitions. A few took up farming. The majority worked in the
fish canneries as longshoremen, or in seasonal occupations such
as lumbering, which provided only a bare subsistence. A few
married whites and merged in the white population, but most of
the survivors clung to their old settlements or to reserves which
were tardily created by the Colonial Government[17].

Authorities such as Macleod have eulogised Governor James
Douglas of British Columbia for interpreting his Imperial instructions to meet what he believed were the needs of the case.
Douglas refused to recognise the Indian title, declared Indian
lands Crown Domain and threw them open for white settlement
excepting where the tribes were actually living on or farming
territory. In the early stages, moreover, the Government failed to
establish adequate reservations or to appoint protectors or agents.
To its credit British Columbia protected its Indians from the
American miner whose unhappy custom was "to shoot an Indian
as he would a dog", but the Province fought greedily with the
Dominion Government which desired to preserve sufficient land
for the Indians. Macleod claims that as a result of its policy
of absorption, British Columbia "had satisfactorily liquidated her
Indian problem" when she entered the Confederation. If the
destruction of two-thirds of the Indians can be regarded as "a
satisfactory liquidation" Macleod's views are certainly correct[18].
Writing in 1937 Jenness estimated that the Haida, Tsimshian,
Bella Coola, Kwakiutl, Nootka and Coast Salish tribes had declined from some 40,000 to 12,000[19]. Disease and social and
economic disruption similarly destroyed the Cordillera tribes,
some of which largely depended upon salmon fishing in the
rivers during the summer. Groups such as the Carrier Indians
found that game became scarcer; that salmon ascended the rivers
in decreasing numbers, and that clan life and organisation were
demoralised by Christianity and European settlement. As in
almost all parts of Canada disease took a disastrous toll, and the
Carriers alone declined to perhaps 8,500 by 1780. Jenness indi-

WHITE SETTLERS AND NATIVE PEOPLES

cates that, as a whole, the Cordillera tribes fell in total from about 27,000 to 10,000[20].

MISSIONARY EFFORT IN THE CENTRE, NORTH AND WEST

As in Eastern Canada the Roman Catholics were first in the field, and were often a century in advance of other religious denominations. Societies such as the Oblates and Gray Nuns carried the Cross to remote regions. Not without justice does the Rev. A. G. Morice quote a Protestant—Malcolm McLeod, of the Hudson Bay Company—"It is no doubt to the noble zeal and effective teaching of the Roman Catholic clergy, ever welcome at every post as brothers of the Cross in a common cause, that the Christian civilisation of the North American Indian is mostly due[21]".

Anglicans, Methodists and Moravians followed the Roman Catholics and in many isolated areas were the pioneers and only promotors of services such as education. Certain Protestant efforts in the West deserve special attention for successes which were based upon sound economic policy—the development of industries that appealed to the Indians. Outstanding was the work of William Duncan, who resigned a remunerative position in England to try and raise the Tsimshian from practices such as cannibalism, human sacrifice and slavery, to which they were rapidly adding white vices. By splendid courage and devotion Duncan, from 1857, built up at Metlakahtla a Christian, civilised and self-supporting community. A narrow-minded Bishop and Church Missionary Society, supported by a greedy Colonial Government, forced Duncan and his Indians to seek a new home and freedom in United States territory in 1857. The American Congress reserved for their use a small island in Southern Alaska, and here evolved New Metlakahtla, a second prosperous settlement[22].

CAUSES OF DECLINE—DISEASE AND DRINK

In spite of differences due to variations in the environment: in the Indian tribes, and in the white Europeans, the moving frontier as in the United States presented more similarities than contrasts throughout Canada. The invaders partly destroyed or

76

absorbed the majority of tribes, the agents being in most cases disease, alcohol, firearms, and a general undermining of Indian religion, culture, tribal organisation, ambition and pride of life.

In Canada, as in the United States, European disease was probably the chief factor. It appeared at a very early date and it carried off the Indians regardless of whether they accepted or resisted the whites. In 1612 the Jesuit Pierre Biard wrote from Acadia, "The Indians are astonished and often complain that, since the French mingle with them and carry on trade with them, they are dying fast and the population is thinning out. For they assert that before this association and intercourse all their countries were very populous and they tell how one by one the different coasts, according as they have begun to traffic with us, have been more reduced by disease[23]". The same story comes from other parts of Canada, often at early dates. Speck, for example, states that by 1650 the Indians at Tadoussac were decreasing from disease[24]. Smallpox seems to have been a very early and very destructive curse. Many observers have described its appalling ravages, and a medical historian, J. J. Heagerty, has traced its path from the time it ravaged the Montagnais until it reached the western tribes both of Canada and the United States. Appearing amongst the Montagnais near Tadoussac in 1635 the disease spread east and south and to the Great Lakes on the west. By 1700 it had covered more than half the continent, leaving a trail of desolation and death. By 1738 it had reached the Canadian tribes of the west[25]. No one can estimate at this date the total number or percentage of Indian deaths, but both were undoubtedly very high. It was reported, for example, that the smallpox epidemic of about 1832 killed from half to two-thirds of the Assiniboine[26].

Diseases other than smallpox also had dire effects. In 1746 typhus carried off a third of the Acadian Micmacs and in 1902-3 this disease wiped out the entire Eskimo population of Southampton island in Hudson Bay[27]. Measles and influenza assisted in the destruction. The latter spared none of the West Coast tribes in the great epidemic of 1918[28]. Social diseases also appeared quite early. Pulmonary afflictions, particularly tuberculosis, were reported at an early date, and became a leading factor in the disappearance of the Indians, particularly under the conditions of reservation life[29].

The English-speaking whites cannot be accused of introducing all these diseases. Macleod believed that the smallpox epidemic, which ravaged New England in 1616, may have come from the French settlements in Canada[30], and Spanish visitors apparently introduced smallpox to the Western Canadian coast. Nor did the English-speaking whites infect the natives deliberately, although Morice gives a shocking instance from Bella Coola in British Columbia about 1864. There, after a smallpox epidemic had killed about a third of the Chilcotins, white men sold to unsuspecting Indians blankets in which other natives had died of the disease. This atrocious action led to a second outbreak which killed another third of the Indians[31].

Although the whites can be acquitted of deliberately spreading disease they were responsible for degenerating the Indians by a disgraceful liquor traffic against which wise and humane elements, such as the French clergy, fought with little effect. The British authorities ceased including rum in their Indian presents in 1829, and the Hudson Bay Company, which dispensed 19,400 gallons a year from 1802-1804, reduced the distribution in later years and terminated the practice about 1860[32].

Alcohol was undoubtedly a leading factor in disrupting Indian life. All over Canada explorers and traders witnessed a decay which lasted until the middle of the nineteenth century. Whisky and brandy destroyed the self-respect of the Indians, weakened family and tribal ties, and made the natives the slaves of the trading posts where liquor was dispensed to them by the keg. It was not until the trade in intoxicants was made absolutely illegal that the Indian began to recover a little of his ancient dignity and independence[33].

CAUSES OF DECLINE—DISRUPTION OF INDIAN LIFE

In addition to disease and alcohol, firearms and other white innovations caused disruption. In Eastern Canada the whites assisted the Micmacs to destroy the Beothuk of Newfoundland. The French armed the Algonkians and Hurons, and the Dutch the Iroquois, these Indian groups then engaging in a bloody and

78

exhausting combat. The French, the English and the American Republicans sowed strife amongst the Indians, enlisted native allies, and, in such practices as the scalp bounties, descended to the level of primitive savages. Franklin, for example, stated in his letters that Indians brought in the scalps of 2,000 white Americans for British bounties. In the North the Chipewyans obtained firearms on Hudson Bay and oppressed the more distant Athapaskans. The effects of firearms and horses on the plains have already been explained.

Not only did the tribes slaughter and exhaust one another, they rapidly destroyed the fur-bearing and other animals in their own territories and then descended on the lands of their neighbours. For several years a tribe might be rich. Then came exhaustion and poverty—perhaps for ever. It was the same story with the fur-bearing animals of the East and North, with the buffalo of the plains, and, when white canneries opened in the west, with the salmon. One by one the tribes surrendered their territories and were confined to narrow reservations. Deprived of their resources and self-sufficiency, their needs became the same as those of the white invaders.

With the decline of economic resources there came a decline in religion, culture and tribal organisation. Christianity overwhelmed the vague nature worship of the Indians, whose few attempts to rebuild their old faiths on the new foundations failed. The fur trade introduced a fresh economic system. The chiefs lost their authority and the community spirit of tribal life evaporated.

Some results of the white-native contacts were, of course, all to the good. The Europeans ultimately ended such practices as warfare, cannibalism, torture, the blood feud, infanticide and the abandonment of the sick and the aged. They gave the Indians better weapons and tools; taught them to build more comfortable houses, and introduced agriculture and stock-raising to replace the vanishing game. Some tribes like the Iroquois, Blackfoot and Kutenai adjusted themselves to the new conditions. Others were largely absorbed by the white community. Others again were unable to effect adjustments. They lost their ambition and will to live and steadily declined[34]. Thus the Canadian moving frontier produced similar consequences to the moving frontier in the United States. The British-French-Canadian story was more merciful and just than the British-American, and the northern invasions destroyed a smaller percentage of natives. Nevertheless, white diseases and other innovations proved disastrous to the Indians in both regions, and palliatives, such as small reservations and missions, in general failed to ease the shock of contact.

CHAPTER V

Canada - The Dominion Administration

THE CONFEDERATION

In 1867 the Eastern Provinces—Canada (Ontario and Quebec), Nova Scotia and New Brunswick—united as the Dominion of Canada. The Confederation spread rapidly. It acquired the Hudson Bay concessions from the company, and admitted this vast region in 1870 as Manitoba and the North-West Territories. In 1871 British Columbia, which had been a Province since 1858, came in, and in 1905 the area between British Columbia and Manitoba was admitted as the provinces of Saskatchewan and Alberta.

The British-America Act of 1867 gave the Dominion power to legislate for "Indians and lands for Indians". The Confederation therefore took over Indian affairs, and placed them under its Secretary of State. In 1873 it attached the Indian Branch to the Secretary of the Interior, and in 1880 gave it the status of a separate department. There is now only one Indian Act and Indian administration in the Dominion, and the simplicity of the Canadian system has won the envious praise of expert observers from the United States[1]

THE OCCUPATION OF INDIAN TERRITORY

From its inception the Confederation worked for the advancement of the natives. The central government absorbed the administrative machinery of Canada, New Brunswick and Nova Scotia, and an Act of 1868 consolidated the previous legislation. Dominion policy progressed along two lines. The Government made treaties with Western Indians to secure land, and at the same time attempted to make them educated and self-supporting. Thus in 1871-5 the Indians of Manitoba ceded large areas in

81

exchange for reservations, annuities and social benefits such as education. In 1873 a treaty secured the passage of the Canadian Pacific Railway, and in 1874-7 treaties began to open up Saskatchewan—a huge region between Lake Winnipeg and the Rockies. In 1899-1900 the Indian title was extinguished over 342,700 miles in the Peace River area, and by 1912 the only land not ceded lay in the far north-west.

The treaties gave the Indians reservations, trust funds, annuities and social services. The Government reserved 640 acres for each Indian family of five—an amount in excess of their agricultural needs. The surplus was, therefore, sold at public auction and the proceeds either given to the tribes or placed in trust funds, which, by 1938, totalled over $14,000,000 and returned a revenue of $1,210,816. The Dominion began to assist education in the Province of Canada in 1875-6 and from 1878-9 there was great expansion in many regions. The Government outlay under this heading rose from $16,000 in 1878-9 to $172,980 in 1889-90, $339,145 in 1910-11, and $1,936,744 in 1935-6.

Canada recognised the Church control of schools and assisted the Churches in their educational activities. There were abuses in the early days. Insufficient attention was paid to Indian health, and possibly 50% of the children died before they gained any educational benefits. Also the school curricula were too academic in character; industrial teaching had disappointing results, and, as no attention was paid to the students when they returned to the reservations, most of them relapsed to pagan life. As time went on, the Dominion remedied many of these evils.

Two difficulties disturbed the even tenor of this peaceful penetration. Foolish and unregulated slaughter decimated the buffalo to such an extent that, when prairie fires occurred in 1879, the surviving herds failed to come into Canada. This threw the majority of the North-Western Indians upon the Government, and, although few perished from starvation, there was acute poverty and suffering.

The second difficulty was the Metis or half-breed rebellion of 1885. For this there was little reason, for, although the crops had failed, provisions were on their way. The Government executed the leaders and temporarily suspended treaty obligations. With the exception of these comparatively minor troubles, the white

THE DOMINION ADMINISTRATION

occupation of central and western Canada presents an amazing contrast to the land robbery, wars, atrocities, and dishonesty on the other side of the American-Canadian boundary. In spite of some mistakes, the Dominion can take pride in her conduct of the white invasions and her treatment of her natives.

For the sound and honest administration of this humane policy much credit is due to the officers of Indian affairs and to the Canadian Mounted Police. In many regions the Indian agents commenced work before all other whites, with the exception of traders and missionaries. They were the pioneers of vast, wild and undeveloped territories, and were frequently the sole agents of law in these then unorganised regions. The Canadian Mounted Police Force was a constructive agency of first importance for the good of the Indians. Established in 1873, the Force gained a remarkable reputation, and, by providing even-handed justice for both whites and natives, won the high respect of the Indians and did much to steady the tribes during the rising of 1885. In the words of Governor Brett, of Alberta: "The manner in which so small a force kept down the liquor traffic, controlled the savage tribes of Indians, and protected the lives and property of the settlers, affords an illustration that is probably without parallel in the world's history²".

DOMINION POLICY

The Imperial Government and the Canadian Provinces did relatively little to improve the lot of the Indians. Nevertheless they conducted a sound and honest land policy and interfered with Indian life to a lesser extent than did the United States. On these solid bases the Dominion of Canada built up a policy and administrative system which, although not without faults, has gained unstinted praise from American experts.

The Canadians sought to assimilate the Indians, but they wisely regarded this as a long term process, and refused to surrender the natives to land grabbers or to misguided philanthropists. The Dominion maintained a fixed policy, embodied in one short Act and administered by permanent officials whose positions were not the spoils of political success. Canadian Indian law envisaged a process of cultural evolution from primitive status to modern conditions. In a first stage it recognised existing tribal institutions; in a second it introduced the principal of elective representation; in a third it visualised Indian groups as self-governing municipal corporations. The American expert, Harper, considered this last a brilliant innovation in native administrative law. The Canadian authorities frequently allowed the Indians to retain their historic organisations, and used this machinery as a bridge by which to approach them. They avoided the mistake of attempting to destroy Indian tribal life and culture, and Indian arts and crafts. Although the Government placed the schools in religious hands, and supported Christian instruction from its funds, it did so at the request of the Indians, and permitted them to choose the denominations which they wished to assist them.

Canadian methods gave considerable power to local superintendents, and avoided much of the massive correspondence and expense incurred by the United States. Another American expert, Abbott, noted for example that .the Canadian liquor control was more efficient than the American, although its cost was only one-twenty-fifth of the cost of control in the United States. Up to 1939 the Canadian Department had not followed the later American practice of giving the Indians a favoured place in their own departmental administration, and Canada might well examine, and if advisable copy, the American example in this respect. On the whole, however, the author thought the Canadian system and its administrative officers wise, successful, and thoroughly up-to-date².

ADMINISTRATION AND FINANCE

The Canadian organisation developed into a Department of Indian affairs—a separate department under control of the Minister of Mines and Resources who became Superintendent-General of Indian affairs. Under him were permanent officials— the Deputy Superintendent-General and the Secretary, with a department organised in five branches — Field Administration, Medical, Reserves and Trusts, Welfare and Training (which included schools), and Records Service. While the Dominion did not finance Indian welfare as liberally as did the United States, she was by no means ungenerous in later years. Shortly after

Confederation her expenditure on Indians was only $50,000, and that on education a meagre $2,600 per annum. In recent times, however, Canada annually spent over $5,000,000 on her natives and her outlay on education rose to $2,000,000. The expenditure for 1937-8 was $4,682,945, of which approximately $600,000 went in administration, $1,800,000 in education, and $1,000,000 each in medical and welfare services. This total of $4,682,945 represented an outlay of about $40 for each of the 118,000 Canadian Indians[4].

LAND POLICY

Canadian native policy proved less destructive than did the policies of the United States, Australia, and New Zealand, mainly because it preserved for most of the tribes an adequate amount of satisfactory land. We have seen that as the whites swept across the country they made, under British traditions, treaties for the liquidation of the Indian title, giving in exchange promises of tribal reserves, and annuities, and guarantees for the provision of social services such as education. In many cases, of course, these concessions were infinitesimal in comparison with the value of the lands which the whites gained. Nevertheless, the Canadian record was clean and honest, in comparison for instance with some of the practices in New Zealand. The Dominion preserved the Indian reservations. It attempted to fulfil its promises, and it tried to make the Indians self-reliant and self-supporting. Even for the unfortunate natives of British Columbia, where the record sank furthest towards the levels in America, Australia and New Zealand, a special committee of the Dominion Parliament recommended in 1927 a number of valuable concessions. While the committee found that Indian claims were groundless, as no aboriginal title had ever existed in British Columbia, it recommended important grants for Indian irrigation, industry, education, and health[5].

Unlike the United States, Canada wisely pursued a most conservative policy in individualising Indian land holdings. The reservations remained closed and unallotted, for the Dominion had no enthusiasm for the patent in fee and granted it only rarely and with the gift of citizenship which took a long and tedious process to secure. The Dominion permitted no allotments to disturb the unbroken continuity of group land. "By placing emphasis on use prior to title, she escaped the terrible malaise of Indian land tenure found in the United States[6]". Individual Indians were located on land which they were able and willing to utilise. If they failed to do this other Indians could pay for the permanent improvements and be located on the same land. The Dominion permitted Indians to sell occupancy and permanent improvements to other Indians but never to whites. The latter could not secure reservation rights by marrying Indians, nor could their children by Indian women secure such rights. If an Indian woman married a white the Government assisted her to terminate her tribal rights and she received their value by commutation. Indians could lease land to white men, but only with the consent of both the Indian Department and the Council of the Band. As a result of this stipulation the Indian revenue from leases was less than a fortieth as much as that in the United States[7].

It is interesting to note in this connection that Canada tried the policy of issuing "location tickets" which recognised individual ownership and in some cases permitted the Indian holders to lease their lands to whites. She soon discovered, however, that, although some cases proved satisfactory, the experiment in general created absenteeism and idleness[8]. On the eve of the World War the Indian Reserves comprised slightly more than 5,500,000 acres or about 47 acres per native. Their capital value was approximately $53,000,000 or $450 per person. Unfortunately these land assets were very unevenly distributed, partly because the reservation areas had been selected for very varied reasons and partly because the transition from primitive to civilised life had, in many cases, completely altered the economic system[9].

INDUSTRY

As indicated above, the Canadian Indian reservations embraced about 5,500,000 acres in 1938. Of this area some 3,000,000 acres were forested, and 2,000,000 acres were cleared but not cultivated. The area under cultivation was about 200,000 acres. The Indians possessed 25,000 horses, 50,000 cattle, and 10,000 other stock, together with a large equipment of motor, sailing and rowing

Canadian Indian woman, Vancouver, British Columbia

Indian Hospital, Brantford Reservation, Ontario
Photo: Author

Tribalised Natives—Central Australia

Photo: C. P. Mountford

Ayers Rock—Central Australia. Tribalised Aboriginal explaining Rock Paintings

Photo: C. P. Mountford

THE DOMINION ADMINISTRATION

boats, canoes, firearms, fishing nets, steel traps and tents. Their total income was assessed at six and a quarter million dollars or about $53 per person as compared with an income of $150 per Indian in the United States. The main sources of this income were approximately: Farm and ranch production ($1,700,000), wages ($1,200,000), Trust interest and annuities ($950,000), hunting and trapping ($870,000), and fishing ($750,000). Obviously the natives, with an annual income of only about £13 sterling per individual, were by no means prosperous".

The Canadian Government deserves credit for its attempts to convert the Indians to a modern economy. The process was difficult but during recent years some tribes showed encouraging improvement in farming and in the management of livestock. The Government provided a certain amount of equipment and stock, establishing a revolving fund to afford loans for community projects, supervised Indian lumbering, and conserved certain territories and fur-bearing creatures for the trapping Indians. The Government also encouraged native handcrafts, particularly in Eastern Canada. In 1938 an official report stated that it was then too soon to gauge the results, but that they seemed encouraging. As in the United States the Indians suffered from white exploitation and from the Japanese forging Indian products. The Canadians, like the Americans, took steps to guarantee and market genuine native wares.

In the period immediately preceding the War, Indian administration still faced two difficult problems—Government relief for the needy, and the diminution of hunting and fishing resources. As previously shown, the British Government had abandoned the system of presents, but the Dominion found it necessary to provide relief, first when the buffalo disappeared, and later in the economic depression of the nineteen thirties. During the latter disaster, crop failures and the downward trend of prices reduced the Indian income by approximately one-third, and threw about a third of the natives on Government relief. To avoid suffering and even actual starvation, the Dominion granted substantial help which amounted to over a million dollars in 1936; but it wisely took measures to discourage idleness, and in 1938 voted funds to provide a special welfare programme, designed to rehabilitate those Indians who were still receiving assistance".

87

WHITE SETTLERS AND NATIVE PEOPLES

The second problem was that of the hunting Indians who were suffering from diminishing resources, and from white competition which was often quite unscrupulous. No Indian, for example was ever reported for laying poison, but white trappers were unhesitating in its use[12]. The British-America Act left the control of game and fish to the Provinces, but the Dominion and Provincial Governments overcame this difficulty in conferences. The gravity of the position was illustrated by the fact that, whereas a large area of Northern Manitoba produced in 1902 over 700,000 muskrat skins, in 1924 the number sold had fallen to 8,600[13]. The only hope of preserving valuable resources and of saving the hunting Indians from destitution lay in the establishment of Indian hunting reservations. On the eve of the World War the Dominion and Provincial Governments were co-operating for this purpose, and they had already established trapping reserves in Ontario, Quebec, Manitoba, Alberta and Saskatchewan[14]. The visiting enquirer notes with great interest how vividly Canadian officials realise the destructive influence of greedy and reckless whites, not only on the Indians, but on resources which are as important to the whites as to the Indians. The Department of Mines and Resources has been pouring out a mass of publications dealing with the preservation of animals, fish, and birds. An important project was the establishment of a Canadian Reindeer Herd which was brought from Alaska by a remarkable trek which lasted from December, 1929, to March, 1935. In under taking this experiment the Government hoped to provide a source of food and clothing, and to reduce the destruction of caribou and game[15].

RELIGION AND EDUCATION

The Canadians avoided the mistake of deliberately attempting to destroy the Indian languages, religion and culture. Abbott stated in 1915 that "in no instance has the Government laid the axe at the root of an Indian language", and pointed out that newspapers were printed in Cree by means of a syllabic character language invented by a Methodist missionary, the Rev. James Evans, in 1840. The Dominion applied the same policy in religious matters. The Government legislated against Indian dances where mutilation of the body was practised, but avoided the American sentimentalism which interfered with Indian ceremonials and art in order to convert the Indian to white religion and culture more quickly. American observers have praised the splendid co-operation between the Government and the religious denominations both on the reserves and in the schools, and have pointed out that, as the Churches were responsible for most of the schools, they have learnt to appreciate the difficulties experienced by officials in managing Indian affairs. The Dominion frankly recognised the value of the religious institutions, but it avoided sectarian squabbles by permitting the chiefs, subject to Government confirmation, to make rules and regulations concerning the denominational colour of teachers in their particular reservation schools. With the consent of the Government religious minorities could also secure their own schools. The system on the whole worked satisfactorily. It protected the Indian from confusion in religious thought and prevented friction between the various denominations. At the outbreak of the World War the great majority of Canadian Indians were at any rate nominal Christians. The census of 1934 recorded that of 112,000 natives, 58,000 were Roman Catholics, 29,000 Anglicans, 17,000 United Church, and 4,000 members of other Christian denominations. The remainder—only about 4,000—were classed as holding aboriginal beliefs. It is difficult to imagine that Christianity is deeply rooted amongst so high a percentage of a people of whom a very large number are still in a nomadic state. Sedentary peoples, such as the Iroquois of Brantford, have included for several generations many sincere Christians. Speck's examination of the Naskapi indicates on the contrary that Christianity has taken little root amongst these nomadic hunters and that, in all probability, it has had some detrimental social effects. During the author's stay in Canada he was unable to discover any adequate treatise on the subject, which clearly deserves further research.

In the Dominion religion and education are closely allied. In colonial days the churches provided most of the few educational facilities afforded the Indians and in the early stages of Confederation the Government gave but a meagre $2600 per annum to educational work. Up to 1928 a substantial part of the educational expenses were met from the accumulated funds of the Indian bands, which exceeded $15,000,000 in 1943. After that year the Dominion adopted a more liberal attitude, and in 1935-6 spent $1,936,000 on education or over $100 for each of the 18,000 children enrolled in the schools. At the time of confederation the Indian office recognised only 50 schools with 1665 pupils—all in Ontario and Quebec. By 1925-6 the number of schools had increased to 341 with an enrolment of 14,782 children and an average attendance of 71.09%. Ten years later—in 1935-6—the number of schools had advanced to 359, the pupils to 18,033 and the average attendance to 76.79%[18].

In recent times the educational system showed many of the excellent features of American Indian education as practised under the New Deal. Efforts were made to improve the health and conditions, particularly in the residential establishments. The curriculum was adjusted to arouse interest, to give vocational training, and to secure correlation with the home environment. The Dominion also improved standards of teaching, increased the number of pupils in the higher grades, and gave grants to Indian students of sufficient promise to warrant advanced education in Universities, Business Colleges or High Schools.

At the outbreak of war Canadian Indian education was partly governmental and partly denominational in character. The Government assisted the churches to support 79 residential schools with an enrolment of 8906 pupils. Of these 44 were Roman Catholic, 20 Church of England, 13 United Church and 2 Presbyterian. The day schools numbered 280 with 9127 pupils.

As noted above American observers have given high praise to this system, which generally places the schools under either Roman Catholic or Protestant patronage. "I am forced to the conclusion", wrote Abbott, "that Canada's school system, by encouraging religious instruction and avoiding the petty quarrels that exist in some of the Indian schools in our country between the different denominations interested, has apparently turned out Indians of superior character who certainly have more religious faith[19]".

The author's observations in Canada and the United States did not altogether support such sweeping claims for the advantages of the Canadian system. For example, the buildings and equipment of the Canadian schools visited were in general below the standard of those inspected in the United States. Nor could one ignore authoritative criticisms that the educational equipment and standards were still comparatively poor in some of the denominational schools, while one even heard allegations that the Roman Catholics deliberately held down standards in order to keep the Indians ignorant and under control. Nevertheless, in spite of such possible faults, Canada is evolving an up-to-date and smooth running system of education, and she has achieved some of her objectives without the high expenditure and political and religious bickerings which have marked educational developments in the United States.

HEALTH AND WELFARE

During recent years the Dominion paid increased attention to Indian health and welfare. In 1927 the Confederation was spending $485,978 on health. By 1937-8 she had increased her medical expenditure to over a million dollars, and, in the same year, spent another million on Indian welfare. In order to improve health Canada maintained full and part time officials on the reserves, supported hospitals, employed field matrons and nurses to conduct educational health propaganda and to inspect Indian homes, and provided medical and dental attention in the boarding schools and day schools. Particularly vigorous efforts were made to combat tuberculosis and trachoma, while the use of alcohol has been prohibited.

The Government soon discovered that the establishment of full time physicians and nurses on the reservations produced both efficiency and economy. For example, the Qu'Appelle Health Unit, which included a doctor, public health nurse and hospital, served 1400 Indians, and in four years reduced the tuberculosis death rate by one half and effected a marked improvement in other respects. The authorities utilised aeroplanes for medical service but discovered that, particularly in winter, air communications brought disease to Indian tribes in remote districts.

In spite of some successes the problem of Indian health remained serious. The Indian population was from ten to twenty times as tubercular as the white; trachoma was very prevalent, and intense local epidemics continued to cause serious loss of life. In a country as vast as Canada there were still large areas in which health control was extremely difficult[13].

INDIAN NUMBERS

In spite of the Dominion's comparatively enlightened and generous policy her Indians long continued to decline in numerical strength. Historical estimates are largely guesses and the current definitions of Indians and "half-breeds" are so loose that statistics can be regarded only as very broad indications of past and present trends. As previously noted figures indicate that a pre-Columbian population of perhaps 220,000 fell to 102,358 in 1871 and 93,200 in 1901. After this came a slow recovery. The Minister of Mines and Resources stated in 1939 that numbers had advanced to approximately 118,000 and were showing an annual improvement of 1%. In 1934 the Canadian Indian census gave a total of 112,510, indicating a steady growth. It, therefore, appears that Canada may confront the same problem of native increase as the United States, Australia and New Zealand, and, although she has been more wise and liberal than these countries in her reservation policy, her reservations in certain regions are already proving insufficient.

Few students have conducted researches on the decline and recovery of the Canadian Indians but the work of Clark Wissler is of considerable importance in this respect. Wissler analysed the statistics for certain Indian groups in the Northern Plains and in British Columbia. He demonstrated that white contacts opened on the plains about 1670 and that by 1690 the Assiniboine and Cree had secured firearms and were raiding southward and westward. In 1780 smallpox decimated Saskatchewan, and the Assiniboine came in from the margin of that area, occupied it and multiplied until 1832, when smallpox carried off two-thirds of their number. The Cree then came in from the margin and repeated the performance of the Assiniboine until the buffalo disappeared and the Crees slumped.

Wissler believes that from 1600-1780 the Indian birthrate was 42 or higher; the deathrate was only about 30; females greatly exceeded males in number and minors exceeded adults, owing largely to the hazards of hunting and war. Reservation life, which

92

opened on the Canadian plains about 1880, effected a great change. The older age groups diminished; the excess of females disappeared; and the total population declined. After some years, however, a number of groups recovered and began to register a slow increase. The United States Indians of the plains reached their lowest ebb about 1895. Of the Canadian Plains tribes the Cree began to advance in 1899, the Assiniboine in 1909 and the Blackfoot in 1924. The majority of the British Columbian groups, studied by Wissler, declined from 1899 to 1924, after which the general trend was upward. The improvement was not due to changes in the birthrate, which remained on the plains "roughly constant, and uniformly high, possibly near the physiological maximum". The deciding factor seems to have been the death-rate, which appears to have risen very sharply under reservation conditions and then to have steadily declined. Wissler quotes a summary of trends in certain Blackfoot reserves, "The general deathrate, as derived from annuity records, rose from 40 per thousand in 1881 to 127 per thousand in 1886, an increase of 87 per thousand in only six years. Vital statistical records for these reserves show that the deathrate for tuberculosis rose from approximately ten per thousand in 1881 to 90 per thousand in 1886—an increase of approximately 80 per thousand in the same six years. Evidently the rise in the general deathrate was due almost entirely to the increase in the tuberculosis death rate". Wissler concluded that the general deathrate on the plains showed a sharp rise to a peak about 1890, followed by a partial recovery and then a steady decline until 1934. "Hence", he says, "the death-rate appears to be the chief variable and probably the most sensitive to mode of life". This means that reservation life with its white diseases produced in the early stages a heavy Indian mortality, but this mortality decreased as the natives accustomed themselves to reservation existence, and, as their birthrate consistently maintained a high level, they began to increase[19].

MIXED BLOODS

It is difficult to estimate how far the recovery of the Canadian Indians is due to an infusion of white blood. In the Dominion the term "half-breed", like the Australian term "half-caste", appears to be a loose definition covering the mixed bloods. Harvard gave the number of these people as 18,000 in 1879, and the Dominion census of 1901 estimated them at 34,481 or 27% of the total full and mixed blood population. Abbott, writing in 1915, said that there were 98,000 Indians on the reservations, 5,000 outside the reservations, and 50,000 half-breeds "who in Canada are not Indians"—a statement which gave a mixed blood figure of 39%. There is little doubt, however, that in Canada there is much white blood in Indian and much Indian blood in white veins, for Indian-white contacts extend over four centuries of Canadian history, and "intermixture has been much more common than is generally assumed[20]".

Opinions vary as to the standards and values of these half-breeds. Some writers have considered them a valuable link between the white and Indian populations. Others have condemned them in unequivocal terms. On the one hand Joseph Brant, who was possibly a mixed blood, provided much of the inspiration and leadership which produced the recovery of the Iroquois; on the other hand half-breeds like Cuthbert Grant were partly responsible for the atrocities on the Red River in 1816, and the French half-breeds—the Metis, actually rose in rebellion in 1885[21].

Abbott reported in 1915 that the status of the Canadian half-breed was the strongest visible argument in favour of the Dominion's closed policy of Indian land tenure and against the American policy of allotment and citizenship. In the seventies, he said, Canada agreed to give the half-breeds freedom from Indian restrictions and gave each individual the choice either of 240 acres of public land or of negotiable scrip. The half-breeds thereupon surrendered their tribal rights and became Canadian citizens, but greedy whites rapidly secured their land or scrip, with the same consequences as those which followed the removal of restrictions from the five civilised tribes of Oklahoma in 1908. "Today", said Abbott, "the word half-breed in Canada is a synonym for the worst type of citizens in the Dominion. While there are many noteworthy exceptions, the Canadian half-breed, speaking generally, is a roving irresponsible individual, a veritable gypsy, his children for the most part being deprived of school facilities because of the nomadic character of the father or of his poverty. Travelling far behind his restricted full blood brother on the reserve, the half-breed, physically, morally and intellectually is a standing warning against the too early removal of Indian land restrictions[22]".

As noted previously estimates of Canadian half-caste numbers increased from 18,000 in 1879 to 50,000 in 1915. These figures are undoubtedly most conservative, and the mixed blood population must be far greater than this at the present time. If trends in Canada resemble those in the United States, Australia and New Zealand, the Dominion would be wise to break the silence which the author encountered on this question and to give it thorough examination. Many Canadian experts deplore the lack of scientific data and statistics in several important aspects of the Indian problem and stress the great need of scientific research.

THE FUTURE

The goal of Canadian Indian policy is the absorption of the natives in the white population, and, although the Dominion has wisely refrained from attempting to accelerate a natural process, the assimilation is already far advanced over much of the country. Eastern reserves, such as Lorette, near Quebec, and Caughnawaga, near Montreal, contain few full blooded Indians and their inhabitants mingle in white industries. The people of Caughnawaga have become magnificent steel workers and earned very high wages in erecting the Golden Gate Bridge and the Empire State and Singer Buildings in New York. Even on the famous Brantford reservation, where numbers increased from about 3,000 to 5,000 between 1910 and 1939, the author was informed that there were comparatively very few full blood Indians, although the Indian language was still spoken in many homes. Here, as previously mentioned, the British rewarded the loyalty of the Iroquois during the War of American Independence by the gift of 750,000 acres of fertile land on the Peace River. Subsequent land sales reduced the area to about 60,000 acres, but the proceeds of the sales provided the Indians with $800,000 of Trust funds. Equipped with fertile lands and agricultural traditions these Iroquois have become comparatively prosperous farmers, the standards of agriculture and housing being as good as many seen in the United States. The celebrated Mohawk

Institute—an Industrial Boarding School—seemed shabby and ill-equipped after American Indian Schools, but the records of this establishment are excellent.

Although there is still some laziness and some liquor troubles, the Indians work well and, in 1939, very few were on relief. Some of the Brantford children do well in the High Schools and others have become doctors and lawyers, or have risen to other positions of prominence. Brantford is clearly a reservation on which the Indians have effected a recovery under native leadership; have accepted Christianity; are rising to white living standards; and are assimilating with the whites.

A similar process can be seen at reservations on the British Columbian coast such as Squamish, near Vancouver. In this part of Canada the Indians have also adopted Christianity, and white industries, and are undergoing absorption. In some places they have formed powerful fishing organisations such as the Native Brotherhood of the Pacific Coast and the Native Fishermen's Association. Some own their own boats and gear; others obtain equipment from the canneries. The shipping companies value their services as long-shoremen, in which vocation they earn from $150 to $350 a month on casual employment which suits their temperament. On the Squamish reservation housing and education, the latter under Roman Catholic supervision, did not appear to be of the standards attained at Brantford. British Columbian Indians, whom the author questioned, were intelligent people fully acquainted with, and anxious to discuss, their racial difficulties. They took the view that absorption was in full swing; that segregation was a mistake and that they should merge as quickly as possible in the white population. It must of course be remembered that Caughnawaga, Brantford and Squamish are reservations situated close to white towns, and offering inducements for the Indians to engage in white industries. On many reservations the natives are far less closely in touch with the whites and there has been comparatively little absorption. Many white Canadians agree with these Squamish Indians. They are opposed to segregation as delaying absorption, and they recognise the danger of creating and increasing minorities where languages and cultures differ widely from those of the majority of citizens. At the same time the success of the Canadian policy of modified

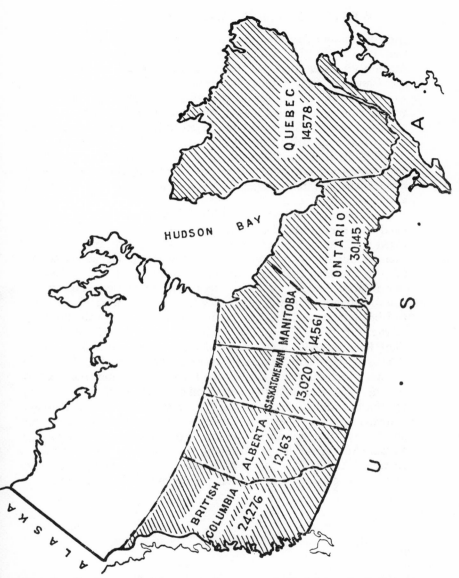

Canadian Provinces containing more than 10,000 Indians in 1938. Statistics from official publications.

and temporary segregation has proved so beneficial to the Indians that its speedy abandonment would be unwise and inhumane. Authorities agree that, whatever happens, the ultimate fate of the Canadian Indian must be absorption. Jenness, for example, wrote in 1934, "Doubtless all the tribes will disappear. Some will endure only a few years longer, others like the Eskimo, may last several centuries. Some will merge steadily with the white race, others will bequeath to future generations only a fraction of their blood[23]". In the broad view this statement is probably true, but, with increasing numbers and improved health, the absorption of the Indians may take longer than Canadian authorities at present anticipate.

There is little indication that the white population of Canada need fear the effects of a further absorption of Indian blood provided that the process of acculturising the Indians and of raising their standards of life and culture continues. Canadian educationists consider that the mental endowment of the Indians is not inferior to that of other races, and these people have frequently demonstrated their loyalty and public spirit in response to liberal treatment. As previously noted they gave valuable help in the wars of 1776 and 1812 and in the first World War more than 4000, or 35% of the males of military age enlisted, although they were especially exempted from conscription. By 1945 2750 Indians, including 56 women, had enlisted during the second World War, and in both great conflicts the record of casualties, promotions and distinctions was highly creditable. Also, although Canadian policy does not incite assimilation, enfranchisement and citizenship, advanced Indians are enfranchised under the Indian Act by Order in Council, and receive full citizenship. Many of them have taken advantage of this opportunity, and some have done well in learned professions and in business[24].

CHAPTER VI

Australia

THE MOVING FRONTIER IN COLONIAL DAYS

The story of white and native contact is, for several reasons particularly interesting in Australia. British peoples formed the vast majority of the invaders, and, up to the coming of colonial self-government in the eighteen fifties, the Imperial authorities carried the ultimate responsibility for native administration. For this reason Australia affords a particularly clear picture of British policy. On their part the primitive Australian aborigines presented to the white invaders exceptionally difficult problems of acculturation and preservation.

The British found perhaps 300,000 natives sparsely scattered over a great continent, two thirds of which consisted of difficult tropics or arid country, where adequate control was extremely hard to secure. Moreover, the religious ideas of the natives bound them particularly closely to lands which the incomers desired, while aboriginal culture differed from white culture to an exceptional degree. Owing to long isolation, and to hereditary and environmental factors, the Australian aborigines were a peculiar people, highly developed and specialised for what were, in many regions, extremely hard surroundings, and hence exceptionally unfitted to adapt themselves to European civilisation. These difficulties to some extent explain the British and Australian failure, but they hardly excuse the whites for a record of destruction and neglect which was considerably worse than the records of their cousins in New Zealand and the United States, and far below the record of Canada. This neglect extends even to historical study in that there has been very little research in the field of white native relations. Considerable work has been done in aboriginal ethnology, but only in recent years have students such as Fox-croft, Hasluck, Tindale and K. Hassell begun to study the historical aspects of Australian native policies and their effects both upon the natives and the whites[1].

NUMBERS

Australia and Tasmania embrace an area of 2,970,000 sq. miles, about two thirds of which consist of tropics or of arid trade wind country. This fact has confined close white settlement to the southern and eastern coastal districts. Pastoralists have, however, occupied almost the whole interior with the exception of the true deserts, while pearl fishers have extended their activities around much of the northern coasts. Estimates of pre-invasion aboriginal numbers are largely guesses, but Radcliffe Brown's close examination indicates that there may have been 300,000 natives on the mainland and 2,500 in Tasmania[2].

Distribution varied greatly with living resources. Population was naturally sparse in the arid regions. In areas such as the lower Murray River and lakes, however, game and fish were plentiful, and the density may have reached two per sq. mile—the maximum which such occupations could support[3].

The invasion quickly showed that wherever the white foot trod the native withered away. Special efforts were made in spite of great difficulties to secure correct figures in the census of 1921 which returned a population of 60,663 full bloods and 16,818 mixed bloods. The census of 1930 gave 61,734 full bloods and 17,797 mixed bloods and the pre-war estimate of 1939 51,557 full bloods and 25,712 "half-castes"—a term which loosely covered the mixed bloods. It seems therefore, that, as in Canada and the United States, the full blood native population is declining while the mixed bloods are registering increase.

Figures clearly indicate that isolation from the whites has been the main factor in native survival. The chief remnants of the aborigines are in the tropical north, which contains very few white people excepting in Eastern Queensland. One aspect of white native contacts is perhaps emphasised by the fact that two-fifths of the half-castes are in New South Wales—the oldest of the States[4].

AUSTRALIA

A few authorities have attempted regional estimates of the rate of decline. Tindale, working from the historical sources of the comparatively merciful colony of South Australia, concluded that the decrease may have reached 50% per decade.

Campbell, using data for the south-east of South Australia, where deliberate slaughter was comparatively rare, wrote that "every five year period saw a reduction of about fifty per cent of the indigenous population". "Half a century and all were gone[5]".

The above figures indicate that the Australian natives are passing through a numerical cycle somewhat resembling those experienced by the American and Canadian Indians. The full bloods are steadily declining and may be absorbed by the whites, probably far sooner than many groups of American Indians. On the other hand the half-castes are increasing, so much so that in parts of the continent they threaten to become a difficult problem[6].

ORIGIN AND CULTURE

It was long believed that the Australian aborigines consisted of two peoples—the Tasmanoids of Tasmania and the Australoids of the mainland. Authorities hold that the Australoids are Caucasians of a highly primitive and unmixed type. Indeed Sir Elliott Smith suggests that they are the representatives of Aurignacian man—the first human being of modern type to enter Europe.

The Australoids appear to have penetrated southwards down the East Indian islands leaving behind them groups such as the Veddahs of Ceylon, the hill tribes of Southern India, the Sakai of the Malay Peninsula, the Toala of the Celebes, and certain tribes of New Guinea.

The Tasmanoids were negritos even more primitive than the Australoids. They probably preceded the latter southwards down the islands, although some students have held that they came from the Pacific by canoe. Tindale and Birdsell have recently conducted highly important researches on these Australoid and Tasmanoid peoples. They conclude that the mainland groups are the result of blending in varying proportions of three discrete ethnic elements—the northern and southern mainland peoples,

101

and the Tasmanoids. These scientists found and examined in the rain forests of North-Eastern Queensland groups of the Tasmanoid negrito type—a discovery which may prove of fundamental importance in Australian anthropology[7].

It is not known how long these people inhabited Australia but their occupation probably extended over a considerable time. Taylor believes that they may have reached the continent during the Wurm Ice Ages, about 50,000 years ago, or even at a more remote period. J. B. Cleland notes evidence that man may have been dwelling in South-East Australia when now extinct volcanic cones were active. More conclusive are the results of archeological research along the Murray. This work indicates that aboriginal life in Australia is at least of some antiquity. Sauer suggests that the Tasmanoids occupied Australia and Tasmania during the Third Glacial period (perhaps 300,000 years ago) when Australia was accessible from Asia during periods of low sea level, and that their culture was an authentic relic of the middle Palæolithic. He considers that the Australoids may have entered Australia during the Wurm glaciation, bringing products unknown to the Tasmanians—the spear thrower, bark canoe, boomerang, bull roarer and shield[8].

Whatever their age and composition the Australian and Tasmanian peoples were highly primitive and hence particularly difficult to acculturise to European civilisation. The Tasmanoids used only the crudest of stone implements without handles. Their weapons were hardwood waddies or clubs and their spears were simply wooden shafts with points hardened by fire. They do not appear to have worn clothes, and their shelters were hollow trees or huts of boughs, bark and grass. They lived by hunting and by gathering shell fish or catching crayfish. Scaled fish they did not eat. The favourite hunting grounds were lightly timbered lands near the coast. The people probably had no canoes or boats, but bound together bundles of bark with cords made of grass. Frail as were such rafts the native paddled them to islands at considerable distances from the Tasmanian coast. White observers, who knew these aboriginals in their primitive state, described them as a simple and kindly people until white brutality drove them desperate. Unfortunately this ill-treatment destroyed the race be-

Tribalised Aboriginal—Central Australia—Taking Part in Rain-Making Ceremony

Photo: C. P. Mountford

Tribalised Native Drinking,—Ayers Rock, Central Australia.

Photo: C. P. Mountford

Aboriginal Boys' Training Home, Kinchela, via Kempsey
Photo: N.S.W. Government

Tribalised Aboriginals—Central Australia—Taking Part in Rain-Making Ceremony
Photo: C. P. Mountford

fore scientists could secure accurate knowledge of their language, culture or organisation[9].

The mainland natives were more "advanced" than the Tasmanians. It is true that in a land which lacked adequate seed-plants or milk-giving animals the aboriginals were poor in worldly possessions and living standards. Nevertheless, their vocabulary was rich, and their social organisation and ceremonial life were in many ways as complicated as those of the whites, while some of their weapons, implements and sacred objects of wood or stone showed fine workmanship and artistic decoration.

Permanent dwellings and clothes were only a handicap to nomadic hunters. Rain evaporated quickly from the skin, whereas the wearing of wet garments quickly produced disease. As was natural in a vast continent the food habits and cultures of tribal groups showed variations. Those who have known the natives best, however, consider them a moral, honest and kindly people. Unfortunately, at the time of the white invasions, and for long afterwards, anthropology was a comparatively unknown science, and many white officials, missionaries, educationists and settlers had little appreciation, or even understanding, of these stone age folk.

The outstanding feature of native life, and that which contributed very largely to its destruction, was the intimate association between the local group and its territory. The natives had divided Australia into tribal areas with clear cut boundaries, and each group hunted its own territory and rarely trespassed on those of others. Even more important was the fact that the tribal lands were the basis of religious and social life, for, according to aboriginal legend, the tribal ancestors had travelled through these lands and established sacred places in them. Members of each local group were bound together in the belief that their spirits had existed in this territory until they were incarnated, and that after death these spirits would return to the same territory, possibly to await re-incarnation. Hence, when the whites robbed the natives of their land, they not only destroyed the living resources to which they were accustomed, but they destroyed their spiritual past and present, and their spiritual hopes for the future[10].

WHITE SETTLERS AND NATIVE PEOPLES

THE BRITISH INVASION

As indicated previously the British occupation reduced the numbers of Australian aborigines from perhaps 300,000 in 1788 to 77,501 full and mixed bloods in 1921, the first year in which a careful census was taken. This reduction was effected by the usual factors of disease, slaughter and land robbery together with the destruction of tribal resources, religion and culture. Owing to the peculiar nature both of the immigrants and the indigenous peoples the whites wiped out the natives more rapidly than those of Canada, the United States and New Zealand. The aborigines were particularly backward and dis-united. Their arms were extremely primitive and, unlike the American Indians or Maoris, they showed little inclination to secure or use white weapons. Britain on her part sent to Australia for the first fifty years some of the most unruly elements in her population—convicts, their military guards, and individualistic, venturesome and widely roaming colonists.

The American revolution ended the British export of criminals to the United States, and in 1788 Britain founded Sydney on the East Australian Coast as an outlet for her convicts. For a time she played with but rejected proposals to despatch in addition to convicts American loyalists with their negro slaves. A little later the first governor—Governor Phillip—disobeyed Imperial orders that he should import Pacific Island women for his criminals. Thus, even in her foundation years, Australia avoided two types of colour problem[11]. In 1803-1804 the motherland founded penal settlements in Northern and Southern Tasmania, and from 1824 to 1838 she established temporary convict posts at Moreton Bay (later Brisbane) on the North-East coast, and at Albany in the south-west of Western Australia. Britain continued to send her worst elements to the Australian mainland up to 1840, and to Tasmania until 1853, and later continued the system in a small, modified and comparatively harmless manner by despatching probationers to provide labour in Western Australia until 1867. Over the whole period the Imperial Government sent 137,161 convicts to Australia. Numbers escaped to debouch the aborigines; others were assigned to remote districts where they caused frequent difficulties with the natives. In many cases the military guards, and later the police, inherited a legacy of brutality from the convict days[12].

Free settlers began to come as early as 1793, and increased so rapidly that by 1821 the free immigrants, the free born and the freed were more than twice as numerous as the prisoners. The exploration of the interior began. Macarthur pioneered the sheep industry. In 1813 Governor Macquarie supported the sheep men in storming the mountain barrier behind Sydney and a flood of pastoralists swept northwards to occupy Queensland, and southward to Victoria in the south-east. In 1829 British officials and free settlers founded the colony of Western Australia; in 1835-6 free Tasmanians forced the New South Wales authorities to open the Port Phillip district. In 1836-7 Wakefield colonising theorists secured the establishment of free settlers in South Australia[13].

DESTRUCTION OF THE NATIVES

The early years of convict settlement and squatter penetration are regarded as the romantic period of Australian colonisation but they provided little romance for the unfortunate aborigines. Facing the menace of a white occupation, conducted in some cases by depraved invaders, the coastal aborigines withered away very rapidly. Few scientific efforts have been made to analyse the causes of this decline, and many factors, such as the loss of ambition and the fall in the number of children, are far from clear. The evidence on slaughter, land robbery and disease is, however, indisputable, and will be summarised. It is particularly necessary to examine the evidence in regard to slaughter as recent research students have tended to minimise this factor on the grounds that most of the settlers treated the natives tolerantly, appreciated their economic value and expressed regret when they disappeared. This, in general, may be the correct view, but it tends to overlook ill-treatment, which, however new and unexpected were the difficulties of colonisation, was discreditable to the British Government, to the colonial authorities and to many of the pioneers.

The coastal explorers generally found the aborigines timid and inoffensive creatures. From the earliest time, however, Dutch navigators tried to kidnap them, and British and French visitors, such as members of the expeditions of Cook and Marion Du Fresne, fired on them.

The inland explorers, the vanguard of the invading hosts, also encountered little opposition considering the small size of the expeditions and the vast areas which they traversed. The aborigines murdered a few explorers for reasons which in general require investigation. It appears that in some cases the natives simply desired plunder, but in most they probably resented the intrusion of their territories and sacred places, or were seeking vengeance for various white misdeeds. Real strife developed when brutal sealers and convicts kidnapped native women and when pastoralists, often employing convict servants, occupied the water holes and drove away or shot the natives' game. When the aborigines retaliated by spearing white men or their stock, the colonial governments, police and settlers organised punitive expeditions, which, up to comparatively recent times, mercilessly destroyed the aborigines. As the historian Rusden wrote in 1884, "The slaughter of any black, whether suspected or not to have been implicated in some deed or of violence against life or property—indeed of every black found by the avenging band—became a common practice under the assumed sanction of government, when bodies of native police were let loose by their hardened officers to slay any and every black who could be hunted down[14]"

As late as 1928, when the natives killed a dingo shooter and attacked a station holder in the Northern Territory, the police "protector" and settlers went out and shot at least 32 aboriginal men and women, a procedure which a court of inquiry found "justified" after an investigation in which the Commonwealth Government refused to appoint legal aid on the aborigines' side[15].

EARLY EVENTS IN NEW SOUTH WALES

When Britain occupied New South Wales in 1788 she made no provision for an aboriginal population which perhaps numbered 40,000; all she did was to instruct Governor Phillip to open intercourse with the natives and to punish any colonists who wantonly destroyed them or disturbed their occupations. Phillip, a great man and humane, did his utmost to secure interpreters and to establish friendly relations with the 1400 natives in the vicinity of Sydney. He flogged a party of whites who set out to attack the natives indiscriminately; offered free pardons to those informing against convicts who murdered aborigines, and, when a native speared him owing to a misunderstanding, prohibited any reprisal[16]. Lesser men unfortunately succeeded the foundation Governor, and the driving of the natives from their fishing grounds, and assaults on native women, rapidly produced atrocities on both sides. When in 1799 an unduly mild sentence of punishment was remitted in the case of free whites who had murdered two aborigines the settlers realised that there would be no more trials for "wantonly killing" natives. Many were thereupon shot and the survivors were driven to the mountains. By 1802 the British Secretary of State was complaining that wise and humane instructions had been so little observed that it was evidently difficult to restore confidence with the natives, alarmed and exasperated as they were by the unforgivable injuries they had only too often experienced[17]. The great and philanthropic Governor Macquarie was well disposed to the aborigines but was unable to prevent murders—even of native women and children while they were sleeping. After native reprisals he sent to the Nepean, Hawkesbury and Grose troops who exterminated the bolder aborigines. There is, unfortunately, ample evidence that during this period 1809-1821, shootings continued along the advancing frontier, and that these were conducted not only by convicts, but by free settlers who "thought no more of shooting a native than shooting a crow[18]".

Governor Brisbane, 1821-25, made no effort to protect the aborigines. In 1824 he proclaimed martial law in the colony west of Cape York and the natives were shot like wild beasts. "The Sydney Gazette", for example, published an account of the killing of sixteen blacks by an overseer and two stockmen, while the "Australian Newspaper" recorded the sorrow of the natives at the slaughter of their women and children, and attributed the atrocities on both sides to the impudent and cruel conduct of certain whites[19].

Governor Darling, 1825-31, told the settlers to take measures for their own defence, and the Attorney General reported that "exceedingly violent proceedings were going on on both sides." In 1827 Lieut. Lowe, of Wallis Plains, was acquitted for having summarily shot a native, but at the same time a native who had murdered a white was hanged[20].

Little relief came until 1838, some fifty years after the foundation, when the effects of the humanitarian revolution in Britain were evident. In that year the Colonial authorities hanged seven whites, who had perpetrated the infamous Myall Creek massacre—the murder of some 28 harmless, innocent and friendly natives of various ages and sexes. At long last the colonists realised that the wanton murder of aborigines was prohibited.

The previous state of affairs is best shown by the intense popular indignation which accompanied the executions, and the murderers' own protest. "We were not aware that in killing the blacks we were violating the law or that it could take any notice of our doing so, as it has (according to our belief) been so frequently done before[21]".

THE DESTRUCTION OF THE TASMANIANS

Britain occupied Tasmania as a gaol for particularly hardened criminals, and the white contacts with the two or three thousand natives in that land were the most terrible in Australia. When the convict parties established stations on the north and south coasts in 1803-4 the natives were peaceable but trouble soon eventuated. At Risdon Cove some 300 to 500 aborigines appeared on a kangaroo drive—clearly with peaceable intentions as they were accompanied by their women and children. Yet the military completely lost their heads and shot about 50 of all ages[22]. This atrocity was the probable cause of native reprisals which became increasingly savage when wild sealers kidnapped native women, and when convicts, bushrangers and even some settlers treated the helpless aborigines with appalling cruelty.

Governors and official commissions unhesitatingly blamed the whites, Governor Daly, for example, reporting in 1813 that native resentment was almost wholly due to a barbarous and inhuman mode of proceeding "under which the whites robbed the aborigines of their children". The same Governor reminded his subjects in the strongest possible terms that the natives were unsuspicious and peaceable when the stockkeepers treated them decently. Governor Arthur repeated in 1828 that the troubles were due to the Risdon massacre followed by the savage action of sealers and stockkeepers in shooting the natives and seizing their women[23]. John West, the author of a "History of Tasmania", gave a fearful account of white atrocities as reported by eye witnesses, "the wounded were brained; the infant cast into flames; the bayonet was driven into the quivering flesh; the social fire around which the natives gathered to slumber became before morning their funeral pile[24]".

In spite of condemning these atrocities the colonial officers made no effort to punish white aggressors. They hanged without any legal proof of guilt a mainland aborigine "Mosquito", who led the Tasmanian native defence, but, according to Melville, who spent many years in the island, "not one single individual was ever brought to a court of justice for offences committed against these harmless creatures[25]". Under Governor Arthur, the natives turned more savagely on their torturers, and a full scale native war took shape.

Arthur established military posts along the frontier; appointed an aborigine protection committee; offered rewards for the capture of unharmed aborigines, and sought British permission to exile the survivors, providing them with clothing and sustenance[26].

Britain gave her sanction. Capture parties hunted the natives like wild beasts, using women as decoys, until the aborigines protection society protested against an indiscriminate killing which made all Christian men shudder. In desperation Arthur in 1830 employed some 4000 whites as a cordon to round up certain groups. Despite an expenditure of £30,000 his farcical effort was unsuccessful[27].

Kindness succeeded where force had failed. George Robinson, a Methodist by denomination and a builder by trade, knew something of the native language, and, going unarmed amongst the embittered aborigines, gained their confidence and brought in some 300 miserable survivors.

Even then, however, the white victors proved incapable of pity. Colonists interfered with the captives, and the Government, refusing to place them on the fertile Maria island, sent them to the barren and repulsive King Island and then to Flinders Island, where all but a handful died under conditions which the following chapter will relate[28].

WHITE SETTLERS AND NATIVE PEOPLES

DESTRUCTION IN THE FREE COLONIES

After the foundation of New South Wales and Tasmania the British founded Moreton Bay (Queensland) 1824, Western Australia 1829, Port Phillip (Victoria) 1835-6, South Australia 1836-7 and the Northern Territory 1863-70. These settlements were made in an age when British colonial policy was coming under the influence of the humanitarian movements. The Governors and the free settlers took in general a more enlightened attitude than in the convict period, but on a moving frontier of continental dimensions the improvement was often very slight.

QUEENSLAND

The vast north-eastern territory of Queensland was part of New South Wales until it became a separate colony in 1859. For very many years little or nothing was done to protect the aborigines whom Radcliffe Brown considers may have numbered 100,000. In the early period New South Wales was occupied with her native experiments in the Port Phillip district and did little in the north, except to establish a corps of native police which began operations in 1848. Northern New South Wales became the colony of Queensland in 1859, but the young colony did not appoint a protector or establish any reservations until 1875, although it continued to maintain the native police corps, a body which had gained "a bad reputation for cruelty and drunkenness". Under such neglect frontier warfare developed and led to the destruction of large numbers of aborigines. In the words of Professor E. O. G. Shann "Queensland seemed to the pastoralists 'their promised land'. Leslies, Campbells and Archers showed the way, and, in the sixties, scores of southern squatters sought safety there from the free selector. Black spearmen ambushed their stock in the brigalow scrub. They besieged even numerous station households with a strength and determination forgotten farther south and murdered isolated shepherds and carters with tragic cunning. In Queensland men went about their daily task with shotgun in hand, and nightly folded their sheep because pastoral occupation was still an invasion of territory held in force by resolute enemies. But native resistance could not stop the

110

invaders. The natural progress of the aboriginal race towards
extinction soon made fences, boundary riders and the 'kelpie'
feasible there too[29]".

VICTORIA

Until 1851 New South Wales administered the Port Phillip
district, which became in that year the colony of Victoria. Here,
amongst the native population of perhaps 11,000, she conducted
at British instigation the most important experiments in
aboriginal administration and welfare made in Australia during
colonial days. It seems, however, that before the British humani-
tarians initiated these experiments there was considerable slaughter on the moving frontier.

In 1853 the administrator, La Trobe, sent to the settlers a
letter of enquiry to which the replies are illuminating. Several
colonists reported that there had been atrocities on both sides
before they arrived, and one at least boasted openly of his share
in the shootings. George Faithfull, of Wangaratta, wrote that in
one conflict the whites had fired sixty rounds and added, "I
trust and believe that many of the bravest of the savage warriors
bit the dust—my name was a terror there ever after". I. G.
Robertson, of Wando Vale, made a terrible indictment of the
constant warfare and shootings and alleged that on one occasion
alone 51 natives perished. There is little doubt that the outstanding causes of these troubles were the white seizure of native
lands and women. Robertson told of a station owner on the
Glenelg River who kept a harem of native women for himself
and his men, who all got "fearfully diseased from these poor
creatures[30]". On the whole it may be said that the whites slaughtered a considerable number of natives in the Port Phillip district but that white-native relations were less violent than in New
South Wales proper, Tasmania and various other areas.

SOUTH AUSTRALIA

In South Australia, which contained perhaps 10,000 natives,
unruly sealers probably made early and vicious contacts. Nevertheless the official and free colonists of 1836 found the aborigines
of Adelaide and the surrounding districts peaceable and even use-

111

ful. When, however, pastoralists pushed inland from the coast, and overlanders brought stock down the River Murray, fierce collisions occurred, due as usual to white destruction of native resources and white interferences with native women. An unpublished research thesis by Kathleen Hassell pictures twenty years of native defence against white penetration, and of white reprisals—both official and unofficial—against that defence.

Britain completely forgot the aborigines when she declared the colony waste and unoccupied in the Foundation Act of 1834. The authorities, however, appointed a protector when the colonists arrived and missionaries were quickly in the field. Unfortunately neither the protector nor the missionaries could offer much restraining influence, as was shown by clashes on the Murray River whither the Government despatched several punitive expeditions, some of which slew thirty or forty natives in revenge for attacks on overland stock parties[31].

A letter from a German missionary—G. C. Teichelmann—written in 1841—throws important light on the underlying causes of these disturbances. Teichelmann complained that the protector had been forced to sanction shooting for the protection of his party but stated that "whatever outrages the natives may have committed on all such occasions the cause of it has been the Europeans". Not only were the whites led into rash and inconsiderate actions through fear of the natives, but stockmen on every opportunity prostituted the native women and then refused the husbands the promised remuneration of food or clothing. The protector, according to Teichelmann had been almost an eye witness to the abominations on account of which the whites had been compelled to resist native attacks[32].

Although the whites undoubtedly slaughtered many aborigines in the Murray basin and Port Lincoln areas, relations improved, as in Victoria, when white settlement increased. While, however, both the authorities and settlers treated the natives better than was the case in certain other colonies official and legal actions were often far from just. In 1840, for example, Governor Gawler greatly disturbed the British authorities by leading a punitive expedition against the murderers of the crew and passengers of the wrecked vessel "Maria" and illegally hanging natives who were suspects. In 1843 the Port Lincoln police shot perfectly innocent

AUSTRALIA

aborigines suspected of murdering a shipwrecked crew who were subsequently found quite safe. In later years the Colonial authorities hauled to Adelaide and left stranded unfortunate natives who were needed as witnesses from far distant parts of the colony[33].

WESTERN AUSTRALIA

The story is worse in Western Australia where, according to Radcliffe Brown, there were possibly 100,000 natives. Those near Perth were at first well disposed to the settlers of 1829, but were soon degraded by distributions of clothes and provisions. Affrays began in 1830, and by 1833 settler and native were in open conflict. In that year Governor Stirling led an expedition, which, in the "Battle of Pinjarra", shot half the males of the Murray tribe and captured several women and children. When the Colonial secretary, Lord Glenelg, censured the Governor from England, and ordered him to punish guilty settlers, Stirling published extracts from this despatch under one of 1832, which ordered the settlers to take measures for their own protection.

The ensuing years saw many conflicts, and both police and settlers slaughtered a considerable number of natives. In the fifties the occupation of the Champion Bay district (Geraldton) saw "frequent and fatal collisions with the squatters". Padbury, who founded the North-West in the sixties, said of two punitive expeditions, "after all they did not shoot many". In 1864 a punitive party, which was instructed to avoid "hostile collisions", received a censure from the British Secretary of State for shooting eighteen aborigines. In 1868 a revenging party of miners slew four, and wounded seven or eight, without arousing protests. In 1893 a police force, encountering opposition while arresting cattle spearing aborigines, shot twenty-three. As late as 1927 an official enquiry failed to unravel the alleged killing of Kimberley natives by the police owing to a settler "conspiracy of silence".

Throughout most of the history of the Western Australian frontier, officials, police and settlers acted without restraint on the assumption that "necessity knows no law". One can appreciate both the outlook of scattered and endangered pastoralists and of the unfortunate natives whose territory they invaded. One has less

WHITE SETTLERS AND NATIVE PEOPLES

sympathy with the colonial authorities, and with the police, who were usually anti-native. Nor can one wholly justify the British Governments, which issued worthy instructions and admonitions but took little action to prevent the slaughter of their native wards. British Statesmen were at a remote distance, and were ham-strung by home difficulties and expense, with the result that they were forced to leave native relations to their local officials and the colonists. Nor did these colonial officials administer the law impartially. The native remained "Black though British". The authorities hanged him not only for murdering the whites but for operating his own tribal justice. Yet when the native became the victim of white criminals he usually received scant assistance. Of this a recent student—Paul Hasluck—gives many deplorable instances. In 1861, for example, a white jury acquitted a settler, appropriately named Death—who poisoned a native child with strychnine[34].

THE NORTHERN TERRITORY

The remote and tropical Northern Territory contained 563,000 square miles of country and, according to the estimate of Radcliffe Brown, some 35,000 aborigines. There, on the northern coasts, Britain established, over the period 1824-49, three temporary convict stations. The colony of South Australia gained the region and administered it from 1863 to 1911 when the Australian Commonwealth took control. No research has been conducted on the aboriginal aspect of the official papers of the South Australian administration, now preserved in the Adelaide Library Archives. Some years ago, however, the author examined these records for other purposes and found that they related the same story as in other parts of the continent.

In the Northern Territory South Australia placed the natives under the nominal control of the Government medical officer, who was unable to prevent constant troubles between Europeans, Asiatics and aborigines scattered over a vast region. In 1901 the Government resident—C. J. Dashwood—created a furore by casting grave reflections on the administration of justice. "It was notorious", he wrote, "that the blackfellows were shot down like crows and that no notice was taken". The position was particularly serious in the districts traversed by miners from Queensland to the Kimberleys. When pressed for an explanation Dashwood quoted incidents in previous years. In 1885, for example, G. S. Little had stated that the blacks on the Playford River had killed a white man without provocation, and that for such actions there was only one remedy which North Queenslanders had never known to fail. L. V. Solomon gave evidence in regard to the way in which the whites had "dispersed" the Daly River natives after an outrage in 1884, and the "Northern Territory Times" then stated that if the right class of men were in pursuit of the aborigines little would be heard of the matter as in such cases "it was far more sensible to avoid complications by the exercise of judicious reticence". Again in 1890 the veteran Police Inspector Foelshe wrote, "The tribe withering away fastest is the Woolwoonga. My private opinion is that a good many have been put out of the way by bullets".

Similarly, Alfred Searcy, who recorded many atrocities by both parties, mentioned a white of the gulf country, who, in revenge for having been speared, had shot on sight 37 natives.

Something should, of course, be said on the side of the whites. It was obviously impossible for a weak and impecunious colony to police so vast a region effectively. In 1905, for example, the Government resident, Herbert, complained that the aborigines had perpetrated some thirty murders for which they had received little punishment.

Nevertheless, South Australia stands condemned for her refusal to amend laws which were unsuited to local conditions, and which for this reason were manifestly unjust.

In 1898 the resident complained that the protector had no powers over the relations between the aborigines and other races, and gave a scandalous example where the Supreme Court of South Australia had quashed the conviction of a Chinaman who had been living with an aboriginal girl of about ten—the Court arguing that there was no legal proof of the unfortunate child's age[25].

Taken as a whole there is ample evidence that the whites slaughtered very large numbers of aborigines, not only in the convict colonies and in the early days, but later, and on many sections of the moving frontier. While due allowance must be made for very great geographical and racial difficulties both Britain and the local authorities must be criticised for their failure to exercise an adequate trusteeship, or to administer the law impartially and with proper regard to the native social system and customs. This does not deny that in many of the settled districts white and native relations were harmonious; that many whites treated the natives with kindness and were sorry when they died away.

LAND ROBBERY

Probably even more important than direct slaughter was the land robbery, which not only deprived the natives of their living resources but destroyed the religious and social organisations that were so closely linked with the territory of each tribe.

When Britain founded Sydney in 1788 she claimed all rights in sovereignty and land, with a total disregard for the aborigines. For many years neither the Home Government nor the Colonial authorities had any anthropological knowledge of native life and, as a result, made little effort to guard native occupancy either in New South Wales or in subsidiary regions such as Tasmania. In 1829 the instructions to Governor Stirling at Swan River contained no specific provisions in regard to the aborigines, and, as previously noted, the Imperial Act which founded South Australia in 1834 completely ignored them, stating that the proposed colony was "waste and unoccupied". Although later British Governments and the Colonial authorities made some efforts to protect their charges and began to proclaim some small and inadequate reservations, the tide of European invasion occupied the aborigines' lands and destroyed their living resources, in almost all the temperate country which could support white industries—the process forcing the natives to enter other tribal territories or to become degraded recipients of white charity.

No anthropologist or historian has yet analysed the various results of these occurrences, nor has an attempt been made to give each cause its proper weight. It appears, however, that the land robberies contributed in a number of ways to the destruction of the aborigines. When the whites seized native territory water supplies and resources, the natives had the choice of resisting, of remaining as trespassers in their own country or of attempting to migrate. If they resisted, even to the extent of spearing stock to replace their lost game, the whites slaughtered them in "punitive expeditions", which were often official in character or at any rate approved by the early Governments.

If the natives remained in the occupied territory they lost their social organisation and customs; degenerated under white charity and vices, and perished from white diseases, at an extremely rapid rate. If the aborigines migrated to other tribal territory, they apparently created, in spite of their generally peaceful nature, the internecine warfare so frequently described by pioneer whites[36] and certainly lost the historic ceremonial connection with their own country. Thus whatsover alternative the native adopted, his ceremonial life, social system and ambitions were stultified, and he fell victim to a despondency which rendered him an easy prey to disease and impelled him to refrain from having children or to destroy his offspring at birth. In the Port Phillip district Protector Thomas showed that after 1836 the aborigines had few children, and that most of those born died during the first month, either from neglect or from deliberate intention[37].

An observant settler reported the same phenomenon from Mildura on the Murray River in 1853. Up to that time the Murray natives had destroyed only half-caste children, but they then began to practise infanticide to such an extent that the greater number of children perished. This was in spite of the fact that the aborigines were fond of their families and that food was plentiful[38].

The psychological reactions of many dispossessed or exiled groups were no doubt typified by one of the gaolers of the Tasmanians on Flinders Island who said that "they died in the sulks like so many bears".

Every morning at sunrise parties of these unfortunates climbed a hill to gaze across the waters to their native mountains, and. raising their attenuated arms, cried with tears streaming down their faces, "Country belonging to me[39]".

DISEASE

Historical material, including an important paper by J. B. Cleland, indicates that, as on other moving frontiers, disease was

117

the most important cause of Australian native decline⁴⁰. While there is little medical evidence in regard to the Tasmanians there are indications of tuberculosis on Flinders Island and alcoholism was prevalent amongst the native survivors in Hobart⁴¹.

Events on the mainland present the usual picture of exotic diseases preceding the moving frontier and destroying a large proportion of the aborigines. As in America smallpox led the van. This disease reached the natives of the Sydney region in 1789, soon after the first fleet arrived, but authorities consider that the epidemic was introduced by Malays on the northern coasts whence it spread through the tribes as far south as Victoria. A second outbreak appeared on the north coast about 1828. This extended to New South Wales and to South Australia, where it probably caused the diminution of the River Murray natives recorded by some observers. Possibly the Malays also caused a third outbreak which in the fifties and sixties affected most of northern and central Australia. It is interesting that the most potent destroyer of Australian aboriginal life in the moving frontier days should owe its origin not to Europeans but to Asiatics.

Cleland, Hasluck and other writers give many examples of the appalling destruction wrought by smallpox, measles and influenza on the natives. To take only two of many instances smallpox in 1836 reduced the natives of Dungog (N.S.W.) from 200 to 60, and in 1865 measles killed half the aborigines of the York District, Western Australia. The Europeans suffered comparatively lightly. When at Nichol Bay (W.A.) the natives fled in terror at the horrors of smallpox the whites cared for the deserted sufferers, yet no European was afflicted save for some unvaccinated children, and these only mildly⁴².

While, as in America, smallpox was probably the most potent of exotic killing diseases in pioneering days, tuberculosis came swiftly to the front, particularly through the natives sleeping in wet clothes.

Medical and other evidence indicates that the high incidence of this disease was due to native attempts to graft on a primitive existence civilised amenities such as clothes, houses and alcohol. Introduced in many cases by the Chinese, tuberculosis rapidly affected up to 20% of some tribes and appeared even in young

Tribalised Aboriginal with Sacred Shield. Central Australia.
Photo: C. P. Mountford

Housing on Aboriginal Reservation, Western Australia
Photo: W.A. Government

De-tribalised Aboriginal—Central Australia

Photo: Author

Aboriginal Children, Government Reservation, Point Pearce,
South Australia.

Photo: Author

persons of sixteen or seventeen. Aboriginal immunity and resistance were low, and lack of stamina led to a rapid abandonment of hope. Native habits such as expectorating freely and herding in airless sick rooms or huts quickly spread the disease. Pneumonia and influenza also caused heavy mortality[43].

Social diseases wrought much havoc amongst a people which seems to have been free from these scourges and which possessed no immunity. There is evidence from many parts of the continent that convicts, sealers and other frontier elements rapidly introduced these diseases which spread with horrible speed and violence. Tribes which were well shaped in body and limb, and which were almost free from disease, contracted venereal afflictions directly they visited towns or stations, and sickness became particularly prevalent where Asiatics encountered the natives in pearling and similar industries. The Asiatics also introduced the opium habit and scourges such as leprosy, many cases of which have been found amongst the northern aborigines[44].

The natives also suffered from diseases which were not necessarily of white introduction. Two of the most common and serious of these were the eye diseases, ophthalmia and trachoma, seeming cases of which were reported in very early days[45].

There is insufficient space to examine the effects of disease on all parts of the moving frontier, and a few illustrations from South Australia and Victoria must suffice. South Australia was occupied from 1836-7 by a good class of free immigrant, though there were rough sealers and whalers on the coast and a number of ex-convicts came in from the east.

At the outset the natives still numbered several thousands in spite of the ravages of smallpox in the eighteen thirties. They were peaceable, friendly and even useful. Unfortunately, they deteriorated rapidly under white charity and vices, and, by 1839, reports showed that their health had become poor and that venereal disease was raging and affecting nearly half of those in contact with the immigrants. The first two decades of white settlement saw sickness spread alarmingly amongst the aborigines living in the white areas, while the bush natives decreased so rapidly that groups which had numbered two or three hundred were reduced to thirty or forty. Venereal disease "communicated by the Europeans" was extensive. The "itch" which apparently resembled smallpox killed many children, and a considerable number of natives died from influenza and chest complaints. By 1850 the Adelaide tribe which had numbered several hundreds in 1836, was nearly extinct. A year or two later it appeared that the natives would be exterminated at Moorundie in the once thickly populated Murray area. "The decrease here seemed steady, rapid and inevitable". In 1857 the Bishop of Adelaide wrote that the settlers were generally kind to the natives, but that pulmonary and mesenteric diseases were carrying them off, even at stations where every care was taken to supply medicinal comforts. Reports of the eighteen sixties and seventies continued to stress the decline, attributing it chiefly to social diseases and tuberculosis. A sub-protector at Wellington, for example, wrote that the native population of his district had declined by half during his twenty-one years of office, and a Governor stated that everywhere he went —south, east, north or west—the natives were disappearing, to the general regret of the squatters, who found them very useful. Even native stockmen, well clothed and well fed, were dying of chest complaints[46].

The same story comes from Victoria which was rapidly occupied by free settlers from 1835-6. Many reports indicate how swiftly white diseases killed off the natives. The Gippsland group, for example, numbered 1800 in 1843, but by 1853 had been reduced to 126. Observant settlers attributed this decline less to slaughter than to the abandonment of an active hunting life for an idleness which fostered catarrhal afflictions, and to vices acquired from the whites, for example drink. In the words of Dr. Manson in 1854, "alas the decrease has been fearful, chiefly from drinking and exposure to all weathers bringing on pulmonary complaints". As mentioned by this officer alcohol greatly increased sickness and immorality. The natives secured drink by occasional work for the settlers, by selling weapons, by staging corroborees and by prostituting their womenfolk. In the South Australia of the forties there were reports of disgraceful drunkenness in spite of liquor prohibitions, and Victorian settlers of the fifties made many references to the havoc wrought by alcohol in causing murderous affrays and in fostering tuberculosis and other diseases. In the year 1851-2 there were eighteen deaths in the Yarra and Westernport groups which numbered 77 persons.

Eight of these deaths were due to murder, three to almost perpetual drunkenness and seven to sickness which the colonial sur-
geon was unable to combat".

In general it can be said that within a very few years of the
establishment of the moving frontier even kindly and well meaning whites were firmly convinced that it was impossible to civilise
the natives and that they would inevitably perish—primarily from
disease and vice. In the words of a Victorian settler of 1853 "the
Australian aboriginal race seems doomed by Providence, like the
Mohican and many other well known Indian tribes, to disappear
from their native soil before the progress of civilisation"". Such
a view was extremely comforting as a blanket excuse for apathy
and neglect.

CHAPTER VII

AUSTRALIA

Reservations and Missions

THE PHILANTHROPIC MOVEMENT IN BRITAIN

We have seen that for nearly fifty years Britain did little for her aboriginal wards. Under such neglect the natives were slaughtered, robbed of their lands and living resources, and riddled with disease and drink. Towards the end of the nineteenth century, however, the official and public conscience began to quicken in Britain, and the Evangelical Revolution led to the foundation of powerful movements for the liberalisation of the political system, for the abolition of slavery, for prison reform, and for the betterment of native colonial peoples.

In 1834 the House of Commons unanimously passed an address that it was deeply impressed with the duty of applying justice, humanity, civil rights and religion to colonial natives and asked that measures should be taken to that end. In 1836 and 1837 a select committee of the Commons under T. Fowell Buxton, who was the brother-in-law of Elizabeth Fry and the co-adjutor of Wilberforce, the promoters of prison reform and the abolition of slavery, issued reports which painted a shocking picture of European injustice and urged reform in fervent language. The committee stressed that the incontrovertible right of the natives to their own soil, "a plain and sacred right" had not been realised. Europeans had entered native lands uninvited. They had acted as if they were the lords of the soil. They had punished the natives as if they were aggressors on their own territories. They had treated them on their own property as if they were thieves and robbers, and had "driven them back into the interior as if they were dogs or kangaroos'".

RESERVATIONS AND MISSIONS

Under the policy suggested Britain and her Governors were to protect the natives as a sacred trust which could not be committed to the colonial legislatures. Colonial revenues were to bear the charge of protection and religious instruction. British law was to deal mildly with native offenders. Missions, and plans for political and social improvement were to be encouraged, and the Australian aboriginals were to be provided with hunting reservations until such time as they became interested in agriculture[2].

These reports were the highlight of British nineteenth century idealism in colonial native administration, but in Australia this idealism produced little practical result. The British Government could neither itself provide the funds to turn precept into practice nor would it extract sufficient funds from the colonists[3]. Moreover, neither Britain nor the Colonial Governments created adequate reservations, nor did they attempt to utilise reservation resources for native welfare. Under such treatment the natives still remained unprotected on the frontier, while, in the settled areas, the survivors received insufficient attention in religion, education, labour conditions, housing or health. It must of course be admitted that white settlement, no matter how philanthropically conducted, inevitably meant the destruction of large numbers of natives by factors such as disease. At the same time Britain and her colonies might have saved many of the outback tribes by the reservation of substantial areas, as was done many years later; and even in the settled regions they could have done considerably more to help the aborigines through the long and difficult period of acculturation. As it was the Motherland and the Colonial authorities made some unscientific and usually parsimonious efforts, and when these failed to transform in one generation stone age hunters into Christian and civilised agriculturists, took refuge in the comforting doctrine that the aborigines were doomed to extinction[4]. In real truth the age was one of an exploitation diametrically contrary to modern ideas, and, despite the greatly improved outlook of the eighteen thirties, no effective change of heart appeared in Australia for nearly a century, by which time the settlers and their diseases had gone far towards exterminating the aborigines.

WHITE SETTLERS AND NATIVE PEOPLES
EARLY WELFARE EFFORTS

The British philanthropic revolution did create some improvements. These assumed the same pattern throughout Australia during the period of British administration until the eighteen fifties; during that of Colonial administration until 1900, and during that of Federal and State administration over the opening years of the twentieth century. The chief threads in the new pattern were the introduction of native administration under officers such as protectors, the enrolment of native police, an improvement in justice and criminal proceedings, the establishment of small reservations and a slight expenditure on religion, education and health. The British politicians who were responsible for the enquiry of 1836-7 associated themselves with the founding of the Aborigines' Protection Society of 1836. Missionary enterprise was to be the basis of the new endeavour. In the the opinion of the enquiry attempts in North America and the South Seas to civilise the natives without the gospel had been "singularly unsuccessful"[5].

TASMANIA

Before this era of philanthropy appeared the gallant resistance of a handful of dispossessed and tortured Tasmanian Negritos had already doomed them to a reservation-gaol-cemetery on Flinders Island. There from about 1834 to 1847 disease and nostalgia reduced these sad remnants from 111 to 44[6]. In 1847 the survivors were removed to the outskirts of Hobart to perish from disease and drink. The last full blood male—a whaler—died in 1869 and the last full blood female in 1876. This woman—Truganini—was born in 1803, the opening year of the white invasions, so that her life of 73 years exactly covered the extermination of her people. She begged the whites to bury her beyond the mountains and not to dissect her body. Despite this pitiful request her skeleton stands in Hobart Museum—an apt memorial to the maltreatment of her race[7]. Some mixed bloods survived on Flinders and Cape Barren Island, at Comeroogunja, in New South Wales, and possibly on Kangaroo Island, to which last place the sealers carried Tasmanian women.

The Commonwealth Year Book of 1942-3 gave the number of

mixed bloods in Bass Strait as 285[8]. Tindale, who visited these groups in 1938, reported that they were mainly "dark whites" of white, Tasmanian and mainland aboriginal extraction. Closely inter-related, they were docile and law abiding and provided in the war of 1914-18 the highest percentage of enlistment in the Commonwealth. Nevertheless, their living standards and housing were poor, and the barren environment and the decline of the mutton bird industry forced them to secure Government aid or to seek better conditions through emigration[9].

NEW SOUTH WALES

In spite of British philanthropic utterances the Mother convict colony--New South Wales—saw, excepting in the Port Phillip district, no native policy worth the name for over a century from its foundation[10]. Governor Macquarie founded a small school at Parramatta in 1814, but it was abandoned in 1823. Lieut. R. Sadler set up another school at Liverpool in 1829. Missionaries were early in the field. In 1814 the Church of England Missionary Society founded a mission which failed through the interference of settlers and from inadequate means. From 1821 the Wesleyan Missionary Society maintained a station at Wellington, and from 1832-41 the Rev. L. E. Threlkeld, supported by the London Missionary Society, gained from the Government a large reserve of land at Lake Macquarie where three or four tribes were located at times. Threlkeld seems to have abandoned the project because the natives died out.

Apart from giving a little help to missions neither the British nor the Colonial Governments did much for the aborigines of New South Wales proper, and the original native population of perhaps 40,000 fell to 11,843 full bloods in 1881 and 3778 in 1901. After New South Wales became a State it established a Protection Board under an Aborigines' Act in 1909. By 1940 this Board had founded 21 stations where some 3,000 natives, almost all of whom were mixed bloods, lived in village communities under resident managers. There were also a number of reserves under the supervision of the nearest police.

The policy of the Board was to make the stations attractive by providing material improvements and social and sporting activities.

125

Something was achieved but much remained to be done. When, in 1939, 300 aborigines struck at the Comeroogunja Mission they alleged that their colony was riddled with disease and malnutrition, that the sustenance rate was quite insufficient and that the children were educated only to the third grade. Foxcroft concluded in 1941 that "the best this State has done for its natives today is yet far short of what is necessary"". Financial statistics support this conclusion. In 1939 New South Wales spent £76,454 or 141/- per person on its aborigines. Although this sum was considerably above the Australian State average of 74/- it compared unfavourably with the 220/- and 460/- spent respectively on the Indians of Canada and the United States.

Meanwhile the aboriginal full bloods declined steadily, while, as in other countries, the mixed bloods registered an increase. In 1921 New South Wales contained 1197 full bloods and 6846 mixed bloods. In 1941 only 594 full bloods remained, but the mixed bloods had increased to 10,616. These figures are of some importance. They indicate that although the full bloods are approaching extinction the mixed bloods and the total number of full and mixed bloods are increasing, the latter at an annual rate of 2.6%".

VICTORIA

New South Wales controlled the Port Phillip district until 1851 when it became the colony of Victoria. It was in this region that the Mother Colony, under the spur of British philanthropic ideals, carried out really important native experiments.

The number of aborigines was the principal factor in frightening away the timid Colonel Collins with a convict expedition in 1803, although a convict deserter—Buckley—lived with the natives until 1835. In the eighteen thirties free settlers and sealers gained an unsanctioned footing in the coastal areas and in 1835 the Port Phillip Association of Launceston, Tasmania, despatched John Batman with Governor Arthur's goodwill to take up land despite the prohibitions of the New South Wales Government.

Historians have dubbed Batman a trickster because he persuaded certain Port Phillip aborigines (who clearly did not understand the transaction) to put their marks on a grotesque ·legal

126

document which ceded him two magnificent tracts of country in return for flour, blankets, knives, tomahawks, looking glasses and the promise of a similar annual tribute. While there is no doubt that the Association intended to use this "piece of grotesque trickery, fantastic and absurd" against the New South Wales Government Batman deserves credit as being one of the comparatively few early British Australian invaders who offered the natives any compensation. The Port Phillip Association seems to have had its tongue in its cheek when it claimed that its objects were the civilisation of the natives as well as pastoral pursuits. Nevertheless it did appoint a missionary in 1836 and it had a praiseworthy record in its dealings with the natives whom it fed and clothed at its own expense. Historians have ridiculed the Port Phillip Association. They might well have remembered that only just previously the British Parliament had declared (1834) that the neighbouring lands of South Australia were "waste and unoccupied"[13].

The New South Wales Government not unnaturally repudiated Batman's treaty with the natives, but his discoveries, and those of other illicit pioneers, forced the Mother Colony to administer the Port Phillip district. Governor Bourke, therefore, appointed Captain Lonsdale as police magistrate; gave him strict instructions to protect the natives, and supplied him with presents which included 200 check suits and 500 red night caps. Lonsdale's administration saw a continuation of the work of the Port Phillip Association in the establishment of a native mission near Melbourne and the enrolment of native police. Neither effort succeeded, partly owing to the roving habits of the natives, and partly through the infinitesimal salaries paid by the Government to secure officers to lead the effort. After a temporary collapse the Government revived the native police force from 1841 to 1853. In spite of some successes the organisation proved "a tragic failure", as the native police became de-tribalised without acquiring the restraints of civilisation. During the first four years of the white invasions (1835-9) certain coastal tribes of Victoria declined from several thousands to a few hundreds. As previously noted births almost ceased and most infants died during the first month either from neglect or deliberate intention. There were also a number of white reprisals resulting in slaughters[14].

WHITE SETTLERS AND NATIVE PEOPLES

Undeterred by these ominous portents the British and New South Wales Governments operated from 1838 to 1850 a "New South Wales Aboriginal Protectorate, Port Phillip District". This protectorate, the outstanding early experiment in Australian aboriginal welfare, attempted to introduce the humanitarian system outlined by the Imperial Parliament. In 1838 the New South Wales authorities appointed a protector with four assistants to supervise various districts. They established central stations to provide schools, to distribute food and to promote agriculture. In twelve years they expended what was then the comparatively large sum of £42,000, denoting £25,000 in the first five years when efforts and hopes were at their peak.

Many factors wrecked the experiment. The Government made little effort to check land robbery and de-tribalisation, and its expenditure was insufficient to provide experienced and satisfactory officers or to deal with the grave problem of native health. The aborigines resented the academic education provided for their children at an age when it was essential for them to learn hunting and bushcraft, and hence they, very naturally, enticed them back to tribal life. White settlers, who frequently considered the natives a menace and nuisance, were unco-operative, while the protectors on their part complained that the New South Wales authorities deliberately thwarted the humane intentions of the British Government. For these reasons both official and private efforts for aboriginal welfare proved unsuccessful. Merri Creek—a Baptist School for the Yarra natives—a Methodist School on the Barwon and other educational experiments were temporarily successful but the natives in these localities soon disappeared or died[15].

In 1849 a select committee of the New South Wales Legislative Council ignored the protectors, took evidence from settlers only —and then mainly from settlers in New South Wales proper— and recommended the termination of the protectorate. In destroying an institution which undoubtedly eased the pillow of a dying people the committee suggested no palliatives of any other type. Nevertheless, some white philanthropists were already beginning to think on scientific lines. Motte, an English barrister, proposed that no lands should be taken from the aborigines without their formal consent and that their sacred tribal headquarters should become reserves. Arden suggested that the Government should create tribal reserves each of twenty square miles in various localities, and should compel the tribes to keep in these reserves in order to maintain group organisation and to prevent evil contacts in the towns[16]

On the whole it may be said that the altruistic British experiments on the Port Phillip district were chiefly valuable in proving the hopelessness of unsound and unscientific efforts. As in other countries the protectorate failed because it assisted detribalisation by gathering the natives on inadequate reservations where worthy missionaries attempted to instil an advanced religion and an academic education tempered by a little agricultural and domestic training. Complete failure again demonstrated the inevitable results of destroying the religious, social and economic life of a stone age people without a scientific examination both of the problem as a whole and of any initial steps which should have been made towards acculturation.

Notwithstanding these early failures Victoria, both as a colony and State, continued to operate the same type of policy. By 1850 de-tribalisation was practically complete. The number of full bloods declined from 2963 in 1851 to 1694 in 1861, and to 53 in 1921. Very recent years witnessed a slight increase and a population of 88 was recorded in 1941. As in other Australian States the number of mixed bloods was advancing; the total having risen from 607 in 1921 to 775 in 1941[17].

In 1860 the colony passed an Act to establish an Aborigines' Protection Board and to permit the Governor to control white-native contacts, prescribe reserves, distribute parliamentary grants and arrange for the education of native children. The Board attempted to initiate a vigorous policy but the wealthy but parsimonious colony cut the 1861 estimates from £11,500 to £5000. Within the next fifteen years small aboriginal stations were established at Lake Tyers and Lake Condah under the auspices of the Church of England, and in other places under the supervision of the Government or religious denominations. Today one-third of the natives is concentrated at Lake Tyers while about a half live on the sites of other, now abandoned, stations.

In 1939 Victoria was spending 187/- per native, the largest sum per head of any Australian Government.

129

WHITE SETTLERS AND NATIVE PEOPLES

A Victorian Chief Secretary claimed in 1938 that his State was dealing satisfactorily with her aboriginal problem and was years ahead of the Commonwealth, Queensland and Western Australia in this respect. Foxcroft blew the bubble of this self complacency with a particularly apt comment. "Victoria in one way alone is years ahead of the other mainland States in meeting the problem, she has gone further towards the extinction of the natives than they"[18].

SOUTH AUSTRALIA

South Australia, founded by the Wakefield colonial theorists and free settlers in 1836, dallied ineffectively with inadequate reservations and impecunious missions. Although Britain ignored the natives in the Foundation Act of 1834, she delayed the first immigrants until there had been discussions on white-native relations, and the first Governor paid much attention to this subject in his first proclamation. Official action was sluggish, however, and clothing rations and disease quickly degenerated the friendly and healthy aborigines of the Adelaide region. Relations became worse as the pastoralists pushed into tribal territory; seized native lands, drove off native game, and interfered with native women. The Murray river stock routes, and the Port Lincoln district in particular, saw mutual actrocities followed by bloody punitive expeditions.

Moorhouse, the protector from 1839, stated that white-native relations passed through three phases. In the first the natives were harmless and usually approached the whites without weapons. In the second they always carried arms. In the third they became peaceable. Thus as the circle of occupation widened there were frequent skirmishes and atrocities on the frontier while in the inside country the de-tribalised natives were dying away peaceably. In many cases the aborigines became quite useful to the settlers, and, when a large proportion of the white male population joined the Victorian gold rushes of the fifties, the natives stepped into the breach and showed that responsibility produced trustworthiness.

Soon after the pioneer settlers arrived the Government appointed an "inefficient protector ad interim" and gave the natives a location near Adelaide. Upon this huts were built. In 1839 the Government appointed Moorhouse protector, and, as settlement spread, established small reservations at Encounter Bay and other places. White settlers protested against even this minor act of decency, but in 1842 Britain granted the Australian Colonial Governments the power to create such reservations under the Waste Lands Act. This Act also provided that 15% of the land sale receipts could be spent on native administration and benefits, but in 1842-3 only the miserable sum of £1000 was allotted to these purposes.

Fighting and slaughters in the Murray river and Port Lincoln areas caused the establishment of aboriginal stations at Moorundi on the Murray and Poonindie near Port Lincoln. The latter, founded by Archdeacon Hale of the Church of England, was a noble experiment to provide young couples with religion and education on a basis of practical farming. Although both Governmental and Church support was insufficient, and the buildings became wet and insanitary, the mission made temporary progress. Nevertheless, in the long run it demonstrated the usual cycle of lack of natural increase, disease and death.

By the eighteen fifties it was clear that the native full bloods were dying out in the settled districts. By 1860 most of the native schools had collapsed; Poonindie was failing, and most colonists considered that the aborigines would soon be extinct. Kathleen Hassell concluded as a result of her careful examination of original documents that British and Colonial native policy in South Australia was conscientious, but desultory, inadequate and unintelligent.

Gradually a few progressive South Australians began to realise that both the protectors and missionaries had made grave mistakes and that scientific enquiry was an essential prelude to a new approach and technique. As the Rev. George Taplin wrote in 1879 "if the missionary does not know the religion of the people to whom he goes—and the superstitions of the aborigines are their religion—he will never grapple with the difficulties that lie in his way—he will not find that aboriginal customs are always to be cast away, some may be usefully retained even after the natives have become educated and Christianised".

Although in later years scientific investigators like Roth, Spen-

131

cer and Gillen provided the knowledge for a new technique, Foxcroft found in 1941 that South Australia had not made sufficient efforts to amend her destructive policies. In 1929 her full bloods numbered 2630 and her mixed bloods had increased to 2197. In the latter year expenditure was 139/- per native as against the Australian State average of 74/-. Although this was far below the Canadian and United States figures it must be remembered that South Australia had only 700,000 white inhabitants.

Foxcroft noted in 1941 that very recently the State had evolved "some sort of policy for its full blooded natives", and had created some reserves in the arid north-west. There, as the chief protector reported in 1936, the full bloods were making their last fight, "not yet degraded by contact with a civilisation they cannot assimilate or understand". The new reserves were to be buffers between white and black to ease the clash. Unfortunately they proved inadequate to contain the natives in seasons of drought, and the police patrols also proved insufficient[19].

NORTH AND WEST

It is clear that the British whites and their diseases exterminated the aboriginal full bloods with great rapidity in the south-east of the continent where settlement on the whole was most dense. By 1929 the full bloods of New South Wales, Victoria and South Australia had been reduced to 3917. By 1939 their numbers had fallen to 3560. In the north and north-west of the continent, however, isolation, tropical climate, seasonal and uncertain rainfall and poor soils provided the aborigines with considerable natural protection and stemmed the white torrent. Although the full bloods declined with great rapidity, Queensland, the Northern Territory and Western Australia still contained 47,997 full bloods in 1939. In these regions, too, the "half-caste" problem threatened to become most acute. From 1929 to 1939 the mixed bloods advanced in numbers from 7278 to 12,379 as against an increase of from 9171 to 12,985 in the south-east of the Continent[20].

The vast State of Western Australia embraces temperate country, deserts and tropics. The South attracted white agriculturists and pastoralists in fairly close occupation. The northern and north-eastern areas proved suitable for only a sparse pastoral

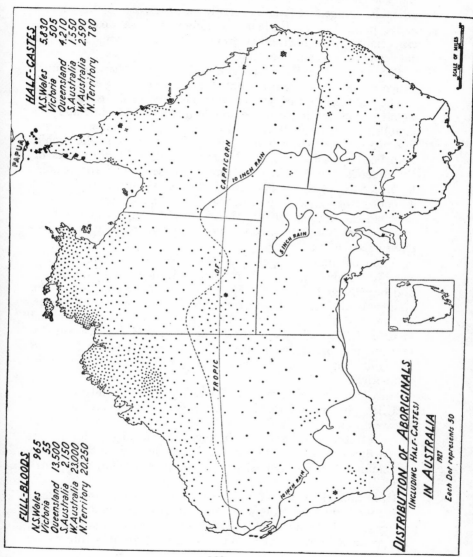

HALF-CASTES

N.S.Wales	5,830
Victoria	505
Queensland	4,210
S.Australia	1,550
W.Australia	2,590
N.Territory	780

FULL-BLOODS

N.S.Wales	965
Victoria	55
Queensland	13,500
S.Australia	2,150
W.Australia	23,000
N.Territory	20,250

DISTRIBUTION OF ABORIGINALS
(INCLUDING HALF-CASTES)
IN AUSTRALIA
1927

Each Dot represents 50

SCALE OF MILES

settlement, but mining parties roamed over much of the State, and the pearling industry of the northern coast attracted considerable numbers of Asiatics. Early estimates placed the original native population at 100,000, and although these were probably exaggerated it is likely that from 1829 until about 1890 the natives outnumbered the whites.

Two recent historians, Hasluck and Foxcroft, have examined native policy in Western Australia, with illuminating results.

The eighteen thirties saw the usual outburst of British idealism, which manifested itself in the appointment of protectors and the establishment of small reserves usually under missionary aegis. For two reasons British native policy in Western Australia should have been specially vigorous. First, until the gold discoveries of the nineties, the natives were the largest section of the population. Second, up to 1897 the British Government maintained its control of native administration. Therefore, theoretically, Britain had the justification and the legal right to apply her doctrine of the Dual Mandate which later proved so valuable and effective in East Africa.

When colonisation opened in 1829 the natives were friendly, but the distribution of food and clothes turned them into thieves and beggars, and the usual affrays followed the occupation of the country lands. The first Governor—Stirling—a former naval officer, was repressive and massacred the Murray natives at the so-called "Battle of Pinjarra". Nevertheless he appointed a native superintendent, interpreter and police corps, and founded near Perth an aboriginal station which collapsed owing to the nomadic habits of the natives[21].

Hutt, the second Governor, a leading British philanthropist, and British humanitarianism, attempted to put philanthropic ideas into practice. The Imperial Government appointed and paid two protectors who promoted pacification, inoculated the natives for smallpox (apparently in the interests of the whites), and helped to establish the Rottnest Island aboriginal prison and some small missions.

Unfortunately when convicts were re-introduced these efforts languished; the protectors were given other duties, and the native police—a body of specially trained whites—were incorporated in a less qualified convict police force. Rottnest became a true prison

Boggabilla Aboriginal Station, N.S.W. View from Tank Stand.
Photo by N.S.W. Government

De-tribalised Aboriginal—Central Australia
Photo: Author

Walgett Aboriginal Station, N.S.W.—School
Photo: N.S.W. Government

Aboriginal Children, Point Pearce Government Reservation,
South Australia
Photo: Author

and native graveyard, while the missions, which were conducted by Anglicans or Methodists at Perth and a few other centres, failed because the natives absconded or died[22].

For a time one mission, New Norcia, like the Californian Missions, seemed to meet with success, and for similar reasons.

Indeed the story is so interesting and the parallelism with California so marked as to warrant detailed research.

New Norcia was established by Benedictine Fathers in the Victoria Plains area, and, like the Californian missions, was conducted on practical and commonsense lines. The founders planted "un villeage du sauvage proprietaires" and trained their converts as farmers and artisans, wisely regarding the A.B.C. as a secondary consideration. While the aborigines were still able to engage in hunting the Fathers made little progress, but from the eighteen seventies to the end of the century they did much for the dispossessed natives. They placed aboriginal families on the land and built decent stone houses to accommodate them. Boys were taught to the age of thirteen or fourteen and were then trained in agriculture or stock raising. Some promising young natives were even sent to Rome to study for the priesthood. As late as 1905 Dr. Roth's inquiry made a favourable report and stated that the mission guarded two hundred natives, and was schooling fifty children.

Nevertheless, in spite of some success and progress, New Norcia exhibited the same cycle of rise and decline as did the somewhat similar missions of California. The Fathers' energetic attempts to civilise and christianise the aborigines contributed to the wrecking of tribal life and the ultimate destruction of the full blood natives. In 1846 the Victoria Plains group numbered some 250 persons. The last full blood died in 1913.

Despite the frequent proclamation of humanitarian aims the British Government did little for the enterprise, even in the years of apparent success. From 1846 to 1858 it gave the Fathers no financial aid, and from 1859 onwards all that Britain or Western Australia gave the mission were parsimonious annual grants of from £100 to £200[23].

Apart from New Norcia there was little effort or progress. The missionary record of Western Australia until the close of the century was "a very sorry one[24]".

WHITE SETTLERS AND NATIVE PEOPLES

After the re-introduction of convictism in Western Australia Britain took little interest in her native trust. The aboriginal was "still black though British" and Hasluck's research has recorded a sorry story of the inequities of British justice over a wide scale of crimes and misdemeanours from murder to absconding from employment.

From 1870 to 1887 successive Pearling Acts tried to control the employment of the natives who proved most useful to that industry, and some remedy of abuses was attempted by the Aborigines' Protection Act of 1886—an act which introduced an Aborigines' Protection Board and sought to establish a census of native employment[25].

Reports of later commissions indicated, however, that employers largely worked their own sweet will. Parliamentary and public opinion was only too often hostile, contemptuous and neglectful of the "niggers", while the British Government, despite occasional protestations, had to let matters take their own course[26].

The Western Australian Constitution Act of 1889 set aside a sum of £5000 per annum for the natives with the further stipulation that if the colonial revenue exceeded £500,000 a year they should receive one per cent per annum for their welfare. Although Western Australia was greatly enriched by the gold discoveries the Colonial Government considered that this moderate provision, which would have provided about £30,000 per annum or 20/- a head for the aborigines, was grossly excessive, and it was rescinded by the Act of 1897 under which the British Government abandoned its control. The Motherland, it is true, made a protest as a last exhibition of her inadequate trusteeship, but she then ended a "rule of uncertainty, inconsistency and neglect, and handed on a charge that was ill-kept, contaminated, hopeless and despised[27]".

In 1904 Western Australia obtained from Dr. W. E. Roth, the Chief Protector in Queensland, a report which exposed a scandalous position in many parts of the State. Conditions of employment were loose and unjust. Along much of the coastline drunkenness, prostitution, opium and loathsome diseases were rife, while the savagery of the police in arresting alleged cattle spearing natives had created, "a most brutal and outrageous condition of affairs". The Government was doing nothing to protect the natives whom the colonists were dispossessing over large areas, and corrupting relief was increasing at an alarming rate[28].

In these circumstances Dr. Roth made sweeping recommendations to give the protector additional powers to establish large reservations in the back country; to curtail rations in hunting areas; to dispense ·better justice; to improve the education of native children and to control employment more effectively[29].

The Aborigines' Act of 1905 gave effect to some of these recommendations, but omitted the most important as certain members of the State Parliament attacked Roth with great bitterness and closed the door to the establishment of adequate reserves in the outback. Later, however, the act was amended and the State created some large reservations although in a very haphazard fashion. Enquiries by G. T. Wood in 1927 and by H. D. Moseley in 1934 indicated that matters were still very unsatisfactory in regard to policy, administration and settler outlook. Moseley considered that even the Missions disrupted tribal life and advised that the tribalised natives should be left alone as much as possible and that much more welfare work should be conducted for the de-tribalised natives and half-castes. He pointed out that the half-caste problem was becoming acute largely through lack of education and vocational guidance. "At the present rate of increase", he wrote, "the time is not far distant when the half-castes or a great majority of them will become a positive menace to the community; the men useless and vicious; and the women a tribe of harlots[30]".

In the pastoral areas the position was more satisfactory. Government cattle stations, established for the natives, were doing good work, although there was need for better medical and educational services[31].

In 1936 a Native Administration Act gave effect to some of Moseley's recommendations, but there were still grave faults and the evidence given at the Canberra Conference of 1937 indicated the pressing need for additional expenditure, particularly on health and vocational guidance. In 1929 Western Australia contained 22,916 full bloods and 2711 half-castes. By 1939 the full bloods had decreased slightly to 21,878 while the half castes had increased to 4688. In the latter year the expenditure was only 31/- per native —the lowest figure of any Australian State. At that time Western

137

WHITE SETTLERS AND NATIVE PEOPLES

Australia had an annual revenue of eleven millions and was spending £10/10/- a year on the education of every child who had the good fortune to be white.

At the Canberra Conference the protector stated that an expenditure of 30/- per native was "a ridiculous sum", but that the State "was not in a position to expend a large amount of money on these people". Such an excuse appeared quite inadequate. The natives still numbered 5% of the population, and were rapidly increasing in the south-west. They were extremely useful in pearling and were vital to the northern cattle industry. With low standards of health and education they formed plague spots in the community while the rapid increase of a low grade half-caste population presented a real menace[32].

QUEENSLAND

Native policy and administration were particularly interesting in the great north-eastern colony of Queensland, because, after a bad beginning, they proved the most successful in the continent. As part of the colony of New South Wales the Queensland region witnessed British philanthropic experiments which, as in the other Australian colonies, secured little success. Missions were established at Moreton Bay (1837), German Station and Stradbroke Island, but these were soon abandoned. A native police force operated for longer than in the other colonies, but, although this institution was the principal Government agency for native welfare, it gained a reputation for cruelty and drunkenness. In 1874 the residents of the Mackay district petitioned that the natives in the area be employed and protected. The Government then appointed to enquire into the condition of aborigines in Queensland a Commission which made important recommendations on the need for protectors, and reservations, and on the suppression of the liquor traffic. The colony began to follow these suggestions, but settler opposition developed in Parliament and for another twenty years little was done to check frequent conflicts between settler and native, white punitive expeditions, and prostitution and exploitation, under which the aborigines declined apace.

In 1896-7 the Government obtained from Archibald Meston,

RESERVATIONS AND MISSIONS

and from W. E. Parry-Okeden, the Commissioner of Police, appalling reports which indicated that the existing machinery of administration was hopelessly inadequate; that white settlement was rapidly exterminating a dispossessed people; that the missions were poorly situated and unsuccessful; that outrages of all kinds were prevalent along the coast, and that the native police had confined their work to retaliatory measures against the blacks.

In 1897 the Government passed the Aborigines' Protection and Restriction of the Sale of Opium Act which still remains the basis of native management. Parry-Okeden, Meston, and Dr. Roth were appointed protectors—the last two as full time officers in the south and west. The native police were employed on native conciliation and welfare. Above all the Government established large reserves in which the natives were to be protected from all racial contacts, the Cairns Reserve becoming the largest then existing in the continent. Later legislation empowered the protectors to control the employment and wages of natives but no major changes were necessary until 1939 when Queensland passed the Aboriginals' Preservation and Protection Act and the Torres Strait Islanders Act.

This policy was administered by capable protectors and was aided by a favourable climate, large unsettled spaces, occupations which attracted the natives, and possibly superior types of aborigines on the coast. On paper the results were satisfactory. From 1933 to 1939 the full bloods of Queensland declined only very slightly from 12,532 to 12,030, while the mixed bloods increased from 3869 to 6778. By the latter year seventy-five per cent of Queensland natives had become self-supporting in the fisheries and on the cattle stations, while the Torres Strait Islanders, who owned a fleet of pearling and fishing vessels which produced a valuable annual catch, had gained a measure of local self-government.

Foxcroft considered that Queensland operated the policy of reservations and missions with far greater success than the Governments of the Commonwealth and of the other Australian States, and this in spite of the fact that her expenditure of 75/- per native was considerably below that of New South Wales, Victoria, and South Australia. He attributed this relative success to the wisdom of the Queensland protectors and to the favourable climate, the reasonably large reservations, the curtailment of white contacts and the direction of industry along lines which conformed to native interests. A further factor may have been the vocational guidance afforded on the reserves and government stations. After the Harvard-Adelaide Universities expedition conducted researches in Queensland, Tindale painted a less optimistic picture. He pointed out that employment was permitted only under contract, the Government keeping 50% of the wages in a trust fund. All people with aboriginal blood were controlled by the Aborigines' Act excepting where they were subject to an exemption which could be revoked at any time. Any person with aboriginal blood, who broke a contract would be removed with his family to a reserve and there restrained temporarily or permanently. Hence, said Tindale, persons of aboriginal blood were tending to become an unhappy and unstable people, the victims of confinement and isolation in settlements such as Palm Island, from which there seemed to be no intention of giving them freedom. Tindale considered that the Queensland system presented elements of the concentration camp, and quoted instances of persons of aboriginal blood who had fled across the New South Wales border to secure freedom[33].

THE NORTHERN TERRITORY

From 1824 to 1849 Britain established some small convict stations on the North Australian coast for fear of occupation by powers such as the French and the Dutch. These stations had some relations with the aborigines, who were regarded as treacherous, but the influence on the natives seems to have been slight, unless, as is now suspected, the settlements introduced disease.

In 1863 the young but ambitious colony of South Australia gained the 563,000 square miles of the Northern Territory—a huge region which the colony was too weak to manage satisfactorily.

The South Australian administration lasted from 1870 to 1910, and the official reports of the period are now housed in the South Australian Public Library. These have not been closely studied in their aboriginal aspect, but when the author examined them for other purposes, he found, as noted previously, the usual Australian

140

story of white neglect, in this case augmented by the influx of
Chinese miners and other Asiatic types.

The South Australian Governments failed to provide adequate
facilities for protection, education or health, and, as few white
women would face isolation in a hot and arid region, the native
lubra became the female pioneer of the North. A police officer
reported from Alice Springs in Central Australia that the practice
of keeping native women was the rule rather than the exception,
a fact which was shown by the number of half-caste children.
Worse than this the lubras were not "kept" in the ordinary or
in any other sense of the word, a practice which reflected no
credit on the fathers of the mixed blood offspring[34]. The South
Australian police, and later the Commonwealth police, were in
most cases fine men who laboured against very grave difficulties,
but their patrols had to cover immense areas of arid country and
were powerless to check many outrages and abuses.

At the beginning of 1911 the Federal Government assumed
control of the Northern Territory. The Commonwealth sang an
opening chorus of pious aspirations; sent up a scientific expedition
to examine the natives and then did little or nothing. As late as
1933 Canberra spent the niggardly sum of £8434 on 19,424
natives or only 9/- per person, a lesser amount than the outlay on
post and telephones for 3300 whites.

After some twenty years of Federal maladministration and
neglect the Australian public conscience became anxious and
forced the national government to act, with the result that in
1929 and 1935-7 Canberra obtained from J. W. Bleakley and Dr.
Donald Thomson most illuminating and distressing reports on
the condition of native affairs in the Territory. Bleakley's tragic
document exposed great evils in native administration, employment, living standards and the prevalence of disease. It condemned the facts that the whites housed the natives like "hounds"
and subjected their women to "gin sprees"—drink and prostitution
orgies—in which Australians even descended to rewarding the unfortunate lubras with bogus money. Bleakley pointed out that
from the economic aspect alone this state of affairs was lamentable. The pastoralists in general fed the natives and their depen-
dents on the offal of beasts killed for station food; housed them
in "kennels", and gave them clothes, and, in some cases, a few

shillings a week. Yet, said Bleakley, the pastoral industry was absolutely dependent upon the blacks, while, according to one opinion, the lubra was "one of the greatest pioneers of the territories for without her it would have been impossible for the white man to carry on"[35].

Thomson reinforced Bleakley's revelations with the statement that the Arnhem Land natives were "already on the road to extinction". He advocated the establishment of reservations; the complete segregation of tribalised natives and other sweeping reforms[36].

The Commonwealth Government adopted the most important of Bleakley's and Thomson's recommendations, and, as in other countries, the nineteen thirties saw Canberra begin to evolve a scientific policy, which, in its aspirations at least, showed some glimmerings of President Roosevelt's New Deal. Under this policy the Commonwealth quadrupled its expenditure, which then approached per person that of Western Australia—the meanest of the States; increased the reservations in Northern Australia, appointed as Commonwealth adviser an officer from the New Guinea Service; stationed an anthropologist as patrol officer in Central Australia; established aboriginal medical benefit and trust funds; improved the supervision of working conditions and wages, and initiated schemes for housing half-castes and for training young natives in arts and crafts, which conformed to their traditions and interests.

The McEwen memorandum of 1939 aimed at raising the status of the aborigines with the ultimate object of admitting them to citizenship. Its framers realised, however, that the task would cover several generations[37]. The World War interrupted this programme, but the Curtin Government made further advances, when it applied to the natives in a modified form pensions, maternity allowances, and child endowment[38].

FEDERAL OR STATE CONTROL?

In 1943 negotiations conducted between the Commonwealth and States indicated that the State Governments were prepared to surrender their natives to Canberra despite the fact that the Federal record was darker and meaner than that of any State.

RESERVATIONS AND MISSIONS

The Federal Government, therefore, submitted the transfer to the nation in a Referendum Act, but as it was combined with highly contentious matters, the proposal met with defeat.

In spite of geographical differences in various parts of Australia there is a case for central and unified control, particularly as this would transfer the bulk of the financial responsibility from sparsely settled States such as Western Australia where large numbers of aborigines have survived—to more wealthy and densely settled regions like New South Wales and Victoria, which have successfully destroyed their natives. Nevertheless, the delay in transfer can do no harm, as it will provide time for the Commonwealth to prove that it is no longer the most incompetent and neglectful Australian Government in matters of native administration. As Dr. Donald Thomson wrote in 1937, "It is desirable that the administration of native affairs should be under one control, but the Commonwealth should initiate action by putting into operation its policy, when it would be in a position to ask the States to come into line"[39]. Dr. Thomson's cautious approach was wise. Eight years later at the close of the war he published the strong criticism that the Commonwealth aboriginal administration had been a dismal record of failure and insincerity, punctuated by hypocritical promises of a "New Deal", the result of which had been nil. As late as 1947 the statement was published that in March of that year the Humber River Aboriginal Reserve in the far north-west of the Northern Territory was sacrificed to mining interests[40].

THE PRESENT POSITION

Australian native problems can be dealt with under several headings such as the tribalised natives, the de-tribalised natives, the half-castes, and the missions. Leading authorities agree that the remaining tribalised aborigines, who are largely in the north, should be segregated from the whites until anthropological research discovers better methods of native management. Under existing conditions de-tribalisation is proceeding apace and has doubtless been greatly accelerated by the war. Moreover, although various governments have increased the size and number of the reservations, these reservations are often insufficiently well policed

143

to keep either the natives in or the whites out. As regards white penetration of the reservations the Australian outlook on native lands is subnormal and immoral as compared with that of more advanced English-speaking peoples, and the Canberra conference of 1937 painted a sad picture of administrative incompetence and settler greed. The United States and Canada rigorously control white entry to reservations and use reservation resources for the benefit of the natives. Yet at the Canberra conference official speakers stated that strong white pressure was still being exercised to secure entry to the reserves (often for the purpose of making immoral contact with native women) and that if minerals were discovered public opinion would enforce the exploitation of the reserves in the interest of the whites[41].

The other side of the picture is the difficulty of confining the aborigines to their reservations, particularly, in some cases, during seasons of drought. Tindale, who studied the problem with the Harvard-Adelaide expedition of 1938-9, pointed out that certain arid country should be resumed from its white occupiers, not only in the interests of the natives, but also in those of the whites. Such action would secure "the control of faunal pests and the effective occupation of a desert area which is a menace to pastoral areas"[42].

As regards future economic development, Canada, the United States, Queensland and Western Australia have shown the way in giving native peoples occupations which conform to their traditions or tastes. The Queensland success in coastal industries, and the progress of West Australian native cattle stations, appear to offer hope.

The author, like other travellers in outback Australia, was horrified by the conditions which existed amongst the de-tribalised natives and half-castes prior to the War, although these natives provided over much of the centre and north an essential supply of labour[43]. Wages, although improved, were still miserably low at the outbreak of war; the food provided largely consisted of offal, and the housing, where it existed, was often scandalous. Even after Bleakley's revelations the sex relations of whites and natives remained a great problem, and the aboriginal and his lubra still coloured every phase of life over vast areas of a continent that claimed to be white.

144

RESERVATIONS AND MISSIONS

After the Harvard-Adelaide expedition Tindale ably outlined the problem of the mixed bloods. He drew attention to the importance of the question; the increasing numbers of these people; the need of education and vocational guidance and the presence of serious malnutrition. He considered that the whites could absorb the mixed bloods without detriment, particularly as the native was close to the white in blood and there were no reversions to the dark aboriginal type. His conclusions were most important, for they indicated that mixed blood groups should not be segregated, as in some States, but should be merged in the general community. He also made the important pronouncement that various grades of mixed bloods varied in their potentialities for absorption".

Tindale made very strong criticisms of the general neglect by Australian Governments of mixed blood education and diet. He stated that the mixed bloods received very little education or vocational training; that the Education Departments of various States took no responsibility, and that on many pastoral properties the educational facilities were "often extremely inadequate". Even more serious was his charge that Australia was permitting many mixed bloods to suffer from malnutrition. He considered that the food which many mixed bloods obtained enabled them to function only at the lowest levels of vitality, compatible with survival. Tindale's conclusions were directed to the feeding of natives both on the reservations and cattle stations. That an Australian-American expedition should find such conditions in a British democracy was a grave indictment of the young nation.

Opinions varied as to the missions which were strongly criticised on the grounds that they destroyed tribal life and organisation without putting anything stable in their place. On the other hand authorities of great experience, such as Bleakley, defended the missions on the grounds that they had done some good work and had proved sympathetic and just. Thomson believed that the proper scope of the missions was to act as buffers on the borders of reservations, while Tindale considered that they could effect their most useful work amongst the mixed bloods. Such opinions seem correct. In spite of much sincere effort the Australian native missions failed to prevent the decline and disappearance of the aborigines and in all probability accelerated that process by their de-tribalising influence. The proper field of the mission appears to be with the de-tribalised native and mixed bloods, and it is certainly vital that every missionary should take an anthropological course.

The war made important changes in native problems as the aborigines and mixed bloods were moved from certain areas and were employed in various types of war service and in labour camps. In much of this work they proved extremely useful, rendering valuable service in finding lost airmen and even playing a worthy part in the fighting units. Unfortunately, however, their services received little recognition. Possessing no votes to buy the attention of Canberra politicians, they remained "Black though British". On the eve of the Second World War Elkin summed up the position very succinctly. "The problem", he wrote, "is the extent to which the aborigines are capable of working out a fresh adaptation to the changed conditions which have come upon them as the result of the settlement of their country by whites. The change has been sudden and all-pervading, going right to the roots of their religious and mental adjustment. The whites, officials and settlers, have not understood this, and neither governments, missionaries nor educational authorities have yet planned and put into operation policies designed to help the aborigines tackle the tremendous task of readjustment which confronts them. The reason for this is our lack of understanding. We have not understood nor appreciated aboriginal social and religious life, nor the significance of that cultural clash which has arisen from the invasion of a primitive food-gathering people's country by a civilised, agricultural and industrial people"[45].

From a variety of causes, of which governmental meanness and neglect seem by no means the least. Australia is the only English-speaking country under consideration in which the total population of full bloods and mixed bloods combined has recently registered a decrease. The total aboriginal population fell from 77,481 in 1921, when a particularly careful count was made, to 77,259 in 1939. The full bloods declined from 60,663 in 1921 to 51,557 in 1939, but the mixed bloods advanced from 16,818 to 25,712 over the same period[46]. This decline of total aboriginal population, like the whole story of white-native relations reflects little credit upon the Australian people, or their present and past governments.

NOTE TO CHAPTER VII

In September, 1948, while this book was in the Press, the author paid a brief holiday visit to Central Australia, during which he called at the missions at Arltunga and Hermannsburg, situated respectively 70 and 90 miles east and west of Alice Springs, the head of the southern railway. Although the time was short and the region covered comparatively small, certain facts were evident.

First, full blood and mixed blood aborigines were present in considerable numbers, and were engaged in a variety of occupations at Alice Springs, at the missions, and on all cattle stations visited. As the Administrator admitted in his report of 1944-5 the native clearly remains essential to the cattle industry in the Australian tropics.

Official figures indicate a slight but steady decrease in the number of full bloods and in the total of full and mixed bloods combined—the latter figure falling from 16,887 in 1937 to 14,153 in 1944. As could be expected wartime conditions decreased the number of nomadic full bloods (8727 in 1937, 4735 in 1944) and increased the number of full bloods in supervised camps (3974 in 1937, 5631 in 1944). In view of the rapid decline in the number of nomadic full bloods the Administrator rightly urged that the native reserves should remain absolutely inviolate. During the war the Government used the natives "steadily and continuously in connection with the Army", and demobilisation created problems, particularly as the Native Affairs Branch was understaffed.

In recent years the Commonwealth Government increased its expenditure on its Northern Territory aborigines and effected some improvements. In his report of 1946 the Administrator claimed that the Director of Native Affairs had inspected all the cattle stations on which natives were employed and had reported on the whole that the treatment of the aborigines was good. The Government also supervised the distribution of rations; drilled bores to supply water to the Central Australian natives, and improved some housing, for example at the Half-Caste Home at Alice Springs, of which a photograph is included.

WHITE SETTLERS AND NATIVE PEOPLES

Unfortunately some of the housing remains inadequate and "kennels", such as those condemned by Bleakley in 1929, are still in evidence, even on Government Reserves, as is illustrated. For this the natives themselves are partly responsible, as their habits are detrimental to the provision of permanent and adequate dwellings. The extension of child endowment has been of considerable value, particularly to the missions which care for native children, but the aboriginal does not yet receive the old age pension. The Federal Medical Service seems to have improved and gained tributes for the rapid despatch of medical supplies during the recent serious outbreak of measles in Central Australia.

As previously noted the author visited the historic Lutheran Mission at Hermannsburg in the valley of seasonal Finke River, and the comparatively new Roman Catholic Mission at Arltunga. Hermannsburg was founded in 1877 under circumstances of great difficulty as it lay in arid country 700 miles from the then rail head, Port Augusta. It now has out-stations at Haast's Bluff and Areyonga in the dry country to the north-west and south-west together with other points of contact, and altogether is in touch with 1,200 natives. It was good to see that the Lutheran missionaries were battling along on scientific lines by endeavouring to develop industries which appealed to the natives, for example, cattle raising; the tanning and working of cattle and kangaroo hides; mulga woodworking, and painting in water colours. In the last-named art several full blood aborigines, notably Albert Namatjira, have been gaining high reputation by their ability in portraying the glorious colours of their rugged desert environment. Recent developments have been the piping of water from a spring some miles distant, which has enabled the mission to grow vegetables; and the appointment of a trained nursing sister. The missionaries claim that, as a result of a balanced diet, births have exceeded deaths in every year save one since 1935. This is a matter of great importance, but it is impossible to decide whether the appearance of a natural increase is due to improved diet; to the natives developing some immunity against white diseases; or to a partial intrusion of white blood. The missioners themselves admit the difficulty of estimating the proportion of mixed bloods

148

in a region where white-native contacts have existed for many years.

The Roman Catholic Church established the Arltunga Mission to care for aboriginal girls during the war, and the missionaries are waging a courageous but pathetic battle on a station which is too small and too arid for the establishment of those industries which make some appeal to the natives, and which at Hermannsburg have met with some success. As at Hermannsburg the Federal Government gives child endowment, together with a similar miserable grant of two or three hundred pounds a year.

In his report of 1944-5 the Administrator of the Northern Territory considered that the assistance granted by the Federal Government to its aboriginal wards was less than that given by some of the States. This seems correct. In 1945-6 the Commonwealth spent, apart from salaries, only £25,410 on some 14,000 aboriginals or about 36/- per native, a more niggardly provision per capita than that of any State excepting perhaps Western Australia, and of course far below the standards set by Canada, New Zealand, and the United States.

As a result of his brief stay in Central Australia the author felt that the Government Trusteeship of the aborigines was slightly more generous and efficient than it appeared on his previous visits but that it was far below what could and should be achieved in a Federal Territory where native wards comprised the majority, and a valuable majority, of the population. In these circumstances the observations of the trained anthropologists, R. M. and C. H. Berndt, set out in the appendix, deserve consideration.

CHAPTER VIII

New Zealand - The Maori Decline

THE MAORI IN PRE-CONQUEST DAYS

New Zealanders claim that their treatment of the Maoris has been exceptionally satisfactory, but the facts of history hardly support this contention[1]. They demonstrate, for example, that the New Zealand record is certainly not as good as that of Canada. Under British-New Zealand contacts the Maoris passed through a period of decline, marked as elsewhere by heart-breaking warfare, disease, land robbery and the destruction of native religion, social life and culture. Also, although the attitude and generosity of the whites improved greatly in later years, and the Maoris entered on a period of recovery, both they and leading white authorities consider that this was largely due to a revival of leadership and morale amongst the Maoris themselves[2].

The fertile and well-watered islands of New Zealand stretch north and south for 1040 miles in the south temperate zone between latitudes 34° and 47° south and are particularly suited to white settlement. It was formerly believed that the aboriginal inhabitants—the Maoris—were a Polynesian people who invaded the islands and conquered an earlier Melanesian race[3]. Very recent archæological discoveries in the South Island indicate, however, a Polynesian culture at the earliest levels—contemporary with the extinct bird the Moa, and that the Maoris were a mixed race before the invasions. At any rate it seems that they were a section of the peoples who roamed the Pacific far and wide with outrigger or double canoes, and that the culminating migrations came from Tahiti and the nearby islands about 1350 A.D.[4]

It is impossible to determine the number of natives in New Zealand when the whites arrived. Captain James Cook, judging

150

Walgett Aboriginal Station. General View
Photo: N.S.W. Government

Boggabilla Aboriginal Station. Aborigines' Cottage
Photo: N.S.W. Government

Aboriginal Humpies on Government Reservation, Central Australia, 1948
Photo: R. B. Lewis

Hospital—Point Pearce Government Aboriginal Reservation
South Australia

Photo: Author

from the coastal tribes which he saw, made a guess of 100,000,[5] but other authorities consider this too high[6]. Dr. Peter Buck on the contrary suggests a figure of from 200,000 to 500,000, but adds, "We shall never know"[7]. The missionaries reported a death roll of 80,000 between 1820 and 1840, when Dieffenbach estimated the population at 115,000, which would give a total of about 200,000 in 1820[8]. With Fenton's census of 1858, which placed the Maoris at 56,049, we reach firmer ground. The figures given by Dieffenbach and the missionaries surmise a pre-invasion populace of 200,000, so allowing for a decline of one-third through disease, and another third from war and other causes, the result approaches fairly closely to this estimate.

The distribution of population varied greatly under geographical influences. The taro and yam were not cultivated as far south as Cook Strait, nor the sweet potato south of Canterbury. It is thought that about a quarter of the population lived north of the present city of Auckland; another quarter were on the Bay of Plenty and in the Ngati-Porou country, and only about a twentieth were in the South Island[9].

All accounts agree that at the beginning of the white invasions the Maoris were a people of considerable intellectual capacity, with well developed agriculture, social usages and arts. Their stone weapons, canoes, fishery, agriculture, dwellings, fortifications, and textiles were of an advanced standard, and, like the Haidas, they excelled in wood carving[10].

Moreover, the Maoris were a healthy people until the whites riddled them with disease. Cook, for example, wrote, "These people enjoy perfect, uninterrupted health". His party never saw any diseased person and was surprised to find the number of well preserved old men[11].

The Maoris had, however, many traits that revolted the incoming whites. They were inveterate fighters and practised slavery and cannibalism, while their squalid and odorous houses, painted and oiled bodies, and love of putrid foods were nauseous to Europeans.

In spiritual matters the Maoris lived in a dream realm which found a unique expression in their language, poetry, art, music, ceremonial and social customs. Their priests worshipped Io, a supreme being, all wise and all good, but the common people obeyed in blind belief an elaborate system of inferior restraints, ceremonials and spells. Fear gripped the Maori in his dealings with spirit things, and his abject humility produced an abnormal savagery together with low moral standards which sanctioned lying, theft, cunning, deceit, treachery, cruelty and revolting orgies. Mentally the Maori was kept in a semi-childhood stage of development by lack of intellectual stimulus—but he probably possessed a cultural potential of considerable height[12].

THE MOVING FRONTIER

Tasman discovered New Zealand in 1642. Cook mapped the islands in 1769 and left pigs and potatoes. On his second voyage he found the Maoris of Queen Charlotte Islands very divided and very ready to trade their wives and daughters for tools, hatchets, and large nails, so much so that George Forster pronounced, "Our intercourse with such sea islanders to be wholly harmful to them[13]". In 1788 the British settled New South Wales, and from 1792 onwards they made attempts to exploit such New Zealand resources as flax, timber, sealing, whaling, and even tattooed heads[14].

The period 1792-1840 presents a terrible example of the effects of a moving and uncontrolled frontier on a primitive people. Frontiersman of many loose types—long separated from female influence—sealers and whalers, shipwrecked and runaway sailors, escaped convicts and traders, degraded the unfortunate natives. In the South the whalers appear to have behaved fairly decently,[15] but the whites created a state of anarchy in Northern New Zealand, particularly in the Bay of Islands, with grievous results[16].

As usual the white weapons of destruction were disease, drink, firearms and miscegenation. Little scientific research has been done on this gloomy period, but the general outline is obvious. Whereas Cook had reported that the Maoris were an exceptionally healthy people, observers on H.M.S. "Dromedary" noted, while visiting the North Island some 40 years later, the presence of consumption, violent rheumatism, sore eyes and inflammation of the lungs and bowels"[17].

Duff states that the muskets of the Maori chief Te Rauparaha, reduced the effective population on the east coast of the South island by one half, and that white contacts, which introduced tuberculosis, measles, syphilis, and rum, then reduced the survivors by another half[18]. The effects of alcohol, and their rebound on the heads of the whites, were shown in resolutions passed by the more reputable settlers of the Bay of Islands in 1835, for example, that the importation and sale of spirits should cease and that the stock on hand should be exported[19].

Keesing notes the results of the indiscriminate gorging on new varieties of food; the over-indulgence in alcohol; the softening effects of clothing, especially of blankets, and the ignorance of the simplest rules of hygiene which gave a new susceptibility and lowered the resistance to disease[20]. Many tribes came down from their hill forts into flax swamps and forests, and the dank river flats had not the healthy atmosphere of the hilltop pas[21].

Equally terrible were the effects of white weapons on a people whose life and amusements were largely centred in war, and in the 20 years following 1816 a series of horrible conflicts altered the face of Maori New Zealand and shook the native social system to its foundations. Tribal boundaries were changed; widespread migrations took place, and it is estimated that anything up to 60,000 Maoris perished[22].

From the very outset white-Maori contacts produced bloodshed. Tasman lost some of his crew, and Cook had to teach the Maoris the killing power of the musket. The French explorers proved tactless, injudicious and merciless, and the voyage of De Surville (1770) and Marion Du Fresne (1772) brought atrocities by both whites and natives[23].

In 1793 Lieut. Hanson was sent with the "Daedalus" to kidnap Maoris to teach the Norfolk Islanders how to work flax, and he seized two young chiefs who were transported to Sydney and Norfolk Island for this purpose. The flax trade began in the following year, and the timber trade in 1798. Whaling opened in the last decade of the century, and many Maoris who joined white crews were abandoned in Sydney. Americans arrived in 1812 and were followed by the French. Sealing started early in the century and soon produced degeneracy[24].

In the tragic native wars which followed the notorious leaders, Hongihika and Rauparaha, were inspired by the example of Napoleon. In 1820 after visiting Britain Hongi secured 300 muskets and ammunition and scourged large areas of the North Island for nearly twenty years[25]. Rauparaha aspired to be the Hongi of the South. He established the island fortress of Kapiti, on the south-west coast of the North Island, conquered large areas and then crossed Cook Strait to devastate far down both the eastern and western coast of the South Island, where he probably killed or enslaved some 4,000 people, about half of the scantv population[26]. A Maori stated in 1844 that Rauparaha and his allies passed over the southern island like a wave, burning, slaying and enslaving hundreds and dispersing hundreds more to die of cold and starvation[27].

In his most atrocious crime, the Sack of Akaroa, Rauparaha was aided by a white man—Stewart of the brig "Elizabeth"—who enticed Arkaroans on board where they were taken prisoner. The village was then sacked and some of the prisoners were murdered and cooked in the ship's coppers for a cannibal feast. Stewart was tried in Sydney for murder but the prosecution failed[28].

Maori marauding expeditions sailed as far as the Chatham and Auckland Islands in 1835-42. In the former group they virtually exterminated the Moriori by slaughter, hardship and disease[29].

MISSIONS ON THE MOVING FRONTIER

Although the great era of missionary enterprise in the Pacific had not yet opened, the inspiring evangelical movement had aroused Britain by the time the whites invaded New Zealand. Hence devoted English missionaries reached the moving frontier even before the establishment of official settlement or administration, and their labours shine as the only light in a dark and horrible picture. Unlike Spain or France Britain did not in general give her missionaries official status and support so that these early missionary efforts were all the more praiseworthy.

Samuel Marsden, Senior Chaplain in New South Wales, proved a born missionary and became the apostle of New Zealand[30]. From 1807 to 1809 he laid in England the foundation of missionary work in New Zealand, which he visited on seven occasions, exploring much of the North Island and receiving an excellent reception from the Maoris[31]. The "Boyd" massacre delayed the enterprise, but in 1814, with the help of the Church Missionary Society, Marsden established a mission under Hongi's protection in the Bay of Islands, where he secured 200 acres of land for 12 axes. Marsden was a man of great vision and his methods showed much of the commonsense evinced by Duncan at Metlakahtla in Canada. He grasped the importance of New South Wales in spreading Christianity in the Pacific area. As he wrote in 1818, "The gospels, humanly speaking, could not be established in the South Sea Islands unless our Government had established a colony in N.S.W."[32] He hoped to see New Zealand a Maori Christian kingdom, united under one ruler, and governed by native law, but in his great wisdom Marsden also realised that any such objective must rest upon a practical economic basis to which the Maoris were accustomed[33]. In his own words, "The arts and religion should go together—to preach the gospel without the arts amongst the heathen will never succeed at any time"[34]. Hence Marsden's first two missionaries were a schoolmaster and carpenter, who not only attempted to convert the Maoris, but taught them agriculture and useful arts and traded with them[35]. The famous scientist, Darwin, paid a high tribute to the splendid results of the missionaries' practical work, "Native craftsmanship has effected this change. The lesson of the missionaries is the enchanter's wand"[36].

At the outset progress was very slow. There were language difficulties and trade was poor as the missionaries refused to supply firearms. Moreover vicious white men had reduced much of New Zealand to chaos. "At Paihia, on one side of the Bay of Islands, the Anglican Mission was endeavouring to introduce an ideal pattern of life, and on the opposite side, members of the same race as the missionaries had established a pattern of debauchery the like of which savages had never imagined"[37]. Nor were the whites alone to blame. At Hongi's stronghold the missionaries could hear the dying shrieks of captives and smell their cooking flesh"[38].

Soon, however, the advance was more rapid and the Williams brothers made progress. The Wesleyans, helped by Marsden, arrived in 1823, and the Roman Catholics in 1838. The Wesleyans attended to the West Coast while the Anglicans concentrated on the East[39]. With the help of Professor Lee of Cambridge the missionaries gave the natives a written language. The first translation of the Scriptures into Maori was published in Sydney in 1827, and a printing press was established at Paihia in 1835[40]. Marsden himself founded a Maori seminary at Paramatta in New South Wales[41].

The Maoris eagerly embraced Christianity and education. By the middle of the eighteen thirties, the faith was spread through New Zealand "like fire in the fern", often by Maori missionaries, and when the New Zealand Company settlers arrived at Port Nicholson at the beginning of 1840 half the population was regularly attending missionary schools and services[42]. By eighteen thirty-eight the Church Missionary Society alone had 37 schools in the North and 17 in the South Island. Congregations numbered 2476 and school pupils 1431[43].

While Christianity became an all prevalent fashion in the New Zealand of the moving frontier, the seeds of future difficulties were already evident. The Maoris had ample intellect to appreciate that Christians included sinners as well as saints, while they were quickly bewildered by the strife of Christian sects. Both the Anglicans and Wesleyans strongly opposed the Roman Catholics, and when Bishop Pompallier arrived in 1838 with a commission from Pope Gregory XVIth, the Protestants represented him to the Maoris as an agent of the French. In point of fact the Bishop proved more interested in the welfare of souls than in white national conflicts, and in 1851 became a British naturalised subject[44]. It is, however, easy to understand the confusion which inter-denominational strife created amongst the unfortunate natives. Te Heuhew made a significant remark to Bishop Selwyn when he said, "I see three ways—the English, the Wesleyan, and the Roman. Each teacher says his own way is the best. I am sitting down and doubting which guide I shall follow"[45].

BRITAIN AND THE MOVING FRONTIER

During the troubled period of the moving frontier Britain showed to little advantage. British governments facing many other and costly claims had no wish to undertake further expensive colonial obligations, while the savagery of the Maoris frightened respectable settlers[46]. Between 1817 and 1836 the British authorities disclaimed possession of the Islands on no less than eight occasions[47].

Nevertheless atrocities in the Pacific were stirring both the public and private conscience, while vigorous organisations were urging colonisation. As early as 1817 a British Act enabled offences in the Islands to be treated as if they had been committed on the high seas, and an Act of 1829 empowered the courts of New South Wales and Van Diemen's Land to take cognizance of offences by British subjects in the Pacific[48]. In 1830 Governor Darling of New South Wales asked that a ship of war should be stationed in New Zealand to restrain the masters and crews of ships. In 1831 came news of Stewart's share in the atrocities at Akaroa and in 1832 Britain ordered Governor Bourke to appoint a Resident in New Zealand, James Busby—the man without guns to support his authority[49].

Busby remained at his post for six years. He was censured by the British Government for his failure to prevent the liquor traffic, and ridiculed for obtaining from Maori chiefs a declaration of independence, which included provision for a Maori Congress, a device by which he calculated to defeat the schemes of the French adventurer de Thierry[50]. His work, however, was far from fruitless, for he interested James Stephen, Permanent Under Secretary of the Colonial Office, who ruled the colonies behind the scenes, and he helped to open the eyes of the British public to the shocking conditions in New Zealand[51]. In 1837 a Committee of the House of Commons stated, "Our penal colonies have been the inlet of incalculable mischief to this whole quarter of the world. It will be hard, we think, to find compensation not only to Australia, but to New Zealand and to the innumerable islands of the South Seas, for the murders, the misery, the contamination which we have brought upon them"[52].

The growth of British conscientious scruples was quickened by colonisation enterprise and by French designs as typified by de Thierry, by the whaling Captain Langlois, and by the Nanto-Bordelais Company which claimed land in the Banks Peninsula of the South Island. In 1839 the powerful New Zealand Association sold 100,000 acres of New Zealand land in London under the nose of the British Government, and on May 7 the same year despatched Colonel Wakefield with the "Tory" settlers.

WHITE SETTLERS AND NATIVE PEOPLES

The Wakefield colonisers had now forced the hand of the British Government and in January, 1840, Captain Hobson reached the Bay of Islands with official instructions to annex all or part of New Zealand for Britain. A French expedition, which reached Akaroa in July-August of the same year, was just too late[53].

LEGALISED LAND ROBBERY

The arrival of a British Lieutenant Governor and official settlers opened a new chapter in white-Maori contacts[54]. On the surface the outlook was promising. In New Zealand Christianity had made substantial progress. In England the great humanitarian movement and the powerful missionary organisations, founded under its ideals, had attracted the attention of English statesmen and the public to the maltreatment of aboriginal peoples.

In 1834 the House of Commons presented to the King an address which prayed that His Majesty would direct colonial officers to secure justice to and rights for colonial native peoples and so lead them to a voluntary reception of Christianity[55].

The 1837 Committee of the House of Commons gave high praise to the British Colonial system, but at the same time published eight hundred pages of evidence from Australia, the South Seas and other regions, much of which was in direct contradiction to the somewhat self-satisfied conclusions of the Committee[56].

In 1837 another Committee of the House of Commons admitted some of the evils of British-Colonial administration, particularly in regard to the penal settlements, and asked that the Government should refuse to countenance schemes for colonising New Zealand and other parts of Polynesia until such schemes had been discussed by Parliament[57]. Following this Lord Glenelg, the Colonial Secretary, stated, "Great Britain has no legal or moral right to establish a colony in New Zealand without the pre-consent of the natives, deliberately given without compulsion and without fraud"[58].

In view of British sentiment Hobson made, in February, 1840, the celebrated Treaty of Waitangi with forty-six head chiefs, and in the presence of at least 500 others of inferior degree. Later he reported that he had secured 56 more signatures[59]. The Maoris

158

appear to have accepted the treaty owing to the growth of European and Christian influences, and to the fact that both the conquerors and captives of the native wars desired outside protection[60].

Under the Agreement the chiefs conceded to the Queen all rights and powers of sovereignty together with the exclusive right of purchasing such lands as the proprietors might wish to alienate. The Crown extended to the Maoris its royal protection, together with the rights and privileges of British subjects, and guaranteed to the chiefs and tribes of New Zealand and to families and individuals "the full exclusive and undisputed possession of their lands and estates, forests, fisheries and other properties which they may collectively or individually possess so long as it is their wish and desire to retain the same in their possession"[61].

No clearer language could have been used to express the sincere desires of British statesmen to give the Maoris a charter of rights which obviously recognised the comparatively novel doctrines that the aboriginal natives of a country possessed the first claim to its soil[62].

Unfortunately words alone were powerless to curb the torrent of white immigration, the unbridled selfishness of the invaders, the moral dishonesty of their political leaders and lawyers, and the childish ignorance of short-sighted natives who were prepared to sell their birthright for a mess of pottage. Thus the Treaty of Waitangi completely failed to effect the worthy objectives of its framers[63].

As far as Maori lands were concerned the colonial lawyers held that until a crown grant had been issued for any piece of land the native owner had no standing in a court of law if dispossessed. He could acquire enforceable rights only by selling the land to the Crown and then buying it back.

If the price which the Crown offered was unsatisfactory he could sell to no one else. The colonial courts refused to listen to native claims in disputes with the Crown and the judges held that if an Assistant Commissioner of Crown Lands claimed that land belonged to the Crown the matter was removed from the jurisdiction of the courts[64]. This was the chief cause of the rising in the Bay of Islands in 1845 and of the wars of 1860 which broke the heart of the Maori race[65].

With the robbing of native lands came as usual the destruction of native resources. Advocates for the Crown secured lakes and beaches which contained or commanded pipi and oyster beds and crayfish and fishing grounds, and, while the whites revolted against the destruction of native birds and plants, they connived at the wholesale destruction of berry-bearing trees by the advance of settlement[66].

The granting of all the rights and privileges of British subjects also proved a farce. For many years after the coming of self-government the Maoris were refused the right to vote. No native districts were even proclaimed, and the Maoris were subjected to laws which they did not understand. Not for 20 years did the Government circulate a summary of English law in the native tongue[67].

In this grave breach of faith both the British and the New Zealanders were at fault. It is true that in 1844 the British Parliament rejected a report by a Select Committee which actually repudiated the Treaty in favour of the New Zealand Company. Nevertheless, Britain made little effort to control the flood of immigrants, as she might have attempted under later ideals such as the Dual Mandate. In 1840 there were only 2000 whites in New Zealand. By 1842 they numbered 11,000 and by 1856 45,000. British financial help also proved inadequate. At a time of great distress at home the Imperial Government refused to give Hobson sufficient funds to execute the Treaty of Waitangi[68]. In later years the Motherland supported well meaning but mistaken native policies such as that of Sir George Grey, and when Britain granted New Zealand a constitution, she failed to provide for the adequate protection of the natives[69].

In New Zealand settlers and lawyers took, as indicated above, a strongly anti-Maori attitude. Christopher Richmond, for example, who was Minister of Native Affairs in the critical years 1850-60, would barely concede that the Maoris were British subjects. Translated to the Supreme Court Bench, he held that the Treaty of Waitangi was not a treaty at all so far as it pretended to transfer sovereignty; it was, he said, "A simple nullity"[70]. If white judges could hold such views it was little wonder that the rank and file of the colonists gave scant justice to the Maoris or paid little attention to their rights.

There were, however, great faults on the Maoris' side. The

native land system had been unsettled by the wars, and many chiefs neglected the customs and courtesies due to the members of their tribes[71]. Moreover, many Maoris were swift to make frenzied bargains for their lands. As early as 1837 speculators began to swarm in, and land fever in all its phases of "sharking", "jobbing" and legitimate purchase raged throughout the country[72]. By September, 1841, there were 38 claimants for 19,280,000 acres in the southern and 339 claimants for 6,250,000 acres in the northern island[73].

Even the missionaries were involved in the land transactions, a fact which created strong native criticism. In this connection and in view of later sad events this old Maori song is significant: "It was in the year 14 that Christianity landed at Oihi and reached the Maori people. It was there that Marsden stood up, and his message was this: God is in heaven, look therefore to the sky. But the Maori people turned and gazed below to the land, the soil of Aotearoa, they beheld it decoyed away with the iron spade, the iron axe, the flaming blanket and the iron jew's harp. Thy goods, Oh Governor! Alas, the land has gone adrift on the great ocean of Kiwa[74]."

For a time, however, the British ideals and the Treaty of Waitangi afforded some protection. Governor Gipps, of N.S.W., proved a tower of strength against speculators, particularly those in Sydney[75]. He issued a proclamation in 1840 announcing that no land claim would be recognised until it had been confirmed by the Government. Hobson was authorised to appoint Land Commissioners, and a Lands Claim Commissioner, appointed by the authorities in England, arrived in 1841 and made progress in settling claims[76]. The Commissioners found that a great many of the claims made by the whites were preposterous and that in many cases the Maoris had had no right to sell, or had signed deeds without understanding or caring about their contents[77].

In spite of the Commissioners, local disputes occurred in several areas. In 1842 Colonel Wakefield was killed on the North Coast of the South Island during a land dispute with Rauparaha in which the whites were clearly at fault, and in 1845 the colonists were at war in the Bay of Islands with Hone Heke, son of the famous Hongi. Sir George Grey was hurried from South Australia, and, after defeating the Maoris, wisely issued a free pardon and restored the chiefs their lands. This action re-established friendly relations and prevented far more serious troubles, which might have led to the necessity of conquering the whole of the islands[78]. Unfortunately, however, Grey's native policy was unsound in principle. The Governor wished to destroy tribal organisation and bring the Maoris to European laws and ways of life whereas a wiser policy would have supported Maori institutions and the Mana or authority of the chiefs. Grey possessed great personal influence with the Maoris, and when he left New Zealand native troubles quickly re-appeared[79].

Even as late as the eighteen fifties Britain could possibly have saved the Maoris from the wars which in the following decade wrecked their tribal organisation and morale with results that almost extinguished the race. Unfortunately, however, the pressure of British and New Zealand land grabbers gained in England influential supporters who included Lord Howick, an advocate of the views of the New Zealand Company. Howick, who became Earl Grey, and, in 1846, British Colonial Secretary, was prepared to surrender the Maori majority to the tender mercies of the white minority and to secure for the Crown all lands that were not actually in Maori occupation. Grey, therefore, passed a New Zealand constitution through the British Parliament and despatched it to the Colony with a set of instructions. Taken together the constitution and instructions meant that the British Crown handed the Maoris over to the colonists, gave them no say in the new government, and claimed from them all land excepting such as they "had been accustomed to use and enjoy, either as places of abode or tillage or for the growth of crops, or otherwise for the convenience and sustenation of life, by means of labour expended thereon"[80]. This to the Maoris was a nullification of the Treaty of Waitangi, and was trickery and deception of the worst kind. Fortunately in the colony Governor Sir George Grey stood firm, and, supported by Bishop Selwyn, the Chief Justice, and strong letters from the Waikato chiefs, took the responsibility of hanging up the Constitution[81]. There then arose on behalf of the natives a storm of protest which staggered Earl Grey, and to his credit he yielded all along the line. Until Governor Grey left New Zealand in 1853 native land was purchased only from the great chiefs, in the presence of the lesser chiefs and tribes, and with the boundaries properly described. So great was Sir George Grey's influence that the government was able to acquire large areas of land with comparatively little friction.

In 1852 Britain granted New Zealand a constitution with better native provisions than those which Governor Grey had suppressed. The new constitution followed the Treaty of Waitangi and tacitly acknowledged the rights of the Maoris to all their lands, although it asserted the pre-emptive rights of the Crown. Moreover, Governor Grey succeeded in withholding Maori affairs from the Colonial Parliament, while the Constitution gave him power to proclaim certain districts as reserves under Maori law[82].

With a Constitution such as this, and in spite of its unpopularity with the white settlers, a strong British policy might have saved the Maoris from the sufferings which followed. Unfortunately the New Zealand lawyers resumed their pernicious efforts and discovered means to deny the Maoris a vote. Thus the Constitution and its interpretation opened a gulf between the Maori and white[83].

THE MAORI WARS

Up to 1856 the Maoris made considerable advance. They accepted Christianity. They established schools so successfully that a larger proportion of natives than of whites could read and write. Although unscrupulous lawyers had denied them the vote the chiefs had shown political ability and wisdom. Accounts of the period depict the natives as a fine progressive people who afforded considerable help to the white colonists. About 1853 an Auckland newspaper stated that the Maori farmers were "clearly becoming more energetic, skilful and successful; as sheep owners, labourers and artisans, they had shown themselves to be the main props of New Zealand"[84].

In spite of this advance the Maoris continued to face great difficulties and grievances. Christianity and white contacts were breaking down their society. Christianity taught the authority of the individual conscience and the equality of all men before God. Hence slaves were freed. Chief and commoner sat together in the schools. People of lowly birth began to lift their voices in the councils. When to these novel doctrines and customs were added novel English ideas of land tenure and law the confusion became even greater. In the words of a chief in 1848, "When we adhered to our native customs we had light—but now the land is confused by the customs of the Europeans".

Similarly the old Maori economy was breaking down. New crops, new methods of cultivation, new appetites, new habits, new ambitions, had altered everything. The old order with its self-sufficient villages had gone forever[85].

Amongst these difficulties the land situation loomed particularly large. The Government was still drawing half its revenues from purchasing native land at 6d. an acre and selling it to the whites at from 5/- to 10/-. In addition to this the natives were paying half the customs revenue. Yet from a revenue of £400,000 per annum, the colonial authorities were giving the Maoris only £15,000 for their needs. The Government failed to proclaim any native districts, and provisions for laws for native trial by jury, for municipal institutions,' and for the granting of one-fifth of the land sales receipts to native purposes remained only promises on paper. A native department did little or nothing. The Land Purchase Commissioners were "like stinging nettles and bayonets", goading the unfortunate Maoris into land sales, and after Grey left there was established a new policy of secret purchase against which lay no appeal[86].

When economic depression added poverty to legitimate grievance the Maori tribes began to unite, and, in 1856, a great council of Maori chiefs near Lake Taupo bound themselves to sell no more land—not even to the Imperial Government[87]. The gathering also evinced a desire for a Maori King, for a Parliament, and even for simple village councils administering English laws adapted to their needs. Seldom did a splendid native people show a more pathetic demand for white leadership and guidance. Seldom did a stupid Governor (Governor Brown), and selfish colonists, fail more ignobly in response[88].

The wars which followed were due partly to land disputes and partly to the King movement which resulted from Maori uneasiness. Precipitated by an act of land purchase, which was clearly unjust but which the Government upheld, the Maoris fought for their lands and national existence. Already by 1860 they reached a desperate state. Christianity had undermined their religion and the law of tapu, and the Government had failed to make any real effort to replace the institutions which had been lost. The Maori plan was to fix the boundaries of European encroachment and to live within their own territories under suitable laws, maintaining friendly relations with the whites and gradually adapting themselves to white civilisation. Yet war was forced upon them, and after a heroic and chivalrous struggle, which aroused in the British General—Cameron—far more respect for the Maoris than for the land-grabbing colonists, they were defeated by nearly 20,000 British and colonial troops[89].

Sir George Grey, who was rushed back to New Zealand, struggled to avert reprisals by the use of autocratic powers, but 3,000,000 acres of Maori land were confiscated in actions which were unjust in their incidence apart from the injustice of the whole policy. As a result of these actions a chivalrous race was embittered and lost its pride of life—its Maori ora or sacred life principle which was necessary to maintain the physical and mental welfare of man. A wave of alcoholism swept over the Maoris and their extinction appeared inevitable. In 1856 Dr. I. L. Fentherston wrote, "The Maoris are dying out and nothing can save them. Our plain duty, as good compassionate colonists, is to smooth down their dying pillow". Dr. A. K. Newman wrote in 1881, "Taking all things into consideration the disappearance of the race is scarcely a subject for much regret. They are dying out in a quick and easy way and are being supplanted by a superior race". As late as 1907 Archdeacon Walsh predicted, "The Maori has lost heart and abandoned hope. The race is sick unto death and is already potentially dead"[90].

LATER LAND ROBBERIES

The decline of the Maori people after the wars is typified and partly explained by the story of Maori lands. In 1865 a Native Land Court was established to determine the title to lands. Condliffe summed up seventy years of its work by saying that throughout its history the Court had been the means of facilitating the separation of the Maori from his lands as equitably and as painlessly as possible. In this way, he added, it has been the chief mechanism in the break-up of Maori economy and the destruction of tribal order and discipline[91]. An Act of 1873 disregarded the communal nature of Maori land tenure and, like the American Allotment Act of 1887, established the principle of individual title to land. A Royal Commission of 1891 roundly condemned direct dealings between the Maoris and private Europeans, and pointed out that the Maoris retained nothing of the purchase money and were rapidly becoming a landless people[92]. A member of the committee, Sir James Carroll, asked the following unanswerable question, "Is it not a melancholy reflection that no single bona-fide attempt has been made to induce the natives to become thoroughly useful citizens in the full sense of the word? No attempt has been made to educate them in acquiring individual knowledge or to direct their attention to industrial pursuits. Whatever progress they have achieved in that direction is owing entirely to their own innate wisdom and energy"[93].

Following the report of this Commission of 1891 an act restored Government pre-emption but the eighteen nineties saw a whirlwind of white settlement, and Maori lands were in various cases exempted from this safeguard. From 1892 to 1900 2,729,000 acres of native land were purchased at a cost of £775,500, and during the same period the Governor-in-Council exempted a further 423,180 acres from pre-emption[94].

The Treaty of Waitangi had acknowledged as Maori preserves about 66,400,000 acres, of which 28,400,000 were in the North Island where native population was most dense. By 1891 the Maoris still possessed in the North Island 10,829,486 acres—about 2/5 of their original lands, and 250,000 acres in the South Island[95]. By 1911 their holdings had fallen to 7,137,710 acres[96]. Later figures show some discrepancies but the Official Year Book gives the figure for 1937 as 4,545,765 acres. Even now the experience of a century affords little guarantee that the figure will not be reduced further. "The fear of such an eventuality is never far from the Maori mind"[97].

Possibly the worst example of white ruthlessness as regards Maori lands occurred in the South Island. Here in 1848 the New Zealand Company purchased 20,000,000 acres from the Maoris for £20,000, that is £1 per ten thousand acres. In 1868 the lawyers found an ingenious method of extinguishing the rights of the Company without fulfilling the promise to the natives, even

166

Quirindi Aboriginal Station, N.S.W.—Medical Unit
Photo: N.S.W. Government

On Half-Caste Reservation, Alice Springs, Central Australia. Modern housing in distance
Photo: Author, 1948

Maori Church at Ohinemutu, Rotorua, North Island, New Zealand
Photo: New Zealand Government

Maori Meeting House, Ohinemutu, Rotorua, N.I., N.Z
Photo: New Zealand Government

those which involved schooling, medical attention and general care[98]. In 1921, after numerous enquiries a Royal Commission recommended £354,000 as a minimum compensation to Maoris deprived of their land by a dubious purchase, and for the non-fulfilment of guarantees. Very recently the matter was settled by the descendants of the claimants accepting a payment of £10,000 per year for thirty years, the money to be administered by a Trust for social purposes. The remedy of this grievance cleared the air considerably.

As a New Zealand writer aptly said, "Injustices such as these are clear indices of the helplessness in a democracy of a section commanding a negligible voting strength"[99]. Only in very recent years have tribal reserves and trust funds been established.

In view of such injustices the period following 1861 was a dark one for the Maoris. The whites rushed the rich lands of the North Island then available for settlement. The discovery of gold in Otago doubled the white population there in three years and by 1870 it reached 250,000. Capital and immigrants poured in. The white prospered but the Maori had lost faith in the Pakeha, his laws, and his religion. Maori leaders were dead or discredited. Maori lands were confiscated. The speculator and the publican found the native an easy prey[100].

THE DECLINE OF MAORI CHRISTIANITY

The period of land robbery and war which almost wrecked the Maori people also saw a grave decline in the progress of Christianity. Although the old and new religions clashed over Maori practices such as cannibalism, polygamy, concubinage, slavery and the vendetta, they had certain common features, for example the Maoris possessed an inner priesthood who worshipped a Supreme Being—Io of the hidden face—and who practised rites such as baptism.

We have seen that by 1840, when the period of missionary enterprise on a moving and uncontrolled frontier had ended, Christianity appeared to have made considerable headway. It seemed that the missionaries had converted two-thirds of the North Island and had gained influence throughout the remainder of that island. In 1842 Bishop Selwyn arrived and began the great work of organising the Church of England in New Zealand and of spreading the Gospel in the Pacific[101].

Unfortunately, as noted above, the Maoris had already become suspicious of a religion professed by a white race which included many rogues and which was divided into a number of warring religious sects. Although in some regions the Anglicans and Wesleyans worked in close harmony Bishop Selwyn's efforts to secure agreement were in general unsuccessful, and particularly in the Southern districts of the North Island, there was considerable religious strife. Such strife soon spread to the argumentative Maoris and a sharp line was rapidly drawn between Haki (Church) and Weteri (Wesley)[102].

Land robbery and the wars of the sixties further awakened the Maoris "to some of the hollowness of the Christianity of civilised man", and when Bishop Selwyn accompanied as official chaplain white forces, who at Waikato burnt Maori women and children in their houses, he damned Christianity in Maori eyes and turned Waikato against the missionaries in a resentment which has smouldered to the present day. The Maoris began to suspect that the clergy were in league with a land robbing government, Selwyn himself writing that the Maoris feared the Missionaries were government agents in a deep plot to subjugate the natives and to seize their lands[103].

Nevertheless, many of the Maoris retained their faith in the new God, but began to suspect that he was not impartial, and that the whites possessed powerful secret prayers which always brought favourable answers. This being so they commenced searching the scriptures for means to counteract the unfair advantages possessed by the whites[104].

The period of Maori despondency which followed their defeats in the eighteen sixties saw the evolution of weird native sects that bear striking resemblances to those which evolved under Indian disillusionment in North America. The first of the Maori prophets, Te Ua Haumene, baptised Zerubbabel, who had studied under the missionaries after learning the magic arts of a Maori tohunga, claimed that the Angel Gabriel had appeared to him and had instructed him in the Hauhau worship and ceremonies which would protect his disciples from British bullets. Religious hysteria, mass emotionalism and atrocities resulted and the Maori wars were prolonged into the middle of the eighteen sixties[105].

This and other cults showed a strange mingling of the bible with the old beliefs together with the usual expectation of a native messiah. In the Hauhau movement, for example, the Maori combined his primitive war dances with biblical depictions of the wanderings of the landless children of Israel, the Angel Gabriel, the Virgin Mary and the Hosts of Heaven[106].

With the foundation motive of resistance to further Pakeha encroachment and with the promise of miraculous deliverances for the Maori people the new seeds fell upon fruitful soil, and Hauhauism spread rapidly soon after the appearance of the King movement. Needless to say white governments in a pre-scientific era saw nothing but evil in these often ferocious but not unusual reactions by a defeated and despondent people, and an official proclamation of 1865 condemned Hauhauism for its "revolting arts . . . repugnant to all humanity", and announced the suppression of its followers "convicted of instigating or participating in such atrocities and crimes"[107].

The first Maori religious movement which deserves the name of a church was the Ringatu Church founded by another fierce zealot, Te Kooti Rikirangi, of Poverty Bay. This creed possessed the powerful keynote of martyrdom, as the Government had unjustly banished the prophet to the Chatham Islands. This Ringatu sect, which combined the cult of Jehovah, the God of the dispossessed and captive Jews, with ancient Polynesian customs and faith healing, spread over large areas where the Church of England once held sway. It has lasted for two generations and survived the death of its founder and the loss of his potent personality[108].

Later years saw the progress of Christian and Morman Churches while another native Church—the Ratana Church—also made great headway and in the nineteen twenties embraced up to 40,000 adherents. Ratana, who was known as the mouthpiece of God, added a hierarchy of angels to the Christian Trinity. His movement was religious, social and political in its aims and embraced many of the old Maori cultural features[109].

As in America these native reactions to white religion and aggression failed to provide any national inspiration or general forces of recovery. Riki and Rura, the gods invoked during the

King movement, were condemned as false deities through whom the Maori lands were lost and the people destroyed, while in 1864-5 the ceremonies of the Hauhaus failed to protect them from severe defeats. As late as 1927, however, Rua, the prophet of the Urewera, foretold the coming of a Messiah in the August of that year, and in response to his call some hundreds of natives sold their farms and possessions at a sacrifice to join the movement[111]. The census of 1926 indicated that in spite of the reactions a majority of the Maoris were Christians. There were then 21,738 Anglicans, 8,558 Roman Catholics, 4066 Methodists, 3804 "Mission" (probably Anglicans), and 3416 Mormans, as against 11,567 members of the Ratana and 4540 of the Ringa-tu sect, the last-named including the Hauhaus[111].

Looking at the history of Maori-white contacts as a whole it must be confessed that neither Christianity nor the cults of despair did much to maintain the race during the critical years of decline, or to promote the recovery which the following chapter will discuss. A deeply religious people, the Maoris eagerly adopted Christianity until they were disgusted by unjust wars, atrocities and land robberies which accorded little with Christian precepts. Many, therefore, sought relief in cults of despair, which proved illusory, while the principal Christian Church—the Church of England—on its side became more orthodox in its worship and departed further from the old missionary services which had adopted the traditional Polynesian invocation and hence had appealed to the Maoris[111].

The religious statistics for 1926 sum up an era during which the natives passed through a period of bewilderment and confusion. A complexity of sects gave little hope of racial progress or unity on any religious basis[111].

THE FAILURE OF EDUCATION

During the period of Maori decline white education in its contemporary character failed as sadly as Christianity, although the mission schools had made progress during the difficult days of the moving and uncontrolled frontier. In 1840 Lord John Russell notified Hobson that education was essential to aboriginal progress and was to be undertaken by the missionaries only, and Fitzroy, the succeeding Governor, began to make land grants to the churches for the establishment of Maori schools. The Native

THE MAORI DECLINE

Trust Ordnance of 1844 set forth the official British policy, which was to utilise education for the purpose of assimilating the Maoris as speedily as possible to the habits and usages of the European population. Both Fitzroy and Grey developed this policy by supporting the mission schools with grants of land and money under conditions of Government inspection and examination; religious and industrial training and instruction in the English language. For a time the Maoris were interested, but sectarian jealousy and inter-racial wars seriously weakened the prestige of the mission schools. Indeed for a time the Maoris withdrew almost completely from the schools and from contact with the Europeans[114].

From 1867 onwards the New Zealand Government continued the attempt to assimilate Maori and white by means of education. In that year an Act instructed the Department of Native Affairs to provide Maori schools, in which, by an amendment of 1871, instruction was to be confined to the English language. Some progress was made and 64 native schools came into operation with an attendance of 1487 children and at an annual cost of £9534 (1874). Administration was, however, haphazard and in 1879 the Education Department took over the schools, the object being to provide European buildings, and European teachers who, with their families, were to present models of desirable living for Maori eyes. Under these provisions educational progress revived, but the syllabi were profoundly academic in type and the whole system was designed "to force the Maori from every aspect of his culture whether good or bad[115]."

As time went on more and more emphasis was placed upon academic education, outwardly with some success but in reality with little result either in training the Maori to use the English language or in improving his housing and home life. Although Maori children could speak English fluently on leaving school the conquerors' tongue was used in only 5% of Maori homes, and the natives continued to live in primitive dwellings and under social patterns which showed little modification. In such a state of affairs white education in New Zealand did little to assist the Maoris during the critical period of despondency and cultural adjustment[116].

THE END OF THE DECLINE

Up to the end of the Nineteenth Century almost every well informed student agreed with the verdict of Archdeacon Walsh

171

who stated in 1907 that the Maori race was sick unto death. Even when the census of 1906 showed an increase of 4000 people Walsh declared that this was simply due to a more accurate survey; finality had been achieved, and the number of natives would soon reach vanishing point[117]. These gloomy predictions proved entirely inaccurate, for numbers, which had long remained about 40,000, increased from 50,309 in 1906 (the first accurate census) to 52,997 in 1916 and 63,670 in 1926. In reporting the last and greatly augmented figure the Government statistician commented, "The position is the more satisfactory in that it presents an almost unique spectacle of a native race living with a white race of overwhelmingly superior numbers and yet able to preserve in no small degree its individuality and strength[118]."

Keesing, writing in 1928, summarised the tendencies of change, which, during the transition years, the Maoris had faced—"the breaking down of the ancient social organisation, customs and the traditional values of the individual and tribe; also the thought system that made them effective; the inability to discover any unified basis of life, or to penetrate the vital meanings of civilisation owing to difficulties of intercourse, physical and mental isolation, and a growing weight of misunderstandings; hence with the old overthrown and the new unrelated to life, there had been an extreme diversity and instability[119]."

Now, however, on the one hand increasing numbers of Maori youth were bridging the cultural gap between the races and gave promise of leading their people after them, while on the other many good features of the ancient system had survived. The Maori tongue, which was still spoken in 90% of homes, had gained stability as a written language, and the heritage of poetry, song, dance and tradition still existed amongst the tribes. In some districts even the "mana" of chieftainship was retained as a rallying point for tribal pride. In 1928 it seemed to Keesing that the issue of Maori survival still trembled in the balance and the stage was set for the climax of the racial drama. In his opinion the salvation of the Maoris depended upon the purposive reorganisation and co-ordination of white and Maori forces. This, very fortunately, the leaders of both races set out to effect[120].

CHAPTER IX

The Maori Recovery

If we disregard knotty problems such as the accuracy of certain census figures and the true proportion of mixed bloods it appears that the Maoris reached their numerical minimum in the period immediately following the wars. Censuses in 1867 and 1871 returned 38,540 and 37,502, after which the population remained slightly in excess of 40,000 until 1906 onwards, when it increased from 50,309 in that year to 82,326 in 1836 and 86,767 in 1939. The census of 1945 placed the Maori population at 97,263 in a total population of 1,702,223[1], and it was estimated that the Maoris numbered 106,492 on June 30th 1947. The 1945 census figure represents only some 5.7% of the total New Zealand population, but the recent advance has been remarkable and the Maoris appear to constitute a rapidly growing section of the community. From 1926 to 1936 the rise was 29.3% as against 10.93% for Europeans. This favourable comparison was chiefly due to a birthrate of 46.64 per 1,000 as against a European birthrate of 17.29. The Maori death rate still remained high (Native 19.29, European 9.08), but this disparity seemed likely to diminish with improvements in Maori hygiene and health[2].

Very striking was the fact that, although Maori death rates actually increased from 14.96 per 1000 in 1925 to 18.29 per 1000 in 1938 infantile mortality declined very strikingly and the natives showed a far higher proportion of young people than did the European population. In 1936 the Maoris in the under twenty years of age groups numbered 54.8% of the native population, while the whites in these groups represented only 34.4% of the European total. Similarly an analysis of the younger groups indicated that 32.5% natives were under ten years of age as against only 16.5% of Europeans.

173

WHITE SETTLERS AND NATIVE PEOPLES

The recovery was, however, by no means limited to numerical increase. As the Board of Native Affairs reported in 1939, "The last two decades have witnessed a renaissance of the native race and this revival of Maori life is manifest in the increasing population, in inter-tribal gatherings, in the revival of arts and crafts of the people, and in the erection of buildings for communal needs, and also in the general feeling of racial pride." By the outbreak of the Second World War the problem facing statesmen was not to provide for a declining race but for a virile people whose numbers were growing rapidly[3]

SOME ASPECTS OF THE RECOVERY—ISOLATION

We have seen that the preservation, and in some cases the recovery, of certain native peoples in English-speaking countries, has been due in some measure to isolation from the whites. Although this factor was less apparent in the comparatively small and highly fertile islands of New Zealand than in the huge areas of hot or cold deserts it was nevertheless existent. The saving effects of isolation were, for example, particularly marked in the mountainous North-East of the North Island, a region in which the Maori population showed particularly rapid growth[4]. It was also significant that the preliminary experiments in economic recovery came from the Ngati-Porou in this area where rugged country and an absence of good harbours protected them from white penetration. Even amongst the Maoris the Ngati-Porou were known as "Nati" or country cousins. In their remote fastnesses they escaped many destructive features of white contact. They were "friendlies" during the wars. They were saved from the worst effects of those conflicts, and the consequent land confiscations together with the resentment and suspicion that resulted. Indeed they even sought white education and white methods of securing practical welfare, but they vehemently refused to sell much of their best country, and they adopted white usages without straining tribal community life and organisation. The census of 1936 clearly indicated the safe-guarding effects of isolation in parts of the North Island as is illustrated by Maps IV and V. In Hawke Bay Province the Maoris then numbered 9% of the population, while in the counties of Matakaoa and Waiapu, in the extreme North East, they

Entrance to Maori Pa, Rotorua

Photo: New Zealand Government

Ruatonia Native School. Maori finishing Panel
Photo: New Zealand Government

Maori School, Whakarewarewa. Organised Games
Photo: National Publicity Studio

Maori School, Whakarewarewa. Stick Games
Photo: National Publicity Studio

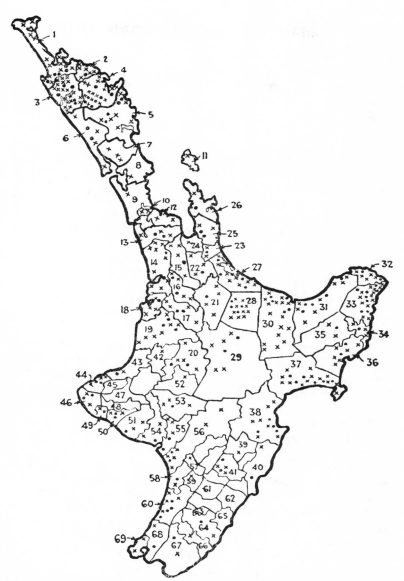

North Island of New Zealand showing location of Maori population. From
N.Z. census, 1936. Full blood Maoris ×. Three-quarter or half bloods ●.
Each cross or dot represents 200 Maoris.

heavily outnumbered all other races, in Matakaoa by 273 to 100 and in Waiapu by 216 to 100.

It also seems probable that isolation assisted in preserving the Maoris in parts of the central districts and north of the North Island, where, as Map IV indicates, they formed over half the population. In 1936 they numbered 12% of the inhabitants of Auckland Province[5].

Unfortunately the majority of Maori tribes were less well situated, for they were scattered in the midst of a rapidly increasing white population which continuously robbed them of their lands and living resources. As some of these peoples began to recover without environmental advantages it is clear that isolation was by no means the only, nor even, in some cases, the predominant factor.

THE WHITE CONTRIBUTIONS

While the Maoris and their sympathisers rightly attribute most of the recovery to the Maoris themselves much credit must be given to the whites both for an improvement in outlook and policy and for the fact that, even admitting the many evils resulting from mixed breeding, some advantages followed an infiltration of white blood. The white contribution to Maori rehabilitation consisted of political and administrative improvements; a more generous financial policy directed towards the provision of health and other social services; a development of conscience in regard to land robbery, and a liberalisation of educational theory and practice on scientific lines.

In some respects, for example in the introduction of Maori members to Parliament, the improvement commenced as early as the eighteen sixties, soon after the Maori wars. In others, for example in the re-orientation of education to meet Maori needs and traditions, the native revival preceded the advancement in white outlook. D. G. Ball, at one time Inspector of Native Schools, condemned the long existing conservatism and unscientific policies of the whites in trenchant words. "Education," he wrote, "even in the first quarter of the present century, appeared to learn nothing from the near tragedy, and, until 1931, persevered with a policy that attempted to divorce the Maori from

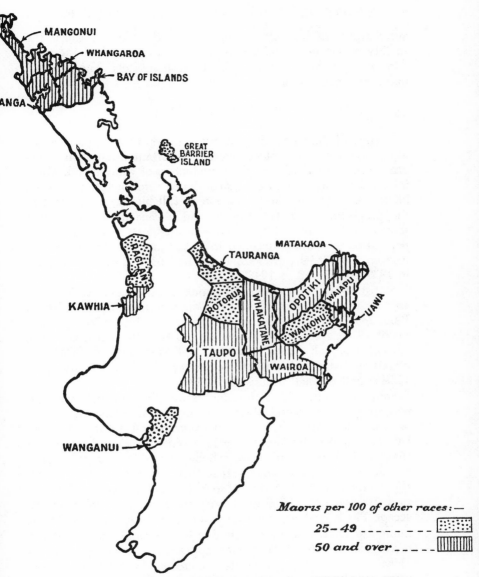

MANGONUI

WHANGAROA

BAY OF ISLANDS

ANGA

GREAT
BARRIER
ISLAND

RAGLAN

KAWHIA

MATAKAOA

TAURANGA

ROTORUA

WHAKATANE

OPOTIKI

WAIAPU

WAIKOHU

UAWA

TAUPO

WAIROA

WANGANUI

Maoris per 100 of other races:—

25 - 49 _ _ _ _ _ _ _

50 and over _ _ _ _ _

North Island of New Zealand showing the proportion of Maoris to other races. From N.Z census, 1936.

177

every aspect of his culture, whether good or bad. Against the mighty waters of established Maori custom was raised the puny dam of a few hours schooling in English subjects. The dam has never stemmed the flood⁶."

RACIAL MIXTURE

In spite of the customary difficulties in census taking and in defining full and mixed bloods certain important racial changes appear to have occurred with the introduction of white blood. These included a rapid growth of the combined total of full and mixed bloods; a decline in the proportion of full bloods; an increase in the proportion of mixed bloods, and a capacity for leadership shown by the mixed bloods. As indicated previously the Maori population as a whole declined to 37,502 in 1871. By 1916 it had recovered to 52,997. In 1926 it reached 63,670; in 1936 82,326, in 1939 86,767 and in 1945 97,263.

Statistics of the mixed blood population are less reliable but it appears that this section of the population numbered 6516 in 1906, 7352 in 1921, 18,241 in 1926, and 26,411 in 1936. The census of 1926 gave 71.35% full bloods, 10.42% three-quarter Maori, and 17.76% half Maori. That of 1936 gave only 67.92% full bloods, and stated that the three-quarter Maoris had increased to 13.84% and the half Maoris to 18.09%.

Some authorities have cast doubts on the comparatively high percentage of full blood Maoris recorded by statistics. Pitt-Rivers, for example, stated that when Buck examined a Maori Pioneer battalion in 1919 he found only 52% pure Maori, and also noted that of 4039 pupils in native schools only 49.9% were of pure blood. Pitt-Rivers considered that there were then only 20,000 full blood Maoris, but the Maoris themselves would have regarded a figure of 30,000 full bloods as unduly low⁷. Whether we accept Pitt-Rivers' arguments or not it is clear that the Maori numerical increase was no little due to the rapid advance of the mixed bloods. This phenomenon appeared to resemble events in Hawaii where the part-Hawaiians increased by 125% in twenty years and showed much more resistance to disease than the pure stock. Scientific research, as conducted in Hawaii, might well es-

178

tablish the fact that some of the Maori increase was due to hybrid vigour.

Another important feature of the white-Maori intermixture was the part played by the mixed bloods in the revival of Maori life and leadership. The Maori-whites, like the Indian-whites, included men of outstanding character and ability, some of whom, such as Dr. Peter Buck (Te Rangi Hiroa) played a leading part in the recovery. Owing largely to inadequate research facilities in the Dominion few students examined problems of intermixture, but it became very evident that New Zealand should examine these questions from the scientific viewpoint—indeed the vigorous growth of the mixed bloods and of the total Maori population made such examination essential. Knowledge was needed as to the real proportion of mixed bloods; their rate of increase; their state of health; and the respective abilities, social and economic value, and assimilation potentialities of the various mixture grades. The visitor to New Zealand quickly realised that many of the whites showed greater racial, social and economic intolerance to the Maoris and mixed bloods than was officially admitted, and that many whites blamed the Maoris for an alleged laziness and squalor which were largely the results of the white invasions, land robberies and wars. In spite of this the Maoris and mixed bloods, with their magnificent record in two world wars, ranked far higher in white eyes than did most native peoples. Intermarriage was common and, at any rate in public, the Maoris suffered comparatively little from discrimination[5].

MAORI LEADERSHIP

Turning to the Maori share in race revival we find that one of the outstanding factors was the Young Maori Party. This party appears to have originated from the past students of the Te Aute College, who founded in 1891 an ambitious welfare organisation. Although this body was greeted at the outset with opposition and contempt it blossomed into the Te Aute Students Association of 1897[6]. In that year a conference, which included later leaders such as Sir Apirana Ngata, discussed the Maori situation with the sympathetic support of the Irish-Maori Sir James Carroll, Minister of Native Affairs, together with that of the first Inspector of

Native Schools, James H. Pope[10]. In spite of white and Maori opposition the Young Maori Party, led by men like Hone Heke, Sir Mauri Pomare, Dr. Peter Buck, Ngata and a loosely organised but intensely purposeful group of young men and women of Maori race and sympathies, brought inspiration and recovery. That this inspiration continued was shown by the Auckland Conference of 1937, when Ngata stated, "I am going home to tell my people that so far as young leaders are concerned, they have nothing to worry about. I will be able to sleep sounder in the knowledge that, for another generation at least, there are leaders to carry on[11]."

RECOVERY OF PRIDE OF LIFE

The chief tasks faced by the young Maori leaders and by their white supporters and sympathisers were to recover Maori pride and ambition; to restore some at least of the Maori organisation; to secure more generous finance for up-to-date services in education and health, and to remedy the very grave situation in regard to Maori lands. As in the other English-speaking countries under examination progress was slow for many years, and, again as in these countries, it was not until the nineteen thirties that New Zealand saw really scientific enlightenment and advance.

Some improvement, both nominal and real, began at an early date. In 1867 the Maoris secured representation in the New Zealand Parliament under an act which divided the colony into four Maori electorates each of which returned one member to the House of Representatives. Five years later two chiefs were added to the Upper House. This liberal reform was one of those which proved of real value as Hone Heke, Sir Mauri Pomare, Dr. Buck and Ngata gave notable service[12]. Unfortunately, however, the Maori members could do little against a Land Court, which as noted above, vigorously transferred Maori lands to the whites[13], or against an educational system which was purposely designed to destroy the native language, religion, organisation and culture.

In view of such facts the young Maori Party and its white supporters could present an unanswerable case that white contacts, white religion and white civilization had produced little but ruin for the Maoris, and that other methods were necessary to save the race. The Young Maori Party therefore rapidly extended its in-

THE MAORI RECOVERY

fluence by means of political and non-political agencies and by the wise and patient use of such forms of Maori organisation as still remained—a work which involved years of strenuous and often discouraging labour in native villages. As a first fruit of its efforts to affect the legislature the Party gained in 1900 "the Maori Councils Act" which dealt with provisions for local self-government in matters relating to social conditions in the villages[14].

The way for the Young Maori Party in Parliament was largely paved by the Irish-Maori, Sir James Carroll, and he was ably followed by other Maori sympathisers, notably Ngata, who was the inspiration and principal mouthpiece of the movement. Although like the American New Dealers these leaders urged a partial return to native culture and organisation, they fully appreciated the value of the better aspects of white civilization, and outstanding in the work of Carroll and others were successful attempts to soften the bitter resentment caused by the wars and land confiscations and to revive the interest of the hereditary chiefs[15].

Perhaps the most pressing of the many problems which faced the reformers was that of the Maori lands which as we have seen had declined by 1937 to some four million acres in spite of the rapid population increase. By 1939 the lands available for development by a Maori population of nearly 90,000 were only about one-third of the area owned by 40,000 natives in 1896[16]. Nor did the New Zealand Government make genuine efforts to assist the Maoris to develop their remaining patrimony in conformity with the changed conditions. In 1911 Carroll complained that Parliament had not made a single bona fide attempt to induce the natives to become useful settlers, and the Young Maori Party long asserted that, while State and Financial organisations assisted European farmers, they would grant the Maoris no aid.

Action at last became imperative and the Ngati-Porou showed the way, for, although their first economic experiments with sheep and storekeeping met with only partial sucess, in the nineteen twenties the Maoris gained some concessions, and at last, in 1929, nearly ninety years after the Treaty of Waitangi, the New Zealand Parliament carried out Carroll's ideas of thirty-eight years before, and assumed direct financial responsibility for encouraging and training Maoris to become industrious settlers under the supervision of the Government[17].

181

In order to secure lands for Maori development the Act authorised the Minister of Native Affairs to step over difficulties of title
and to bring under the scheme lands which then could not be
privately alienated.

The Government provided money for development. State officers controlled expenditure and, with certain exceptions, the
jurisdiction of the Native Land Court was exerciseable only at the
instance, or with the consent, of the appropriate government department. Over a period of ten years the plan acquired 840,000
acres and established 1700 settlers with 16,000 dependants. By
1939 the scheme had involved a net expenditure of £1,615,551,
but the revenue from produce had already reached an annual total
of £257,408 and the Dominion was reaping a reward in the form
of improved Maori industry, housing, health and child physique
and alertness. "The policy so long and patiently advocated is now
a common element in political platforms, and is as thoroughly
incorporated in the policy of the State as settlement of Crown
lands and State advances to settlers[18]."

There remained the grave question of the landless Maoris, for
the lands which were still available at the outbreak of the World
War could occupy only two-fifths of the increasing population,
and the development plan had taken the last, best, and only land
of many Maori communities[19]. Some authorities considered that
the natives made good manual labourers, fencers, bushmen,
ploughmen and farmers, and that their ancient manual dexterity
appeared in the skilled trades[20]. Nevertheless apprenticeship was
difficult for a people of communal culture and many Maoris had
little interest in manual work, domestic service, nursing or trade.
Thus D. G. Ball could write in 1939, "For the majority of landless
Maori youths the prospects are almost hopeless[21]." The obvious
solution was for New Zealand to follow the enlightened example
of the United States and to make some atonement for past robberies by re-purchasing Maori lands for the descendants of their
previous owners. A minor palliative was for the Dominion to copy
the United States further and to make greater use of Maori personnel in the native services, even if the Maoris "may at times be
less efficient by conventional administrative standards[22]."

A third and perhaps the most important possibility lay in education—particularly in technical education, as was stressed by

Ruatonia Native School. Handcraft and Designing
Photo: New Zealand Government

Making Piu-piu (skirts) at Whakarewarewa, N.I., N.Z
Photo: New Zealand Government

Maori Weaver at Work, Rotorua, N.I., N.Z

Tooth Brush Drill at Te Kaha Native School
Photo: J. D. Pascoe

authorities such as Ngata, Belshaw, Turbott, and Ball from the respective angles of sociology, economics, and health[23]. Precious decades had been lost in endeavouring to make bad Europeans out of good Maoris, and it was largely due to this erroneous policy that the Maori race was not self-supporting, decently housed, and provident.

EDUCATION

We have seen that the whites designed the earlier system of Maori education to wreck the language, culture and organisation of the natives. As in other English-speaking countries scientific reform began to appear in the nineteen thirties. In 1931 the head teachers of native schools answered a comprehensive questionnaire on health, housing, and similar topics. They indicated that Maori health and sanitation were unsatisfactory; that housing was poor; economic opportunities limited; social coherence weak, and provision for recreation and the use of leisure time inadequate[24]. After this exposure and indictment New Zealand re-orientated her native educational system under the new scientific ideas. The Native School was now to radiate a healthy pride in the Maori history and race, and the Maori child was to continue as an adult in active participation in school affairs. In other words the Native School was to become, as in the United States, an integral part of Maori community life—an institution which trained the children for Maori home life and which taught them to improve Maori homes[25]. This was all to the good. At the Young Maori Conference in 1939 D. G. Ball emphasised that the Maori School should be a Maori institution in a Maori community[26]. In recent years strenuous efforts were made to break away from the traditional type of education, and, although teaching was still in the experimental stage, there was definite and consistent progress[27].

Unfortunately certain obstacles retarded the advance. Only about half the Maori children were educated in the Native Schools. The other half was educated in Education Board Schools which still inflicted upon them an inappropriate academic syllabus. In the words of Turbott the result of Education Board training was for the Maori a "surface Europeanisation with unsettlement and maladaptation beneath[28]."

Maori children had the same right as Europeans to attend the secondary schools, and the Government also provided scholarships at Denominational Schools for Maoris from remote districts under a system which was greatly liberalised in 1936. Unfortunately from the viewpoint of Maori children, the syllabi of many of these schools were largely academic. Recent writers have held that these institutions should face up to realities and give their pupils a practical training that would equip them for life[29].

The problem of adult education was also of great importance. A number of Maoris reached the universities, where some gained world wide distinction, but there was great need for the schools to take up adult education as those of the United States did for the Indians. Another pressing need was for the establishment of a Maori journal like the American "Indians at Work" which would unite the scattered Maori communities and keep the race in touch with the services rendered both by the Maori leaders and by the New Zealand Government.

Some progress was made in the restoration of Maori arts and crafts when an Act of 1926 provided for a Board of Arts and Crafts to foster and encourage these interests. Under this plan a school was established at Rotorua where trained experts and students concentrated on the famous Maori woodcarving. Tribal projects resulted, and by 1939 some four or five hundred young Maori men and women had taken up various aspects of the work[30].

The provision for training the Maori youth in agriculture was never really adequate. In recent years the Government gave a few scholarships at various colleges but in 1939 "the only facilities for organised training were at Flock House and on the Maori land development schemes." At the outbreak of the World War the position was one in which there was urgent need for the New Zealand Government to take matters in hand on New Deal lines, for the future of the Maori race and its contribution to New Zealand life probably depended more upon education than upon anything else[31].

HEALTH, HOUSING AND DIET

Over the period under review problems of health, housing and diet continued to be very serious. Some progress was made, but

THE MAORI RECOVERY

in many cases the advance was far from adequate. In body and mind the pre-European Maori was perhaps as fine a race as ever lived, and the people still retained much of their old stamina and physique[32]. Such health troubles as arose were mainly due to primitive living conditions and to faults in personal and community hygiene which were largely preventable. Changed living conditions produced scourges such as scabies, impetigo, common sores, and eye infections. The Maoris also showed less resistance to epidemics than did the whites. In 1938 for example, measles caused 212 Maori deaths as compared with 107 white, and, although in 1939 there were no published statistics, social diseases appeared to be affecting the Maoris seriously in certain areas. On the other hand the natives seemed to possess a higher immunity than the whites from diphtheria and scarlet fever[33].

By 1939 Maori health was in the hands of a Health Department which contained 13 District Health officers together with Inspectors and District Nurses. Good work had been done, but it was stated that certain hospitals exhibited racial antipathy towards the Maoris, while statistics indicated that more institutional care and more district nurses were needed. Figures presented at the Young Maori Conference of 1939 showed that the natives suffered far more severely from tuberculosis, pneumonia, diarrhoea, enteritis and influenza than the whites. The Maori death rate from tuberculosis was 35.71 per 10,000 as against a white rate of 3.92, and pneumonia 19.41 as against .73. Although the infantile death-rate had improved it was still 92.17 per 1000 births as against 31.21 for the whites. Dr. Turbott noted that four Maori babies died for every one white, and added that this was "surely a disgrace to a country renowned for the lowest European infant mortality rate and the Plunket system of infant care." "European mothers," he wrote, "receive, through the Plunket system, education in correct care and management, but the system does not cover the Maori areas[34]."

As in Australia and other regions of native habitation much of the sickness and inefficiency was due, apparently, to unsatisfactory diet. In pre-European days the Maori diet was soundly balanced. After the invasions this diet was replaced by an unbalanced white diet which was high in carbo-hydrates, but short in first class proteins and vitamins. Where children were supplied with milk

185

twice a day their health improved immediately[35]. White diet with a deficiency of Vitamin D produced tooth diseases, and New Zealand health authorities considered that this trouble followed the extension of European shops and stores[36]. There appeared to be a crying need for better health education, together with campaigns against alcohol, for the Maori communities which indulged in drinking were rarely progressive. In this connection the results obtained by Ngata and the Princess Te Puea Herangi were object lessons on progress[37].

Housing was another serious problem. Belshaw stated in 1940, "All too large a proportion of the existing dwellings are miserable hovels, overcrowded and insanitary, and either badly ventilated and lighted, or draughty and affording scant protection against the weather[38]." At the Young Maori Conference of 1939 Campbell estimated that half of the 86,000 Maoris were inadequately housed, and that hundreds and hundreds all over New Zealand were living under appalling conditions[39]. Until 1937, which saw the first advance in native housing, the Maoris were generally left to provide for themselves. Then came schemes for Native Development and housing assisted by special grants and loans with the result that by 1939 some 2,000 houses had been erected or authorised[40]. By that time the Princess Te Puea had shown that it was possible to build a four-roomed cottage with Maori materials and in Maori style for £50[41].

By 1939 the Maori people had reached a very interesting position. They had made an amazing recovery and were increasing very rapidly, even although the assimilation with the whites was considerable. So rapid was the progress produced by such factors as Maori leadership, anti-acculturation developments, the infusion of white blood, and the improvement in Government outlook, that the nineteen thirties witnessed what Maori sympathisers hoped was an era such as President Roosevelt's New Day for Indians. In spite of the fact that the New Zealand Government and white public still fell far short of the American New Dealers in idealism, policy, and action, the continued increase of the Maoris, and the resulting problems, seemed likely to force the Maoriland whites to pursue further the task of remedying the injustices which their fathers had perpetrated on a splendid race.

THE MAORI RECOVERY

The census of 1945 indicated still further how necessary it was for the Government to appreciate the gravity of the outlook, as the statistics revealed that the white population was increasing far more slowly than the Maoris, and was evincing a very rapid drift to the towns. It was now quite clear that the Maoris were a people of high cultural potentiality who had adjusted themselves to white culture contacts, and, in a pure or mixed form, might well become the predominant rural population over considerable areas of New Zealand.

In 1945 Professor I. L. G. Sutherland summarised Maori affairs in two very striking pamphlets. He emphasised the rapid growth of Maori population, which doubled between 1895 and 1936 and may double again by 1976. An important factor in this phenomenon was the comparative youth of the Maori population. In 1941, for example, the Maoris under twenty one made up 57.8% of native population while the Europeans under twenty one numbered only 33.06% of white population.

The Maori gave magnificent war service both in the Armed Forces and at home, where, since 1942, they possessed for primary production and other services their own organisation, directed by a Minister and by nearly four hundred tribal committees.

The war had a profound effect upon the Maori peoples particularly through the exodus of young Maoris from the country districts to the cities and city industries despite the fact that government land schemes had made rapid and successful progress and that in 1943-4 returns from nearly two thousand Maori farms were the highest on record.

Questions of health, housing and diet still offered grave difficulties, but the outstanding problem was that of finding new and varied vocational outlets for the increasing number of young Maori people. In this matter Vocational Guidance Officers were giving some assistance. Authorities such as Sutherland and Buck agreed with the opinion of the late Sir James Carroll that the Maoris must hold fast to their Maoritanga (Maori-hood), even if this involved a danger of growing colour feeling as the natives advanced in numbers and as racial contacts and intermingling increased.

At the moment, however, there lay between the races no issues which could not be resolved by tolerance, mutual understanding and active good will. It was particularly important for New Zealanders to realise that their rate of population growth was declining at a time when the world situation urgently demanded an increase. Under such conditions the Maoris might well prove as fine an asset in peace as they had proved in war.

Professor Sutherland's analysis clearly showed that the Maoris and their white supporters had conducted a recovery on similar lines to that effected by the Indians of the South-West United States with the guidance and help of the New Dealers. The success of these parallel recoveries by native minorities in English speaking democracies is one of the most interesting of the minor phenomena of racial history[42].

CHAPTER X

Conclusion

THE IMPORTANCE OF THE WHITE INVASION

The invasion by English-speaking whites of the vast territories of North America and Australia and of the fertile islands of New Zealand forms one of the most important chapters in the story of the human race for it saw the creation of nations which now include 150,000,000 whites, who lead mankind in the promotion of democratic liberty and scientific progress. In this chapter the relations between the white incomers and the aborigines played an important part, particularly in the early stages when reciprocal reactions had many, and in some cases permanent effects (for example the white adoption of Indian corn and tobacco), and when concerted native resistance could have greatly delayed and perhaps in a few cases frustrated white settlement.

From the broad view point there can be no regret that the invasions took place. Without them the world would have lost some of the most valuable and healthy of English speaking influences. Certain features of the invasions, however, cause deep regret. First the earlier generations of white invaders were usually ruthless, selfish and unscientific in their dealings with the natives, with the result that these peoples declined from perhaps a total of one and a half to two millions to the six hundred thousand full and mixed bloods remaining today. Secondly some white governments, for example the government of the Australian Commonwealth, are still treating the surviving aborigines with meanness and neglect. Thirdly the white invaders destroyed the historic balance, which the natives had established with their environments, and wrought grievous harm to both native and white. The energetic efforts of the Americans to meet their erosion prob-

189

WHITE SETTLERS AND NATIVE PEOPLES

lems; of the Canadians to revive their fur bearing animals and other game, and of the Australians and New Zealanders to restore their forests are only some of the many attempts now being made to remedy the mistakes of the earlier generations of invaders.

THE GENERAL PICTURE

The preceding chapters indicate that the story of the invasions is one of similarities rather than of contrasts. With very few exceptions it everywhere presents the same tragic picture of the destruction of native life and resources in spite of differences in environment, in the type of incomer, and in aboriginal intelligence, physique, capacity in warfare and cultural development. In the pioneer stages the Home and Local governments had little strength to preserve the aborigines from disease, alcohol, warfare, land robbery, the exploitation of resources and destructive cultural contacts. Even when the Philanthropic Movement in Britain brought a more enlightened outlook, which later spread to some American and Colonial Governments, the chief result was the adoption of well meaning but ineffective palliatives—the herding of the unfortunate natives in meagre reservations, where they were usually placed in charge of Christian Missions, which under noble but mistaken policies, subjected them to religious, educational and other influences that destroyed their tribal organisation and culture without assimilating them to white civilization. Only in very recent times have scientifically minded white administrators assisted the surviving aborigines of full or mixed blood to swing back towards their former social systems and cultures in movements which have been very effective and beneficial in regions such as New Zealand and the South-West of the United States. In some of these areas the natives are now increasing rapidly, but, although some white governments, particularly the American, have greatly improved aboriginal health, hygiene, education and other social factors, many aboriginal peoples still suffer from lack of land, lack of practical education, ill health, bad housing, poor diet and social discrimination, which produce grave problems that deserve the most serious and scientific attention.

Maori School, Whakarewarewa. Hot Dinner for Underweight Children

Photo: J. D. Pascoe

Maori School, Whakarewarewa. Open Air Class Rooms
Photo: National Publicity Studio

Maori School, Whakarewarewa. "Haka"
Photo: National Publicity Studio

Maori School, Whakarewarewa. Youthful Carvers
Photo: National Publicity Studio

CONCLUSION

ENVIRONMENTAL FACTORS

Generally speaking the chief factors which protected the natives were environmental, particularly when these factors prevented white-native contacts. Tropical Australia—a vast, hot, infertile and still partly isolated region—proved unsuitable for close settlement either by whites or Asiatics, and hence contains the great proportion of surviving aborigines. The arid regions of the American South-West contain a substantial Indian population which is now registering a vigorous increase. Mountainous and isolated country similarly protected some of the Maoris, and much of the driving force of their remarkable recovery came from the rugged North-East. This of course is a usual and historic phenomenon; for from the dawn of history the more powerful peoples have driven the weaker peoples into marginal areas which have favoured resistance to racial and cultural impacts.

Returning to white-native contacts we find many cases in which industries resulting from particular environments influenced the destruction or preservation of the natives. The Indians of the Eastern United States for example were of comparatively little value to the white settlers and were virtually exterminated. The Canadian hunting Indians on the contrary were essential to the white fur traders and hence received more tolerant treatment. Again, although the Australian governments permitted many of the northern cattle raisers to exploit the aborigines unmercifully, there was growing recognition that the aborigine and half-caste were essential to the northern cattle industry with the result that supervision and justice made some slight progress in the Australian tropics. From the environmental aspect it may be said that the whites are likely to assimilate most native groups in regions of close white settlement, with perhaps the exception of the Maoris, but that in some marginal regions, particularly in the South-West of the United States, assimilation will be a very long process and in some cases may never take place.

BIOLOGICAL FACTORS

It is extremely difficult to determine the superiority or inferiority of human races or groups as regards their moral, mental or physical characteristics. The early white invaders treated all the

191

native peoples as savages, although many of those peoples, including even the Australian aborigines, had highly complex social organisations and were far more law abiding and humane than a large proportion of the incoming convicts and settlers. Also many of the natives of the hot and cold deserts were far better adjusted to their environments than the whites and existed in conditions under which the whites perished. What the aboriginal peoples lacked was resistance to white diseases and alcohol, and the organisation, social cohesion and weapons to resist white force. The natives must, however, be condemned for the failure of their groups to unite against the whites, and for their consuming desire for alcohol and for trade goods. Only too often, peoples such as the Iroquois and the Maoris secured and utilised white weapons for internecine warfare of the most murderous and revolting type.

In racial contacts and admixture the weight of population numbers is often a highly important factor, although it is sometimes difficult to disentangle this factor from environmental controls. North European whites have never effected permanent settlement amongst the vast population masses of China or Japan, although the climates are favourable. Southern Europeans gained a strong footing in Mexico, Peru and other regions where the Indian population was fairly dense, but, after initial setbacks from disease and warfare, the Indians recovered, and in later times the Indian and mixed blood populations have shown a very great increase. In Northern America, Australia and New Zealand the aboriginal populations were small and the climates of vast areas highly favourable to the whites, who poured in and increased in immense numbers. In these circumstances the incomers, their diseases, and their cultures destroyed or assimilated the native civilisations in a ruthless but not unnatural process which resembled the destruction by exotics of native animals and plants.

No comparative work has been done on the relative abilities of the various native peoples to resist invasion and extermination and little on the results of the variations that existed amongst the invading peoples. It is clear, however, that the more vigorous and culturally advanced groups like the Iroquois and Maoris, showed greater powers of survival and adaptation than highly primitive peoples such as the Australoids and Tasmanoids. Variations in the invading peoples were of importance. Macleod noted that in North America the French were never guilty of a massacre nor of a design for the extermination of a native; whereas the Dutch attempted to exterminate the coastal Algonkians. He considered that amongst the English colonists the Quakers alone had their hands free from the blood of innocent women and children and old men. They never deliberately schemed for the extermination of the natives, but they came from a better grade of selected English stock than perhaps any other group of colonists and under no conditions would have degenerated into murderers as did the Puritans, Scotch, Irish, and many others on the frontier[1]. Like the Quakers many of the New Zealand whites were free immigrants of a good type, and, dealing as they were with the courageous and advanced Maoris, neither side perpetrated many atrocities. On the other hand the early invaders of Australia were convicts, uncontrolled and individualistic free settlers, and military—the last named being sometimes undisciplined as was the New South Wales Corps. Hence in some parts of Australia the extinction of the natives was rapid, but even in free and comparatively peaceful colonies like South Australia the rate of decrease was very high, reaching, according to Campbell, a fifty per cent reduction every five years[2]. It is, however, almost impossible to disentangle biological factors from those of environment and culture. Macleod, in noting that the Indian rate of survival was probably higher under French and Spanish contacts than under British, emphasised the fact that the Indians were of greater economic use to the first two peoples than the last[3]. It was for this reason, combined with the constant fear of Indian reprisals that the English speaking frontiersman demanded the extermination of the natives whose lands he had appropriated.

CULTURE CONTACTS.

Of all aspects of the earlier invasions the most difficult to assess is that of cultural contact. The white destruction of native culture was generally rapid, although Elkin's researches in Australia indicated that even in that country the aboriginal culture was often highly tenacious[4]. The rapidity of deterioration probably varied with the degree of cultural development which the native had achieved. Thus in the important sphere of religion relatively advanced groups such as the Maoris eagerly adopted Christianity which had certain features akin to their own religion, and, in spite of the appearance of "cults of despair," many Maoris are still Christian. On the other hand Elkin states that the Australian aborigines rarely seemed able to obtain a grip of the Christian faith, although this may have been due to the fact that few missionaries understood the natives' secret life and hence presented Christianity as a revelation quite unconnected with the beliefs, ritual or conduct of the aborigines.

Elkin's criticism of the Australian missionaries seems generally applicable, as these well meaning but often destructive pioneers of white culture broke down the native systems too rapidly and without adequate replacement. There were, however, exceptions both Roman Catholic and Protestant, for men such as Marsden in New Zealand and Duncan at Metlakahtla realised that religious and other acculturation must rest upon a sound basis of new economics. Usually, however, the missions created a cycle of destruction, remarkably uniform in type. The Spanish missions in California and Australian Missions such as New Norcia and Poonindie saw the full bloods disappear in about fifty years, with the result that the missions closed, unless fresh native groups appeared or work amongst mixed bloods gave the enterprises renewed life.

Some of the most remarkable similarities in all the countries under consideration were the revivals of native religions and anti-acculturation movements connected with those revivals. These movements were partly due to a growing detestation by the aboriginal peoples of all things white and foreign; the knowledge that many of the conquerors failed to practise their own religious precepts, and a realisation that the missionaries were rent into antagonistic sects which waged religious warfare on abstruse problems. As a result North America saw Prophet Dances, Ghost Dances and the Peyote cult; New Zealand Te Kootie's movement and the Ratana Church, while, according to Elkin, even the Australian full blood and half-caste aborigines endeavoured to return to the secret life of their ancestors with modified beliefs and rites. with biblical characters equated to the old heroes, and with the belief that the old teaching contained all that was valuable in the new[5].

These religious reactions have been called "cults of despair,"

CONCLUSION

originating from visions, delusions and the mental confusion which followed the inrush of European ideas. Most of them combined Christian and native influences—the coming of a Messiah; the return of the dead, and the expulsion of the whites. Most of the revivals brought disillusionment when the Messiah failed to appear or his apostle failed to protect the faithful from white bullets. Some, however, like the Peyote cult in North America and Ratana Church in New Zealand, still persist.

The results of educational differed little from those of religious contacts. In the early stage both the governmental and missionary teachers offered an academic training largely contradictory to native tradition and interests, and used that training to ridicule and destroy all that the aboriginal peoples valued in life. Children were torn away from their parents and confined to schools during the period which was essential for training in such pursuits as hunting, and it was small wonder that peoples such as the Australian aborigines made frequent and successful efforts to regain their children. Here and there the whites attempted to establish a technical education in conformity with native industries and arts, but the history of education in the United States and New Zealand indicates that these attempts did not appear until comparatively recent dates.

Margaret Mead has made one of the few close and scientific studies of the acculturation periods as applied to a comparatively small group. According to this student the Antler Indians passed through a trading stage when the dislocation of aboriginal life commenced; a settler stage when an Agency and Presbyterian mission were established, and when the buffalo disappeared, and a period when, under governmental and missionary pressure, and native leadership, a movement towards white culture commenced. It appears that the Antlers had at this stage made for themselves some sort of existence although this existence lacked the rich complexity of their former life. Unfortunately they were then overwhelmed by a fresh rush of settlers, and were robbed of much of their remaining lands with the resulting deterioration that Mead disclosed and analysed[6].

Paul Radin in a similar examination of the influence of the whites on the culture of the Winnebago Indians demonstrated that the influence of the European culture took four lines. It ob-

195

literated completely the Winnebago customs. It introduced customs, utensils and ideas of European origin. It brought into contact with the Winnebagos Indian tribes that had had no previous intercourse with them, and it stimulated contacts which had existed before the coming of the whites[7].

Writing of the Australian aborigines Elkin outlined three stages of cultural adjustment. During the first the natives showed opposition to the whites, and bewilderment, resentment, and a sense of loss of their historic social systems and culture. This stage was also noted by Protector Moorhouse of South Australia who considered that it followed an opening period during which the aborigines were peaceable and approached the whites without weapons[8]. Elkin postulated a second period during which the natives developed a feeling of scorn for and inferiority towards their historic culture, a dangerous outlook liable to result in despondency and depopulation. The third stage according to Elkin was one of contra-acculturation. In this stage the aborigines returned to their old faiths in a somewhat modified form and regained a sense of worth for their historic arts, crafts, literature, law and customs[9]. Research in North America and New Zealand indicated that the Indians and Maoris passed through similar stages. Where native groups reached the third stage they tended to survive, but, unless they reached this stage, they perished or were assimilated by the white population.

DESTRUCTIVE FACTORS

Authorities would probably agree that Mooney's list of destructive factors in North America would be fairly accurate for the majority of regions. Mooney gave priority of place to smallpox and other epidemics, and followed these with tuberculosis, social diseases, whisky and attendant dissipation, removals, starvation and subjection to unaccustomed conditions, low vitality due to depression, and wars. All these evils with the exception of wars and tuberculosis he considered came from the whites[10]. In Australia smallpox, apparently introduced by the Malays, was probably the chief killing agent although it was quickly succeeded by tuberculosis, social diseases and other complaints. Slaughter by the whites, alcohol, and the seizure of native lands particularly

196

CONCLUSION

as these contained historic sacred places, were also important agents. In New Zealand the chief destructive factors were disease, alcohol, and warfare conducted with white weapons. As a result of these three factors it was estimated that some 60,000 Maoris perished. Following on initial periods of disease, alcoholism, warfare, land robbery and the destruction of resources the majority of native groups entered upon periods of despondency and decline against which the palliatives of small and inadequate reservations and Christian Missionary enterprise were rarely effective.

NUMERICAL DECLINE

It is impossible to estimate in any of the English speaking countries the exact degree of numerical decline which resulted from the above mentioned factors. This is due to the fact that pre-conquest estimates are largely guesses, while census estimates, even in recent times, are far from satisfactory owing to a number of complications, such as the difficulty of distinguishing between full and mixed bloods. It seems that in the United States the aboriginal population declined from a possible 845,000 before the conquest to 244,000 in 1880; in Canada from a possible 220,000 to 93,200 in 1931; in Australia from a possible 300,000 to 77,481 as recorded by the careful census of 1921, and in New Zealand from a possible 200,000 to 37,500 in 1871.

Thus it appears that the white invasions reduced these aboriginal peoples from a problematical total of about a million and a half to less than half a million, a figure including mixed bloods. Some authorities consider that the pre-conquest figures given for North America and New Zealand are far too low. If so the percentage of destruction was considerably greater than that indicated.

NUMERICAL RECOVERY

In presenting the figures of the numerical recoveries, which were comparatively recent, allowance must again be made for certain census difficulties such as the correct estimation of the number of Australian aboriginal nomads, and, in all countries considered, the difficulty of classifying accurately the mixed bloods. Taking the statistical figures at their face value, however,

197

it appears that in the United States the total native population—full and mixed blood—increased from 244,000 in 1880 to 270,544 in 1900 and 351,878 in 1938. It was reported that this advance had become consistently higher than that of the whites and was greater than that of any other major population group in the country. In Canada the Indian population fell to 93,000 in 1901 and then increased to 115,000 in 1939 when numbers were showing an annual improvement of 1%. In New Zealand the Maoris, who had declined to 37,502 in 1871, remained less than 50,000 until 1918 after which they increased to 86,767 in 1939 and 97,283 in 1945 and 106,492 in 1947, when they were advancing far more rapidly than the white population. Only in Australia did the total native population continue to register a decline, although this was slight, the figures falling from 77,481 in 1921 to 77,259 in 1939.

Very important was the fact that the increase of native population in the United States, Canada and New Zealand, and the small extent of the decline in Australia, were undoubtedly due to the rapid advance of the mixed bloods. Thus, although the total Indian population increased in the United States, the ratio of full bloods fell from 62% to 52% in 1920-30 and from 1930 to 1937 the mixed bloods increased by 22½% and the full bloods by only 3.5%. In 1937 the United States Bureau of Census published in "The Indian Population of the United States and Alaska" comparative tables, which showed that between 1910 and 1930, in twenty selected states, the Indian full bloods registered an average decline from 61.9% of the native population to 46.16%, while the mixed bloods increased from 35.36 to 41.28%. Moreover the Bureau stated that as a result of scientific investigations the proportion of full bloods seemed considerably lower than that recorded in the census of 1930 or 1910. In 1915 the Bureau of Census published in "Indian Population in the United States and Alaska" a map which indicated that the highest percentages of full blood (85% to 100%) were mainly confined to Nevada, Utah, Colorado, Arizona and New Mexico—a solid block of semi-arid states in the South-West and it is here, perhaps here only, that the Indian full bloods seem likely to hold their own or even increase.

In a report of 1937 Mr. John Collier analysed the difficult, and

CONCLUSION

sometimes contradictory statistics, covering these questions. He agreed that the total Indian population was increasing by 1.2% per annum but stated that, whereas the reservation population was increasing, the non-reservation population was being merged in the white population or was dying away. In his opinion over 60% of the Indians enrolled at the Agencies were full bloods, but much of the increase was due to white admixture, and, if consideration could be given to the full bloods alone, the figures might show a decline. The tables which he presented gave a clear and important picture of hybrid vigour: 8.6% of all marriages were sterile, but for full blood marriages the figures were 10.7% as against only 6.7% for mixed marriages, the proportion of issueless marriages decreasing directly as the amount of white blood in mixed marriages increased. The statistics for child mortality gave the same picture of hybrid vigour. For all marriages the proportion of surviving children was 74.7%, for pure blood marriages 64.7% and for mixed marriages 79%.

Very unwisely Canada published no statistics of her mixed bloods, but Abbott estimated that these numbered some 50,000 in 1915, and there is no doubt that the country contains many persons with an admixture of Indian blood, and that in many areas absorption is proceeding apace.

It seems that in New Zealand the mixed bloods are playing an outstanding part in the Maori increase as their numbers rose from 7,352 in 1921 to 26,000 in 1936. The full bloods are also increasing but their percentage in the rapidly advancing native population is registering a slight decline. In 1926 they numbered 44,794 or 71.35% of a population of 62,781, and in 1936 55,916 or 67.92% of a population of 82,326.

In Australia the fact that the aboriginal population as a whole registered only a slight decline over the period 1921-39 was almost wholly due to the increase of mixed bloods. In 1921 these numbered 16,818 as against 60,663 full bloods, and in 1939 25,712 as against only 51,556 full bloods.

In summary it can be said that the native population (full and mixed blood) is increasing in the United States, in Canada and in New Zealand, but is declining slightly in Australia. The full bloods are decreasing in all countries excepting New Zealand, but the number of mixed bloods is everywhere on the advance.

199

WHITE SETTLERS AND NATIVE PEOPLES

THE MIXED BLOOD PROBLEM

Unfortunately extremely little scientific work has been done on the highly important problems of the increase of mixed bloods and of their assimilation in the white populations. In this field the work of Tindale is outstanding and opens up a number of serious but unexplored questions[11]. It is, for example, highly important to both the white and native populations of New Zealand, the South-West of the United States and Western Australia that scientific examination should be made of the various grades of mixed bloods, and the potentialities of the various grades for acculturation or absorption, on the lines opened up by Tindale's pioneering researches.

Such scientific examination will have a most important bearing upon whether or not the aim of white policy should be the building up of native minority populations or alternatively the assimilation of such groups in the white communities. Broadly it may be said that the amalgamation of widely different ethnic stocks often produces grave short time problems but may produce satisfactory results in the long run.

CAUSES OF RECOVERY

The causes of the recovery of some of the aboriginal peoples in the twentieth century were of several types—environmental, biological, cultural, administrative and economic. Broadly speaking the century saw certain white governments acquiring and applying anthropological knowledge to native problems, thus producing great advances on the reservations—advances in administration, health, education, social organisation and economic life, with consequent improvement in native psychology and outlook. On their part some natives appear to have developed a resistance to white diseases, a tolerance of reservation conditions and occupations, and some acculturation to white civilisation. This last was accompanied in certain very striking cases, such as the Maoris and Navajos, by an evolution of native or mixed blood leadership and a partial restoration of the former social systems and cultures. As Clark Wissler pointed out, however, many groups had been almost wholly born and bred on reservations or in close contact

200

CONCLUSION

with white civilization. They were in the process of becoming bilingual and literate and had no first hand knowledge of the former life. Wissler believed from his study of Indian groups on the Northern Plains—in Alberta, Saskatchewan and Montana—that the lowest level of population was reached about 1904, and that from that time onwards the Indians appear to have adapted themselves to reservation conditions. This accounted for the fact that their death rate, which in 1884 had been possibly as high as 70, fell to 52 in 1904 and 33 in 1934[12]. Unfortunately scientific studies such as Wissler's are very rare. The Phelps-Stokes Enquiry on the rapidly increasing Navajos admitted that no vital statistics were available.

In New Zealand the Maoris appear to have begun their recovery early in the Twentieth Century, and from about 1918 they increased in numbers very rapidly.

In this case the death rate actually increased from 14.96 in 1925 to 18.29 in 1923, but the birth rate was extremely high and there was a very satisfactory fall in infant mortality. In the case of the Maoris, the Navajos and other groups recovery and progress were undoubtedly assisted by the great improvement in white outlook, policy and administration. This new outlook fostered anti-acculturation, although somewhat paradoxically combined with certain acculturation processes, for example the acceptance of white services for health, hygiene and technical education, together with the adoption of certain white industries and industrial methods.

The outstanding example of the changed white-native relations was President Roosevelt's "New Day for Indians" which at long last provided a reasonable approach to and expenditure upon Indian problems. The Governments of Canada, New Zealand and some of the Australian States were making progress on similar lines and the Australian Federal Government was talking the same language with little action or result.

THE FUTURE

It is unwise to generalise in regard to the future. It appears, however, that in most regions the full and mixed blood natives will continue the present process of acculturation and will be gradually assimilated by the white majority populations. In a few

WHITE SETTLERS AND NATIVE PEOPLES

regions, however, particularly on the margins, as in North-Eastern New Zealand and the South-West of the United States, he aboriginal populations will continue to exist for very long periods, perhaps even indefinitely. On present statistics New Zealand faces a particularly serious problem for the Maoris now number nearly 6% of the population and are rapidly increasing that percentage. In regard to many other regions one cannot accept Macleod's airy dictum that, as the Indians of the United States total only about the population of a small city, the problem has ended[13].

Although comparatively few in numbers the native peoples are scattered over vast territories. They are still of great value to important industries such as the North Australian cattle industry, and they present grave problems as islands of ill health, undernourishment and social inferiority, or as in part responsible for such evils as American soil erosion.

A final problem which is of fundamental importance is the relative merits—ethnical, biological, social and economic—of the old harsh policy of assimilation as compared with its young and successful rival the policy of assisting native peoples in movements which to some extent oppose acculturation and which maintain or even increase native minority groups. Both types of policy have ardent supporters. There are still many whites who would hasten assimilation and end the problem, notwithstanding the fact that the former unscientific systems created mixed peoples who in many cases suffered from mental and physical disharmonies and from social inferiorities and disabilities. On the other hand the advocates of the new methods rightly claim that the policy of fostering aboriginal minorities has proved much more merciful and successful where the reservations have been of adequate size and wealth, and where it has been possible to sustain or revive a substantial measure of native pride of life, organisation and culture, and that these successes far outweigh any alleged disadvantages. The results achieved in a comparatively short time appear to justify the advocates of the new and scientific methods, but it also seems that local variations may demand certain variations in policy. For example Australian authorities such as Tindale believe that Australia should adopt widely different methods in dealing with her tribalised natives, de-tribalised natives, mixed bloods, and Torres Strait islanders[14]. Similarly in North America different

CONCLUSION

policies appear necessary in the handling of the tribalised and de-tribalised Indians.

In conclusion it may be justly claimed that the English-speaking invasions of North America, Australia and New Zealand were only some of many population movements and clashes which occurred throughout pre-historic and historic times, and that the decimation and degradation wrought by the invaders upon the invaded were, in all probability, less extensive and ruthless than in many other instances. It is clear, however, that the English-speaking peoples increased, to some extent unnecessarily, the destruction of the conquered natives, and of their cultures, by inhumanities and errors which are clearly portrayed in the history of every country that we have considered. Whether the future policy should be to hasten the absorption of the remnants, or to foster their continuance and increase as minority groups it is the duty of the English-speaking Governments and peoples to deal humanely, generously, and scientifically with the descendants and heirs of the dispossessed.

APPENDIX TO CHAPTER VII

The following notes on Australian Native Policy and Social Anthropology were kindly contributed by Ronald M. and Catherine H. Berndt, Research Fellows in Anthropology under the Australian National Research Council and the Department of Anthropology, Sydney University. The Berndts' notes re-emphasise two matters stressed by the author in Chapter VII. The first of these is the comparatively slight use still made of an anthropological science by those responsible for Australian native administration. The second is the grave state of affairs still existing in the Northern Territory where native policy is the direct responsibility of the Australian Federal Government at Canberra.

The picture painted by the Berndt's as a result of their eight months' survey of native life on the northern cattle stations reveals unsatisfactory diet, housing, education, medical attention, hygiene, and sanitation, and working conditions under which the aborigines are disappearing as rapidly as they did in the days of the moving frontier.

The Berndt's criticise the lack of Australian anthropological work during the war, but while this book was in the press the Arnhem Land Expedition, led by Mr. C. P. Mountford, of Adelaide, and sponsored by the Commonwealth Government and the National Geographical Society of Washington, U.S.A., conducted, during eight months of 1948, field research on aboriginal diet and other problems important to native administration. The party included anthropologists, nutritionists, biochemists, a medical scientist, and four naturalists.

SOME NOTES IN REFERENCE TO AUSTRALIAN NATIVE POLICY AND SOCIAL ANTHROPOLOGY, BY RONALD M. AND CATHERINE H. BERNDT, 1946[1]

The dependence of Native Policy—its formation and execution—on actual field work in applied anthropology and acculturation has been recognised in most countries where an indigenous

WHITE SETTLERS AND NATIVE PEOPLES

minority is dependent on alien administration. But in Australia this is unfortunately not the case; anthropological knowledge, which is ideally based on a scientific and disinterested approach, has not been made use of to any noticeable extent by Government bodies and administrators. This attitude is apparent in the fact that there is at present only one Chair of Anthropology in Australia (under Professor A. P. Elkin of the Department of Anthropology, Sydney University) and no Chair of Sociology (although there has recently been formed a Sociological Institute in Sydney).

The most noticeable feature, however, is the lack of any co-ordinated native policy for Australia; that is, each State has its own regulations, which are administered in accordance with its own wishes and desires, without the sanction or check of a Commonwealth body of experts. Formation of the latter is an essential feature where native administration is concerned; such a body should be composed of educationalists, social anthropologists, colonial administrators, and medical doctors specialising in nutrition, hygiene and certain prevalent diseases. One must consider the fact that today there are but very few officers employed in Native Affairs and Welfare Departments, in the various States of the Commonwealth who have had any training in Anthropology and the administration of native peoples; through the endeavours of Professor A. P. Elkin and Mr. E. W. P. Chinnery (late Director of Native Affairs) this position in the Northern Territory has to a small extent been modified—but lack of Government support has so far prevented their full plans from materializing[2].

---

[1] Research Fellows in Anthropology under the Australian National Research Council and the Department of Anthropology, Sydney University.

[2] In regard to Native Policy, see A. P. Elkin, *Citizenship for the Aborigines* (Sydney 1944); this summarised general legislation and individual State policies. With regard to South Australia and the Northern Territory see two works by the writers, mentioned in the main body of this Appendix, together with the monograph, *A Preliminary Report on Field Work in the Oldea Region, Western South Australia*, Oceania Reprint, Sydney 1945, particularly pp. 27-46, and *Some problems of the Mixed Blood Aborigines in the Southern Part of South Australia*, Social Horizons, July 1945 (Sydney 1946) pp. 40-45. Also reference to acculturation by various writers in the Journal *Oceania*.

APPENDIX

Apart from Professor Elkin and the writers, only three other female research workers into problems of aboriginal-white culture contact, native policy etc., have been carrying out field work during the war years in Australia; all these anthropologists are currently continuing their investigation under the Australian National Research Council and the Department of Anthropology, Sydney University, etc. The extreme paucity of social research workers in various fields of anthropology in Australia is particularly lamentable. It is an excuse for continuation of the present unsatisfactory administration of Australian aborigines, and the localised autonomy of State policies.

In this brief Appendix, however, only brief mention may be made of general tendencies and conditions.

Between 1941-1944 the writers (under the Australian National Research Council and the Department of Anthropology, Sydney University) carried out field work in South Australia. This consisted of a study of the culture contact situation in an urban area, as well as in country, pastoral and "outback" regions. The results of this work have been included in a volume entitled "Acculturation in Southern Australia" (for publication, 1946). This covers most aspects of native-white acculturation in that State and certain parts of New South Wales; and from the basis of original research a general native policy (with local variations) has been postulated. This is too wide in scope to be summarised here.

Between August 1944 to April 1946, the writers carried out a survey of native employment in the Northern Territory, having been engaged as anthropologists for the Australian Investment Agency (popularly known as Vestey Bros.); this was made possible under an arrangement with Professor Elkin and Mr. E. W. P. Chinnery on the one hand and the general manager of the firm concerned on the other. It was a unique experiment, as it was the first instance in Australia of anthropologists being engaged by a commercial firm for the purpose of carrying out investigations into specific conditions and recommending a general policy.

The results of this survey have been set out in a volume entitled "Native Labour and Welfare in the Northern Territory," (to be published by the Department of Anthropology in conjunction with the Association for the Protection of Native Races). This describes actual conditions in central western Northern Territory and the upper Northern portion of the Northern Territory on pastoral stations, Army settlements (a wartime innovation, during the employment of aborigines by the Military authorities). Buffalo camps, a Civil compound, and an "uncontrolled" region etc.; it further outlines the general terms of a native policy to be adopted in the regions under discussion.

In order to widen the scope of the distribution of such information to the public, concerning conditions on certain Northern Territory pastoral stations, the following summary of data has been prepared[3].

(a) Unsatisfactory and inadequate diet, which is quite insufficient both in type and quantity to maintain a reasonable standard of health. This state of affairs is more intensified in some areas than in others.

The continued under-nourishment, over a long period, of local tribes (i.e. with the consumption of only relatively small quantities of "bush tucker") has been to a large extent responsible for the situation noted under the following heading.

(b) Low birth rate, and high percentage of deaths among infants and young people.

This high percentage of deaths applies particularly to the local station tribes, among whom the birth rate is alarmingly low. Detailed tables relating to Vital Statistics and Depopulation demonstrate that the birth rate is not a replacement rate. The practice of abortion is not carried out on a sufficiently wide scale, nor to a sufficiently large extent, to make an appreciable difference over a long period, while it was not a feature of these areas that infants were destroyed at birth.

(c) Inadequate and spasmodic medical attention. Consideration of the presence of venereal disease among native men and women is another important factor. The presence of gonorrhea in the individual is recognised to have an impairing action on his reproductive organs, directly or indirectly causing sterility.

(d) Absence of any facilities for hygiene and sanitation. No

---

[3] Summarised from *Native Labour and Welfare in the Northern Territory* by the writers, pp. 153-165.

encouragement was given to natives, either children or adults, to improve on their indigenous habits in this respect. Water supplies often inadequate.

(e)   No adequate shelters provided for the use of station employees (or other natives) during the wet season except such as they had themselves put together in their spare time from old scraps of material.

(f)   Unsatisfactory working conditions, with no choice or consideration accorded to the individual concerned. In remuneration for his labour the native receives the minimum of food, clothing, tobacco etc., the cost of these being cut down as much as possible to save expense, his family is not adequately fed or provided for.

(g)   No educational facilities of any kind are provided or desired. No organised training exists in the areas under discussion; e.g. in domestic duties and in stock work.

(h)   Excessively high degree of cohabitation between white men and native women, the incidence of this increasing with the absence of supervision.

(i)   Mutual intolerance and hostility between the two groups. Since neither group understood—except in a very small and superficial degree—the life, customs and ways of the other, it is not surprising that so little sympathy and tolerance existed between the two. Violence and the threat of violence are considered by a large number of people in these areas, to be the only effective means of exercising authority over natives.

(j)   Consistent breaches of the regulations governing native employment; that is, apart from the above mentioned aspects, these regulations are consciously evaded. This also refers to the employment of children under 12 years of age.

Perhaps a greater awareness of such facts will precipitate some action in relation to Native Policy, more particularly on these cattle stations in the Northern Territory. But such statements have also a general application, since conditions of native administration throughout Australia are far from satisfactory. A greater diffusion of knowledge in this respect is an essential prerequisite to the general formulation and carrying out of Native Policy in Australia.

NOTES

CHAPTER I

[1] There is a considerable literature on the origin and pre-Columbian numbers of the Indians: A. L. Kroeber *Anthropology*, London 1923, Ch. 13; *Native American Population, American Anthropologist*, Jan.-March, 1934; Clarke Wissler, *Natural History*, Sept. 1934; and in F. J. Brown, *Our Racial and National Minorities*, New York, 1937; D. Jenness, *Indians of Canada*, Ottawa, 1934, Ch. 16; J. Mooney *Aboriginal Population of America*, Smithsonian Misc. Coll., Vol. 80, No. 7, Washington 1928; *Handbook of American Indians*, Washington, 1910, Vol. 11. p. 287; E. Anteos, *The Spread of Aboriginal Man to North America*, the *Geog. Review*, April, 1935; For an estimate of 3,000,000 Indians in pre-Columbian times, W. C. MacLeod, *The American Indian Frontier*, London, 1928, pp. 15-16.

[2] A. L. Kroeber, *Anthropology*, ch. 13; Clarke Wissler, *Ethnological Diversity in America and its Significance*, Am. Museum of National History, pp. 175-185; Ellsworth Huntington, *The Red Man's Continent*, Yale, pp.4 seq. p. 152; D. Jenness, *Indians of Canada*, chs. 3, 4, 5, Ottawa, 1934, and *The Indian Background of Canadian History*, Ottawa, 1937, pp. 18 seq.; *Handbook of American Indians*, Vol. 1, p. 540; Edna Kenton, *The Indians of North America*, New York, 1929, (2 vols.) for Jesuit Relations; E. L. Hewett, *Ancient life on the American South West*, Indianapolis 1930, Part 1.

[3] A. L. Kroeber, *Native American Population*, and *Handbook of Californian Indians*, Am. Bureau of Anthropology, Washington, 1925, pp. 886 seq.; A. C. Wilgus, ed. *Modern Historic America*, Washington, 1933, pp. 139-169, and *The Carribean Area*, Washington, 1933, pp. 210-227; Report of the President's Research Committee, New York, 1933, p. 561.

[4] Kroeber, *Anthropology*, Ch. 13; Wissler, *Ethnological Diversity*, p. 194.

[5] Authorities quoted above—Kroeber, Hewett, Jenness, Huntington, Kenton, and *Handbook of American Indians*. For effects of Indian culture upon white civilisation, Clarke Wissler in F. J. Brown, pp. 725 seq. and Jenness Ch. 17.

[6] *Cambridge History of British Empire*, Vol. 1, p. 9 and Vol. VII, Ch. II; H. A. Innes *The Fur Trade in Canada*, Yale, 1930, Ch. II.

[7] *Annual Report American Bureau of Ethnology*, 1896-7, Washington 1899, pp. 527 seq.; J. T. Adams, *Epic of America*, Boston, 1932, pp. 77-8; J. P. Kinney, *A Continent Lost, a Civilisation Won*, Baltimore, 1937, Ch. 1.

[8] Quoted by Macleod, pp. 49-50.

[9] Macleod, p. 244.

[10] Kinney, Ch. 1.

[11] *American Bureau of Ethnology Report*, 1896-7, pp. 562 seq. for Colonial

WHITE SETTLERS AND NATIVE PEOPLES

attitudes to the Indians; also *Cambridge History of British Empire;* Vol. 1, Chs. 3, 5, 8, 10; Macleod Parts, 3, 4, 5; Kinney, Ch. 1; J. G. Leyburn, *Frontier Folkways,* Yale University Press 1935, Ch. 1.

[12] Kinney, p. 15 seq.

[13] A. Nevins, *A Brief History of the United States,* O.U.P. 1942, p. 21; *Cambridge History of the British Empire,* Vol. 1. pp. 544 seq.; Kinney, Ch. 1; Macleod, Chs. 12-27; *Handbook of American Indians,* pp. 617 seq.; J. T. Adams, Ch. II.

[14] L. F. Schmeckebier, *The Office of Indian Affairs,* Baltimore, 1927, Ch. 1, and Kinney, pp. 130-1.

[15] *Office of Indian Affairs,* pp. 12-17

[16] A. Nevins, *Brief History,* p. 71, and *Office of Indian Affairs,* pp. 20 seq.

[17] *Office of Indian Affairs,* pp. 28 seq.

[18] *Office of Indian Affairs,* pp. 37 seq.

[19] Quoted by Macleod, p. 468.

[20] Macleod, Chs. 32-3.

[21] Clark Wissler, *Indian Cavalcade,* New York, 1938, p. 22.

[22] Quoted by Macleod, p. 487.

[23] A. G. Harper, *Human Dependency—an Economic Survey,* unpublished report, 1939; A. L. Kroeber, *Handbook of Indians of California,* Washington, 1925, p. 890.

[24] *Indian Cavalcade,* Ch. V.

[25] *Office of Indian Affairs,* pp. 4 seq.

[26] For relations between the Americans and Indians, L. F. Schmeckebier, *The Office of Indian Affairs;* Kinney, Ch. II; Macleod, Part V and conclusion; Clark Wissler, *Indian Cavalcade; Handbook of American Indians;* A. L. Kroeber, *Handbook of Indians of California.*

[27] For numerical decrease—*Indian Population in the U.S. and Alaska,* Washington, 1915, pp. 10 seq.; *Handbook of American Indians,* Vol. 1, pp. 540 seq.; A. L. Kroeber, *Native American Population,* American Anthropologist, Jan.—March 1934, and *Handbook of Indians of California,* pp. 880 seq.; Clark Wissler in F. J. Brown, *Our Racial and National Minorities,* New York, 1937, Part III, pp. 37 seq.; Annual Report of Secretary of the Interior, Washington, 1938, pp. 258 seq. The lowest figures given in *Indian Population* (p. 10) are 228,000 from Report of Commissioner of Indian Affairs 1890, and 237, 196 by Census 1900.

[28] *Handbook of American Indians,* Vol. II, p. 286

[29] A. Townsend, *Disease and the Indian,* Scientific Monthly, Dec. 1938, pp. 482 seq.

[30] S. F. Cook, *The Extent and Significance of Disease amongst the Indians of Baja California,* 1697-1773, Berkeley, 1937.

[31] P. Meigs, *The Dominican Mission Frontier of Lower California,* Berkeley, 1935, pp. 153 seq.

[32] Macleod, Ch. III, and pp. 41 and 307; Leyburn, p. 53; *Cambridge History of the British Empire,* Vol VI, Canada, references to liquor traffic; Jenness, *Indians of Canada,* pp. 253-4; Roy Nash, *Survey of the Seminole Indians of Florida,* Washington, 1932, pp. 46 seq.

NOTES

[33] *Handbook of American Indians*, p. 286; Macleod, pp. 284 seq., 487 seq.; Jenness, pp. 254 seq.

[34] *Handbook of American Indians*, Vol. I, pp. 569 seq.; Jenness pp. 129 seq.

[35] C. Wissler in F. J. Brown, pp. 725 seq., and Jenness, *Indians of Canada*, Ch. 17.

CHAPTER II

[1] For the Spanish Missions, A. G. Keller, *Colonisation*, Boston, 1908 pp. 287 seq.; Macleod, Ch. 9; P. Meigs, *The Dominican Mission Frontier of Lower California*, Berkeley, 1935.

[2] *Handbook of American Indians*, Vol. 1. "Missions," pp. 874 seq.; W. C. Macleod, *The American Indian Frontier*, pp. 104 seq.

[3] Handbook, Vol. 1, pp. 892 seq.; Macleod, note p. 109.

[4] A. L. Kroeber, *Handbook of the Indians of California*, Am. Bureau of Anthropology, Washington, D.C., 1925, pp. 889 seq.

[5] Meigs, p. 153.

[6] Paul Hasluck, *Black Australians*, M.U.P. 1942, Ch. VII, note 19, Ch. VII of this book.

[7] Meigs, pp. 155-6.

[8] Macleod, p. 171.

[9] ibid., pp. 389 seq.

[10] ibid.

[11] ibid., Ch. XXII, and *Handbook of American Indians*, "Missions," pp. 874 seq.

[12] Handbook, p. 898.

[13] Macleod, pp. 342 seq. and Handbook.

[14] Macleod, Chs. XXVI, XXVII; L. F. Schmeckebier, pp. 42 seq.

[15] Kinney, pp. 19. seq.

[16] Schmeckebier, pp. 24, 25.

[17] ibid., pp. 43 seq. and p. 84.

[18] ibid., pp. 60-61. A *Birdseye View of Indian Policy*, House of Representatives, Dec. 30th, 1935.

[19] Kinney, pp. 333 seq.

[20] Schmeckebier, pp. 66 seq.; Kinney, Ch. V.

[21] Kinney, p. 207; Schmeckebier, pp. 78 seq.; D. S. Otis, *History of the Allotment Policy*, H.R. 7902, Washington, 1934.

[22] Kinney, Ch. VI, A *Birdseye View*; Lewis Meriam, *The Problem of Indian Administration*, Baltimore, 1928, p. 468; Annual Report of Indian Commissioners, 1929, p. 25.

[23] Schmeckebier, p. 48.

[24] Macleod, p. 450.

[25] Kinney, p. 172.

[26] Macleod, pp. 445-6; *Handbook of American Indians*, "Missions," pp. 874 seq.; Schmeckebier, p. 54 and Ch. XIV.

WHITE SETTLERS AND NATIVE PEOPLES

[27] Kinney, p. 159; Macleod, Chs. XXXIV, XXXV.
[28] Meriam, p. 823.
[29] *Handbook of American Indians*; Meriam, Ch. XIV; Schmeckebier, Ch. XIV; *Christian Missions Among the American Indians*; U.S. Board of Indian Commissioners, Bulletin No. 280, 1927; G. E. E. Lindquist, *The Red Man in the United States*, New York, 1923.
[30] Meriam, Ch. XIV.
[31] M. Mead, *The Changing Culture of an Indian Tribe*, New York, 1932, p. 222.
[32] Clark Wissler, *Indian Cavalcade*, New York, 1938, p. 197.
[33] Macleod, Ch. XXXIV.
[34] Meriam, p. 629.
[35] Kinney, p. 264.
[36] ibid., p. 336.
[37] Kinney, p. 334.
[38] ibid., p. 335.
[39] Schmeckebier, pp. 227 seq.
[40] ibid., pp. 197 seq. and D. S. Otis in H.R. 7902, pp. 452 seq.
[41] Kinney, pp. 300 seq.

CHAPTER III

[1] Report of Secretary of the Interior, Washington, 1938, pp. 258 seq.; C. T. Loram and others, *The Navajo Indian Problem*, New York, 1939, p. VII; *Indians at Work*, July-Aug. 1944, p. 21; Clark Wissler, Scientific Monthly, July, 1936; Anthropological Papers of American Museum of National History, Vol. 36, Part 1, New York, 1936; and *The Rebirth of the Vanishing Indian*, "National History," Sept. 1934. The student will find many minor contradictions in U.S. Indian statistics. The Meriam report pointed this out (Ch. VIII) and urged the need for more accurate details and methods.
[2] C. T. Loram, above, p. 118.
[3] Meriam Report, pp. 3-21 and (for land) pp. 466-7.
[4] Kinney, pp. 300 seq.
[5] Author's interviews with John Collier, Washington, 1939; John Collier, *A Birdseye View of Indian Policy*, submitted to Sub-Committee of Appropriation Committee of House of Representatives, Dec. 1933; Clark Wissler, *The Rebirth of the Vanishing Indian*, Natural History, Sept. 1934; Loram, *The Navajo Indian Problem*, pp. 119-120; Kinney, p. 310.
[6] M. Mead, *The Changing Culture of an Indian Tribe*, pp. 123-129.
[7] *Birdseye View*.
[8] Annual Reports of Secretary of Interior, Washington, D.C.
[9] *Birdseye View*, p. 8.
[10] *Birdseye View*, p. 9; *New Day for the Indians*, 1938, p. 28.
[11] *Birdseye View*, p. 5.
[12] Report of Secretary of Interior, 1938, pp. 211, 214; *New Day*, p. 30.
[13] Report of Secretary of Interior, 1938, pp. 217 seq.
[14] ibid., pp. 233-4.
[15] Report of Secretary of Interior, 1938, pp. 238 seq.; Jas. G. Townsend,

NOTES

Disease and the Indian, Scientific Monthly, Dec. 1938, pp. 479-495; Loram, *Navajo Indian Problem*, pp. 87 seq.

[16] Secretary of Interior, Report, 1938, pp. 244 seq.; Loram, Ch. IV; *Progressive Education*, Washington, D.C., Feb. 1932.

[17] Loram, p. 107.

[18] *New Day*, p. 12.

[19] Loram, p. 103; For Navajo native religion, K. Luomala, *Navajo Life Yesterday and Today*, Berkeley, 1938.

[20] Loram, Ch. VII.

[21] Author's notes, 1939.

[22] *The New Day*, pp. 35 seq.

[23] In *Saturday Morning Post*, April 1st, 1939.

[24] Loram, pp. 120-121.

[25] *Indians at Work*, May—June, 1944, pp. 4 seq., pp. 17 seq.

[26] *Indians at Work*, May—June, 1944, p. 11.

[27] John Collier in *Indians at Work*, July—August, 1944.

[28] *Indians at Work*, May—June, 1944, pp. 23 seq.; July—Aug., 1944, pp. 21 seq.; Jan.—Feb., 1945, pp. 1 seq.

[29] *Indians at Work*, Jan.—Feb., 1945.

[30] President Roosevelt in *Indians at Work*, Jan.—Feb., 1945.

CHAPTER IV

[1] C. L. Andrews, *The Story of Alaska*, Idaho, 1938.

[2] H. A. Innis, *The Fur Trade in Canada*, Yale, 1930; D. Mackay, *The Honourable Company*, Toronto, 1938.

[3] Canadian figures from Annual Report, Dept. of Indian Affairs, 1926; The U.S. figures from *Indian Population*, Washington, 1910, p. 10, show discrepancies but suggest a minimum of about 240,000.

[4] D. Jenness, *Canada's Indian Problems*, Smithsonian Report, 1942, Washington, D.C., p. 367.

[5] Jenness, *Canada's Indian Problems*, above; *The Indians of Canada*, Ottawa, 1934, Ch. 19, and *The Indian Background of Canadian History*, Ottawa, 1937. J. G. Leyburn, above, Ch. 3.

[6] Jenness' publications above.

[7] *Cambridge History of British Empire*, Vol. 1, Chs. 1, 2, 10, 12, 13, 16, 18; Vol. VI, Canada, Chs. 1-4; H. A. Innis, above, Chs. 1, 2 and Part 2; Jenness, *Indians of Canada*, pp. 259-260; J. G. Leyburn, above, Ch. III.

[8] Jenness, *Indians of Canada*, pp. 259-260 and Ch. 18; *Canada's Indian Problems*, pp. 369 seq.; J. G. Leyburn, above, Ch. 3.

[9] For French contacts, *Cambridge History of British Empire*, Vol. VI, Canada, pp. 44-5, 118-9, 154, 167-8; Macleod, p. 118; Edna Kenton above, pp. 24 seq., for Jesuit Relations; F. G. Speck, *Naskapi*, Oklahoma, 1935. American Bureau of Ethnology, Report 1896-7, pp. 545 seq.

[10] Report of Office of Indian Affairs, Ottawa, 1936, p. 8; I. R. L. MacInnes, *The History and Policies of Indian Administration in Canada*; F. H. Abbott, Secretary, Board of Indian Commissioners, Washington, Report of

WHITE SETTLERS AND NATIVE PEOPLES

Investigation made in 1914. Washington, D.C., 1915, p. 45. United States officials informed the author that this Survey was largely the basis of the American New Day for Indians.

[11] For British Administration and British Indian Contacts:— *Cambridge History of Empire*, Vol. 1, Chs. 1, 2, 10, 12, 13, 16, 18; Vol. VI. *Canada*, Chs. 2, 3, 5; *Canada and its Provinces*, A. Shortt and A. G. Doughty, Editors, Toronto, 22 volumes, Vol. IV, Indian Affairs, 1763-1841, Vol. V, Indian Affairs, 1840-1867; R. B. Mowat and P. Slossan, *History of the English Speaking Peoples*, O.U.P. 1943, Chs. 18, 19; American Bureau of Ethnology, Report, 1896-7, pp. 549 seq.; H. A. Innis, *The Fur Trade in Canada*, Parts 1-4; D. Mackay, *The Honourable Company*, Toronto, 1938, Chs. 1-16; Report of Dept. of Indian Affairs, 1936, and F. H. Abbott, above.

[12] *Canada and its Provinces*, Vol. 4, pp. 721 seq.

[13] *Report*, Dept. of Indian Affairs, Ottawa, 1927, pp. 7 seq.

[14] Jenness, *Indians of Canada*, Ch. 20, and pp. 256 seq.; *Canada's Indian Problem*, pp. 369 seq; and *Indian Background of Canadian History*, Part 11, p. 44.

[15] Jenness, *Indians of Canada*, Ch. 23, and *Canada's Indian Problem*, pp. 375 seq.

[16] H. D. Anderson and W. C. Eells, *Alaska Natives, A Survey*, Stanford U.P. 1935, p. 88, and C. L. Andrews, *The Story of Alaska*, Chs. 1-17.

[17] D. Jenness, *Canada's Indian Problems*, pp. 372 seq., and Indians of Canada, Chs. 21-23.

[18] Macleod, pp. 481 seq., and Papers Relative to the Indian Land Question, 1850-1875, Govt. Printer, Victoria, B.C., 1875, pp. 12 seq.

[19] Jenness, *Indians of Canada*, Ch. 21.

[20] Jenness, *Indians of Canada*, Ch. 22.

[21] Rev. A. G. Morice, *The History of the Northern Interior of British Columbia*, Toronto, 1904, p. 220.

[22] *Handbook of American Indians*, Vol. 1, pp. 895 seq., and pp. 905-6 seq.; *Cambridge History of British Empire*, Vol. VI, *Canada*, pp. 573 seq.; H. S. Wellcome, *Story of Metlakahtla*, New York, 1887.

[23] Edna Kenton, *The Indians of North America*, Extracts from the Jesuit Relations and allied documents, 1610-1791. Vol. 1, pp. 41-2.

[24] F. G. Speck, *Naskapi*, pp. 27 seq.

[25] J. J. Heagerty, *Four Centuries of Medical History in Canada*, Toronto, 1928, pp. 56 seq., quoted by Jenness in *Indians of Canada*, pp. 251-2.

[26] Clark Wissler, *Changes in Population Profiles among the Northern Plains Indians*, Anthropological Papers of American Museum of Natural History, Vol. 36, Part 1, p. 36, and Jenness, *Indians of Canada*, p. 316.

[27] Jenness, *Indians of Canada*, p. 253.

[28] ibid.

[29] ibid., and Annual Reports, Dept. of Indian Affairs, Ottawa, e.g. 1926, pp. 8 seq.

[30] Macleod, p. 43.

[31] Morice, p. 320.

[32] D. Mackay, *The Honourable Company*, Toronto, 1938, Ch. 14.

NOTES

[33] Jenness, *Indians of Canada*, pp. 253-4; *Canada and its Provinces*, Vol. IV, p. 720.

[34] e.g. Jenness, *Indians of Canada*, p. 261.

CHAPTER V

[1] Report Dept. of Indian Affairs, Ottawa, 1936, pp. 8-9; F. H. Abbott, above; Dr. A. G. Harper, U.S. Bureau of Indian Affairs; *What other Nations may learn from Canada's Administration of Indian Affairs*, M S. Report, 1939.

[2] R. G. Macbeth *Policing the Plains*, London 1921, Ch. 11; *Canada and its Provinces*, Vol. III 1867-1910, pp. 593 seq.

[3] *Cambridge History, Canada*, pp. 576-7; Harper, MS. 1939; Abbott, 1915; Reports, Dept. of Indian Affairs, 1927-1938; *Canada and its Provinces*, Vol. III, 1867-1912; *The Treaties of Canada with the Indians of Manitoba and the N.W. Territories*, Toronto, 1880.

[4] Reports, Dept. of Indian Affairs, 1927-1937-8.

[5] Dept. of Indian Affairs, Report, 1927, p. 10.

[6] A. G. Harper, MS; and Abbott, p. 23.

[7] Harper, MS; Abbott, p. 23; Report, Dept. of Indian Affairs, 1936, p. 23.

[8] Annual Report, Dept. of Indian Affairs, Ottawa, 1936, p. 23.

[9] Reports, Dept. of Indian Affairs, 1936, pp. 22 seq; 1938, p. 210.

[10] Indian Affairs Branch, Report, 1938, pp. 205 seq.

[11] Indian Affairs Branch, Report, 1938, pp. 192-3.

[12] Dept. of Indian Affairs, Report, 1936, pp. 13 seq.

[13] Minister of Mines and Resources, Broadcast, 23/2/37.

[14] Minister of Mines and Resources, above, and Report of Indian Affairs Branch, 1938, pp. 187 seq.

[15] Amongst many of these publications are *Canada's Reindeer Herd*, Ottawa, 1938; *Conserving Canada's Musk-Oxen*, Ottawa, 1937. See also Dept. of Indian Affairs, Report, 1936, pp. 13 seq.

[16] Dept. of Indian Affairs, Report 1936 p. 20; Abbott above; Speck, *Naskapi*, above.

[17] Abbott, Report 1915; Dept. of Indian Affairs, Reports, 1927-1937-8.

[18] Indian Affairs Branch, Reports 1927-1938-9.

[19] Dept. of Indian Affairs, Reports, 1927-38; Clark Wissler, *Changes in Population Profiles among the Northern Plains Indians*, in Anthropological Papers of the American Museum of Natural History, Vol. 36, Part 1, New York, 1936.

[20] *Handbook of American Indians*, pp. 913 seq.; Canadian Year Book, 1939; F. H. Abbott, above.

[21] D. Mackay, above, Chs. 9, 18.

[22] Abbott, above, pp. 4, 8, 9.

[23] *Indians of Canada*, p. 264.

[24] I. R. L. MacInnes, *The History and Policies of Indian Administration in Canada*, Indian Affairs Branch, 1939, and *Report of Indian Affairs Branch*, 1944.

WHITE SETTLERS AND NATIVE PEOPLES
CHAPTER VI

[1] For discussion and bibliography on aboriginal mentality and adaptability, H. K. Fry, *Aboriginal Mentality, Medical Journal of Australia*, March 23rd, 1935, pp. 353 seq. For Foxcroft, Tindale and others see references below.

[2] A. R. Radcliffe Brown in *Commonwealth Year Book, No.* 23, 1930, pp. 687 seq.

[3] J. B. Cleland, in *Centenary History of South Australia*, Adelaide, 1936, pp. 22 seq.

[4] Commonwealth Year Books, 1930-1942.

[5] J. B. Cleland, in *Centenary History of South Australia*, above; T. D. Campbell, *Notes on the Aborigines of the S.E. of South Australia*, Part 11. Trans. Roy. Soc. S. Aust. Vol. 63, pp. 27-35, 1939.

[6] *Aboriginal Welfare*, Conference of Commonwealth and State aboriginal authorities, April, 1937. Commonwealth Parl. Paper F., 1939.

[7] N. B. Tindale and J. B. Birdsell, *Results of Harvard-Adelaide Universities Anthropological Expedition*, 1938-9; *Tasmanoid Tribes of North Queensland*, S.A. Museum, Vol. 7, No. 1, Adelaide, October, 1941. There is considerable literature on the origin, age and dispersal of the Australian aborigines, e.g. Sir Edgeworth David in proceedings Pan-Pacific Science Congress, Australia, 1923, p. 224; R. Pulleine, Aust. Assoc. Advancement of Science, Vol. 19, Hobart, 1928, pp. 294 seq.; A. P. Elkin, *The Australian Aborigines*, Sydney, 1938, Ch. 1; S. D. Porteus, *The Psychology of a Primitive People*, London, 1941, Ch. 14; Griffith Taylor, *Environment, Race and Migration*, Oxford 1937, Chs. 6 and 7; Carl C. Sauer in Geog. Review, Am. Geog. Society, New York, Jan, 1947.

[8] Griffith Taylor, Elkin and Sauer above and J. B. Cleland in *Centenary History of South Australia*, Adelaide, 1936, p. 17.

[9] C. Lord, in A.A.A.S., Vol. 17, pp. 456 seq.; and R. Pulleine, A.A.A.S. Vol. 19, p. 301; *Australian Encyclopaedia*, Vol. II, pp. 539 seq.

[10] Elkin, Chs. 1, 2; Porteus, Ch. 14; Foxcroft, Ch. 1; Fry, *Aboriginal Mentality*.

[11] *Historical Records of Australia*, Series 1, Vol. 1, pp. 14, 23, and A. Grenfell Price, *Australia Comes of Age*, Melbourne, 1945, Chs. 1-3.

[12] Price, above, Chs. 1-4.

[13] A. Grenfell Price, *Australia Comes of Age*, Chs. 1, 2, 5, and *Foundation and Settlement of South Australia*, 1924.

[14] G. W. Rusden, *History of Australia*, London, 1884, Vol. 1, pp. 130 seq.

[15] M. M. Bennett, *The Australian Aboriginal*, London, 1930, pp. 78 seq. with references.

[16] H. K. Fry, *The Problem of the Aborigines*, Australian Rhodes Review, 1936, pp. 33 seq.; Hasluck, p. 46.

[17] *Cambridge History of British Empire*, Vol. 7, Australia, p. 91; Rusden, Vol. 1, pp. 130 seq.

[18] Rusden, pp. 530 seq., and T. Dunbabin, *The Making of Australasia*, London, 1922, pp. 109 seq.

[19] Rusden, Vol. 1, pp. 575 seq.

NOTES

[20] Dunbabin, p. 110.

[21] Dunbabin, p. 111.

[22] *Historical Records of Australia*, Series 3, Vol. 1, p. 242.

[23] Turnbull, C., *Black War*, Melbourne, 1948, for detailed account of the extermination, with references.

[24] Scott, E., *Short History of Australia*, London, 1936, p. 167.

[25] Rusden, Vol. 1, pp. 625 seq.

[26] Rusden, ibid.

[27] Scott, p. 171.

[28] Rusden, pp. 328, seq.; Scott, pp. 171 seq.; Dunbabin, pp. 129 seq.

[29] E. O. G. Shann, *Economic History of Australia*, C.U.P. 1930, p. 236; *Cambridge History of Australia*, p. 306; Foxcroft, *Australian Native Policy*, pp. 115, seq.

[30] *Letters from Victorian Pioneers*, p. 31.

[31] For official accounts, *Papers Relative to South Australia*, London, 1843, pp. 267 seq.

[32] Teichelmann to G. F. Angas, Sept. 1841, in Angas Papers, S.A. Public Library Archives, quoted by A. Grenfell Price, *Founders and Pioneers of South Australia*, Adelaide, 1929, pp. 215 seq.

[33] K. Hassell unpublished thesis, South Australian Public Library Archives.

[34] Paul Hasluck, *Black Australians*, M.U.P. 1942, pp. 47 seq., 63 seq.; 175-190; J. S. Battye, *History of Western Australia*, O.U.P. 1924, pp. 132 seq. *Story of a Hundred Years*, Perth, 1929, pp. 110 seq.

[35] A. Grenfell Price, *History and Problems of the Northern Territory*, Adelaide, 1930, pp. 26 seq.; A. Searcy, *In Australian Tropics*, London 1907, p. 174.

[36] Foxcroft, p. 53; Elkin, Ch. 11; Porteus, *Psychology of a Primitive People*, London, 1931, pp. 239-42, 383; *Letters from Victorian Pioneers*, p. 7.

[37] Foxcroft, p. 54.

[38] *Letter from Victorian Pioneers*, p. 272.

[39] M. M. Bennett, p. 39.

[40] J. B. Cleland, *Disease amongst the Australian Aborigines*, *Journal of Tropical Medicine and Hygiene*, 1928.

[41] Aust. Assoc. Advancement of Science, Vol. 18, p. 523; Dunbabin, p. 130; Turnbull, Ch. 10.

[42] J. B. Cleland, pp. 317, 28-9; Hasluck, pp. 103 seq.

[43] J. B. Cleland, pp. 28-9.

[44] J. B. Cleland, pp. 17-21.

[45] J. B. Cleland, pp. 38-9.

[46] K. Hassell, Thesis in S.A. Public Library Archives, pp. 41, 135 seq., 140; *South Australian Aboriginal Folklore*, G. Taplin, Ed., Adelaide, 1879, pp. 44 seq., 78 seq.; *Centenary History of South Australia*, Ch. II.

[47] *Letters from Victorian Pioneers*, pp. 43, 78 seq, 251-2.

[48] ibid., p. 275.

CHAPTER VII

[1] Hasluck, pp. 51 seq.

[2] ibid., pp. 55 seq.

[3] ibid., p. 59.
[4] ibid, pp. 198 seq.
[5] ibid., pp. 54-5.
[6] E. J. B. Foxcroft, Australian Native Policy, M.U.P. 1941, p. 29.
[7] Turnbull, Ch. 10; Aust. Assoc. Advancement Science, Vol. 18, p. 523.
[8] Commonwealth Year Book, 1942-3, p. 315.
[9] N. B. Tindale, Survey of the Half Caste Problem in South Australia. Results of Harvard-Adelaide Universities Anthropological Expedition 1938-9. R.G.S. of Aust. (S.A. Branch), Proceedings 1940-41, pp. 129 seq.
[10] Foxcroft, p. 30.
[11] Foxcroft, pp. 30-31, 109-110, 157.
[12] Statistics from Commonwealth Year Books.
[13] E. Scott, Short History of Australia, O.U.P. 1943, Ch. XIV; T. Dunbabin, The Making of Australasia, London, 1922, Ch. XII; Foxcroft, Ch. III.
[14] Foxcroft, pp. 39-54.
[15] Foxcroft, pp. 79-86, 91-99.
[16] Foxcroft, pp. 55-78.
[17] Commonwealth Year Books, No. 22, pp. 914-5, No. 35, p. 315.
[18] Foxcroft, Ch. VII.
[19] Hassell, MSS., pp. 77-8, 119, 124, 129, 170-1; Foxcroft, pp. 112, 114, 157; Tindale, pp. 74 seq; Geo. Taplin, South Australian Aborigines, Adelaide 1879, p. VII.
[20] Statistics from Commonwealth Year Books, tabulated in Foxcroft.
[21] Hasluck, pp. 47-51; 69-71.
[22] Hasluck, pp. 69-96.
[23] Hasluck, pp. 121-3; Foxcroft, pp. 96-99; A Story of a Hundred Years, Perth, 1929, pp. 122 seq; H. N. Birt, Benedictine Pioneers in Australia, London, 1911, Vol. 11, pp. 468 seq.; Cardinal Moran, History of the Catholic Church in Australasia, Sydney Vol. 11, pp. 555 seq.
[24] Hasluck, p. 89.
[25] Foxcroft, p. 123.
[26] Hasluck, Chs. V and VI.
[27] Hasluck, p. 203.
[28] Foxcroft, pp. 124-5.
[29] ibid.
[30] Foxcroft, p. 129.
[31] H. D. Moseley, Report of Royal Commission, Perth 1935.
[32] Canberra Conference, 1937, pp. 11, 12; A. Grenfell Price, What of our Aborigines, Adelaide, 1943, p. 4; Tindale, above, pp. 94 seq., 124 seq. and in conversation with the author.
[33] Foxcroft, pp. 115 seq.; Price, above, p. 4.
[34] A. Grenfell Price, History and Problems of the Northern Territory, Adelaide, 1930, pp. 26 seq.
[35] J. W. Bleakley, The Aboriginals and Half-Castes of Central Australia, Canberra, 1928-9, pp. 7-9.
[36] D. Thomson, Recommendations of Policy in Native Affairs, Canberra, 1937; Foxcroft, pp. 145 seq.
[37] Foxcroft, p. 149.

NOTES

[38] Price, *What of our Aborigines*, p. 4.

[39] Quoted by Price, *What of our Aborigines*, p. 13.

[40] Adelaide *News*, 8/4/46 and 9/4/46; and Dr. C. Duguid quoted by the *Australian Intercollegian*, May 1947, p. 36.

[41] Canberra Conference, 1937, p. 29.

[42] N. B. Tindale, in *Proceedings R.G.S. of S.A.*, 1940-1, pp. 77-80.

[43] A. Grenfell Price, *White Settlers in the Tropics*, Am. Geog. Society, New York, 1939, p. 119; and *Pioneer Reactions to a Poor Tropical Environment*, Am. Geog. Review, New York, July, 1933, pp. 361-3.

[44] N. B. Tindale, in *Proceedings R.G.S. of S.A.*, 1940-1, pp. 120-1.

[45] A. P. Elkin, *The Australian Aborigines*, Sydney, 1938, p. 20.

[46] Statistics from Commonwealth Year Books.

CHAPTER VIII

[1] I. L. G. Sutherland, (Ed.), *The Maori People Today*, Auckland, 1940, p. 27.

[2] ibid., p. 11.

[3] Elsdon Best, *The Maori as He Was*, Dominion Museum, Wellington, 1934, Chs. I, II.; I. L. G. Sutherland in correspondence with author.

[4] Best, Ch. II, and I. L. G. Sutherland, *The Maori Situation*, Wellington, 1935, Ch. II.; Dominion N.Z. Census, 1936, Vol. III, Maori Census, p. 1.

[5] Sutherland, *The Maori People Today*, p. 19; *Cambridge History of the British Empire*, Vol. VII, Part II, *New Zealand*, p. 143; Maori Census, 1936, p. 1.

[6] H. D. Skinner, in *Camb. Hist. N.Z.* above, p. 143.

[7] *The Maori People Today*, p. 19.

[8] Skinner, above, p. 143; Maori Census, 1936, P. 1 and p. 1.

[9] *Camb. Hist. N.Z.*, pp. 18-19.

[10] Sir Apirana T. Ngata in *The Maori People Today*, p. 307; E. Best above; F. M. Keesing, *The Changing Maori*, Board of Maori Ethnological Research, Vol. IV, New Plymouth, 1928, Ch. I; *Camb. Hist. N.Z.*, pp. 13-14.

[11] H. B. Turbott, in *The Maori People Today*, p. 229.

[12] Keesing, pp. 22 seq., 39 seq.

[13] *Camb. Hist. N.Z.*, p. 28.

[14] T. Dunbabin, *The Making of Australasia*, London, 1922, p. 160.

[15] D. G. Ball, in *The Maori People Today*, p. 270.

[16] *The Maori Situation*, pp. 16 seq.

[17] Turbott, in *The Maori People Today*, pp. 229 seq.

[18] Roger Duff, in *The Maori People Today*, Ch. XI.

[19] A. J. Harrop, *England and New Zealand*, London, 1926, p. 15.

[20] Keesing, pp. 55-6.

[21] ibid., p. 56.

[22] H. Miller, in *The Maori People Today*, pp. 75 seq.

[23] *Camb. Hist. of N.Z.*, p. 31; A. W. Jose, *History of Australasia*, Sydney, 1921, pp. 272-3.

[24] *Camb. Hist. of N.Z.* pp. 32 seq.

[25] *Camb. Hist. of N.Z.*, pp. 49-50; *The Maori Situation*, pp. 75 seq.;

Ngata, in *The Maori People Today*, pp. 104 seq.
[26] R. Duff, in *The Maori People Today*, p. 375.
[27] ibid., p. 376.
[28] Jose, above, p. 278; Dunbabin, above, p. 166.
[29] *Camb. Hist. of N.Z.*, p. 21; Maori Census, 1936, pp. I, V.
[30] Dunbabin, p. 162; For Marsden. See E. Ramsden, *Marsden and the Missions*, Sydney, 1936.
[31] *Camb. Hist. of N.Z.*, pp. 35 seq.
[32] *Camb. Hist. of British Empire*, Vol. VII, Part I, *Australia*, p. 332; and Part II, *New Zealand*, pp. 35 seq.
[33] D. G. Ball, in *The Maori People Today*, p. 270.
[34] *Camb. Hist. N.Z.*, pp. 45 seq.
[35] ibid.
[36] *Camb. Hist. N.Z.*, p. 54.
[37] Ngata and Sutherland in *The Maori People Today*, pp. 336 seq.
[38] ibid.
[39] *Camb. Hist. N.Z.*, p. 52.
[40] ibid., p. 51.
[41] ibid., p. 49.
[42] H. Miller, in *The Maori People Today*, p. 77.
[43] Harrop, *England and New Zealand*, p. 58.
[44] ibid., pp. 101-8.
[45] *Camb. Hist. N.Z.*, p. 53.
[46] ibid., Ch. IV; Harrop, pp. 6-9.
[47] *Camb. Hist. Australia*, p. 327; Dunbabin, p. 161.
[48] *Camb. Hist. Australia*, p. 326.
[49] Harrop, pp. 12-16.
[50] *Camb. Hist. N.Z.*, p. 64; Harrop, pp. 16 seq.
[51] Harrop, pp. 20 seq.
[52] ibid., p. 26; Parl. Paper of 1837, VII, 425, pp. 1-304.
[53] Harrop, Ch. V; Dunbabin, Ch. XIV.
[54] Harrop, Ch. VI; Hobson was Lieut. Governor under the Governor of New South Wales until November 1840, when Britain separated these colonies, and appointed Hobson Governor of New Zealand with an Executive Council.
[55] Harrop, p. 23.
[56] ibid.
[57] ibid., p. 25.
[58] ibid., p. 26.
[59] ibid., Ch. VI.
[60] *The Maori People Today*, p. 108.
[61] ibid., pp. 110 seq., and *Camb. Hist, N.Z.*, pp. 74 seq.
[62] Harrop, pp. 139 seq.
[63] H. Miller, in *The Maori People Today*, pp. 81 seq.
[64] ibid., p. 82.
[65] ibid.
[66] Ngata, in *The Maori People Today*, p. 112.
[67] Miller, above, pp. 78-95.
[68] *Camb. Hist. N.Z.*, p. 80; Harrop, pp. 148 seq.

NOTES

[69] *The Maori People Today*, pp. 85 seq.; and Sutherland, *The Maori Situation*, p. 29.

[70] Miller, above, p. 83.

[71] Ngata, above, p. 109.

[72] ibid.

[73] ibid., p. 110.

[74] *The Maori People Today*, pp. 345, seq.

[75] Jose, p. 286.

[76] Harrop, pp. 154 seq.

[77] Jose, p. 285.

[78] *Camb. Hist. N.Z.*, pp. 86-7; Jose, pp. 298 seq.

[79] ibid., Harrop, pp. 223-8.

[80] Harrop, pp. 263 seq; *The Maori People Today*, pp. 116 seq.

[81] ibid.

[82] Jose, pp. 298 seq.; Miller, above, pp. 85 seq.

[83] Miller, above, pp. 85 seq.

[84] Miller, above, p. 80.

[85] Keesing, above, Ch. III; D. G. Ball in *The Maori People Today*, pp. 276 seq.

[86] H. Miller in *The Maori People Today*, pp. 81-95; Ngata, ibid. pp. 115-124; *Camb. Hist, N.Z.*, Ch. VII; I. L. G. Sutherland, *The Maori Situation*, Ch. IV.

[87] ibid.

[88] ibid.

[89] *Camb. Hist. N.Z.*, p. 140; Sutherland, *The Maori Situation*, pp. 30 seq.

[90] *The Maori Situation*, p. 40.

[91] Quoted by Sutherland above, p. 36.

[92] ibid., p. 37.

[93] Ngata, in *The Maori People Today*, p. 125.

[94] ibid., p. 126.

[95] Ngata, in *The Maori People Today*, pp. 126-7.

[96] ibid., p. 129.

[97] ibid.

[98] R. Duff, in *The Maori People Today*, pp. 391 seq.

[99] ibid., p. 393.

[100] Elsdon Best, quoted by Ngata and Sutherland in *The Maori People Today*, pp. 336 seq.

[101] *Camb. Hist. N.Z.*, p. 56.

[102] ibid.

[103] Ngata in Sutherland above pp. 347 seq.; Keesing *The Changing Maori*, pp. 49 seq.

[104] ibid.

[105] ibid., and *Camb. Hist. N.Z.*, pp. 137 seq.

[106] Ngata in Sutherland above, pp. 351 seq.; Keesing above pp. 49.

[107] Ngata in Sutherland above, p. 353.

[108] ibid., pp. 354 seq.; *Camb. Hist. N.Z.*, p. 139.

[109] Ngata in Sutherland, above, pp. 364 seq.; Keesing, above, pp. 149 seq.

[110] Keesing, above, p. 146.

WHITE SETTLERS AND NATIVE PEOPLES

[111] ibid., pp. 143-4.
[112] Ngata in Sutherland, above, pp. 368-9.
[113] Keesing, above, pp. 151-2.
[114] D. G. Ball, in *The Maori People Today*, pp. 261-273.
[115] ibid., p. 276.
[116] ibid., pp. 249-253; Keesing, above, pp. 134-143; Sutherland, *The Maori Situation*, pp. 109-110.
[117] Keesing, above, p. 80 and note.
[118] ibid., p. 83 and Maori Census, 1936, p. 1. (There is some slight discrepancy between the figures given by the Maori Census and Keesing.)
[119] ibid., p. 86.
[120] Keesing, above, Part II, Ch. 1 and Part III. Ch. 2.

CHAPTER IX

[1] The low figure of 34,854 recorded for 1896 was "almost certainly due to omissions on the part of the enumerators." The high figure of 1926 includes all half-castes whether living with the natives or the whites. *Camb. Hist. N.Z.*, p. 143; Keesing, *The Changing Maori*, p. 83; Maori Census, 1936, p.1. Report of Dominion Population Committee, 1946, p. 15.
[2] Report of Young Maori Conference, Auckland, 1939, p. 22.
[3] Sutherland, in *The Maori People Today*, p. 21.
[4] Sutherland, in *The Maori People Today*, pp. 404-5; Keesing above, pp. 168-9.
[5] Sutherland, above, pp. 406-7; Maori Census, 1936, pp. 111, IV. Report of Dominion Population Committee, 1946, p. 15.
[6] Ball, in *The Maori People Today*, p. 276.
[7] Belshaw, in *The Maori People Today*, pp. 187 seq.; *Camb. Hist. N.Z.*, pp. 143-4, quoting G. H. L.-F. Pitt-Rivers, *Clash of Cultures and Contact of Races*, p. 279; Maori Census 1936, p. III.
[8] *Camb. Hist. N.Z.*, pp. 145-6; P. H. Buck, in *The Maori People Today*, pp. 14 seq.; and Belshaw, ibid., pp. 193 seq.; W. B. Bariska, *Where the White Man Treads*, Auckland, pp. 289 seq.
[9] Sutherland, in *The Maori People Today*, pp. 399 seq.
[10] ibid., and pp. 182 seq.
[11] Young Maori Conference, p. 39; Belshaw, in *The Maori People Today*, p. 403.
[12] *Camb. Hist. N.Z.*, p. 142; Sutherland, in *The Maori People Today*, p. 403.
[13] Ngata, in *The Maori People Today*, pp. 121, seq.
[14] Sutherland, in *The Maori People Today*, pp. 402 seq.
[15] ibid.
[16] Ngata, in above, pp. 148 seq.
[17] ibid., pp. 143 seq., and Sutherland in above, p. 405.
[18] ibid., p. 146.
[19] ibid., pp. 148-154.
[20] Turbott, in *The Maori People Today*, p. 235.
[21] Ball, in *The Maori People Today*, p. 303.
[22] Belshaw, in above, pp. 221-2.

NOTES

[23] *The Maori People Today*, pp. 220 seq., 229 seq., 317 seq., 320 seq.
[24] Ball, in *The Maori People Today*, p. 283.
[25] ibid.
[26] Young Maori Conference, p. 25.
[27] Turbott, in *The Maori People Today*, pp. 264 seq.
[28] ibid., p. 264.
[29] Ball, in *The Maori People Today*, pp. 292 seq.
[30] Ngata, in above, p. 325.
[31] Ball, in above, pp. 301 seq.
[32] Turbott, in above, pp. 233 seq. For a comparison of European and Maori health, Young Maori Conference, 1939, p. 22.
[33] Turbott, above, pp. 230 seq.
[34] Turbott, above, pp. 253-4.
[35] ibid, p. 234; and Young Maori Conference, 1939, pp. 34 seq.
[36] Turbott, above, p. 258, and Young Maori Conference, p. 23.
[37] Turbott, above, p. 260 seq., and Sutherland, in above, pp. 434-5.
[38] Belshaw, in above, pp. 217 seq.
[39] Young Maori Conference, p. 20.
[40] ibid., pp. 20-21.
[41] ibid.
[42] I. L. G. Sutherland in correspondence with the author, and N.Z. Armed Forces, Bulletin, Vol. 3, Nos. 7 and 8, May, 1945.

CHAPTER X

[1] W. C. Macleod, *The American Indian Frontier*, pp. 375-6.
[2] T. D. Campbell, *Notes on the Aborigines of the South-East of South Australia*, Trans. Royal Society of S. Aust., July, 1939, pp. 27-35.
[3] Macleod, Chs. VIII, XII, XXIV.
[4] A. P. Elkin, *Civilised Aborigines and Native Culture*, Oceania VI, pp. 117-146, quoted by M. J. Herskovits, *Acculturation*, p. 74.
[5] A. P. Elkin, *The Australian Aborigines*, Sydney, 1938, Ch., VII.
[6] Margaret Mead, *The Changing Culture of an Indian Tribe*, New York, 1932.
[7] Paul Radin, *The Influence of the Whites on Winnebago Culture*. Proceedings of the State Historical Society of Wisconsin, 1913, pp. 137-145. Quoted by Herskovits, above, pp. 53 seq.
[8] K. Hassell, Thesis in S. Aust. Public Library Archives.
[9] Elkin, *The Reaction of Primitive Races to the White Man's Culture*. The Hibbert Journal, 1937, XXXV, pp. 537-545. Quoted by Herskovits above, p. 74.
[10] *Handbook of American Indians*, Vol. II, p. 286.
[11] N. B. Tindale, A *Survey of the Half Caste Problem in South Australia*. Proceedings R.G.S. of Aust., S.A. Branch, 1941, pp. 66-161.
[12] Clark Wissler, *The Effect of Civilisation upon the length of life of the American Indian*, Scientific Monthly, July, 1936, pp. 5-13.
[13] Macleod, pp. 541, seq.
[14] N. B. Tindale, above.

INDEX

Abbott, F. H., 68, 84, 90, 94, 199 (notes), 215, 216, 217.
Aborigines, Australia: Chaps VI, VII.
Arnhem Land, 142, 205; cattle stations, 137, 144; child endowment, 142, 148, 149; culture, 101-3; destruction of, 99, 103-106, 110-142, 146, 196, 197; diet, 126, 144, 145, 202, 208; diseases, 117-121, 136, 208; economic value of, 138, 142, 147, 191, 202; education, 126, 146, 209; expenditure upon, 126, 129, 132, 137, 139, 141, 142, 149; future policy towards, 143 seq.; health in Northern Territory, 141, 142, 208; housing in Northern Territory, 141, 144, 148, 208; in World War II, 146; isolation of, 99, 132; lands, 103; liquor, 118, 120, 136, 141; numbers, decline in, 100, 125-127, 132, 137, 139, 146, 147, 197-199, 208; numbers, pre-conquest, 100, 110-114, 134; numbers, recent, 197, 198; origin of, 101, 102; prostitution, 120, 137, 141; religion of, 99, 103, 131.
Aborigines' Protection Society (British), 124.
Aborigines, Tasmanian: Culture, 102, 103; destruction of, 108, 109, 117, 124; diseases, 118, 124; liquor, 118, 124; numbers, 100, 109; origin, 101.
Acadia, 62, 66, 77.
Acculturation, 191-196, 201-203.
Adams, J. T. (notes) 211, 212.
Akaroa, 154, 157, 158.
Alaska, 73, 74.

Algonkian Indians, 61, 78.
Alice Springs, 141, 147.
Allotment and Citizenship (U.S.), 23, 31-34, 40, 43.
Altunga mission, 147-149.
American Revolution, 67, 104.
Anderson, H. D., and Eells, W. C., 74, (notes) 216.
Andrews, C. L. (notes) 215.
Anteos, E. (notes) 211.
Antler Indians, 36, 37, 44, 195.
Arthur, Governor, Tasmania, 108, 109, 126.
Asiatics, introduction of disease to Australia, 118, 119, 134, 136.
Assimilation, 57, 64, 79, 83, 93-95, 98, 125, 126, 137, 138, 176-188, 191-196, 201-203.
Assiniboine Indians, 72, 73, 77, 92, 93.
Australian Colonial Governments, attitude to aborigines, 124 seq.
Australian Government, expenditure and policy in Northern Territory, 141 seq.; fails to gain control of aborigines in States, 142, 143.
Australian physiography, 99, 100.

Ball, D. G., 176, 182, 183 (notes) 221-225.
Bariska, W. B., (notes) 224.
Batman, John, 126 seq.
Battye, J. S., (notes) 219.
Bay of Islands, 152, 155, 159, 161.
Belshaw, H., 183, (notes) 224.
Bennett, M. M., (notes) 218, 219.
Beothuk Indians, 64, 78.
Berndt, R. M. and C. H., 149, 205 seq.
Best, Elsdon (notes) 221, 223.

226

INDEX

Birt, H. N., (notes) 220.
Blackfoot Indians, 61, 71, 72, 79, 93.
Bleakley, J. W., 141-2, 144, 148, (notes) 220.
Brantford Reservation, 67, 69, 70, 89, 95, 96.
Brisbane, Governor, 107.
British America Act, 81.
British Columbia, 68, 74, 75, 78, 81, 85.
British Government, attitude to Indians, 11-13, 27, 29, 30, 59, 68 seq.; to aborigines, 105-109, 116, 123, 125, 128, 134 seq.; to Maoris, 156 seq.
Brown, Radcliffe, 100, 110, 113, 114.
Buck, Dr. Peter, 151, 178, 179, 180, 187.
Buffalo, 9, 22, 61, 72, 79, 82, 195.
Busby, James, 157.

California, 16, 17, 20, 73.
Californian Indians, 8, 10, 16, 17, 20, 21, 24-27, 30, 33.
Campbell, T. D., 101, 193, (notes) 218, 225.
Canada, Dominion of: Indian policy, Ch. V; Indians of North-West, 61, 72, 73; Mounted Police, 83; Preservation of game, 88.
Canberra Conference of 1937, 137, 138, 144.
Carroll, Sir James, 179, 181, 187.
Caughnawaga Reservation, 95, 96.
Cherokees, 16, 23, 29, 33, 34.
Chilcotin Indians, 78.
Chipewyan Indians, 73, 79.
Church Missionary Society, 76, 125, 154-5.
Civilian Conservation Corps, 47, 52.
Cleland, J. B., 102, 117, 118, (notes) 218.
Collier, John, 3, 43 seq., 50, 52, 54, 56, 57, 198, (notes) 214, 215.
Cree Indians, 64, 72, 73, 88, 92, 93.
Creek Indians, 9, 16, 25.

Darling, Governor of N.S.W., 107, 157.
Darwin, Charles, opinion on Maori health, 155.
Dashwood, Government Resident, N.T., 114, 115.
David, Sir Edgeworth, (notes) 218.
Delaware Indians, 34, 37.
Disease, 5, 6, 11, 12, 18-22, 25, 70, 72-74, 76, 77, 111, 117 seq., 134, 136, 140, 141, 151-153, 185, 186, 192, 196, 197, 200.
Douglas, James, Governor of British Columbia, 75
Duff, Roger, 152, (notes) 221-223.
Du Fresne, Marion, 106, 153.
Dunbabin, T., (notes) 218-222.
Duncan, William, of Metlakahtla, 76, 155.
Dutch, 65, 78, 105, 140, 193.

Eliot, John, missionary, 28, 36.
Elkin, A. P., 146, 194, 196, 206, 207, (notes) 218, 219, 221, 225.

Firearms, 21, 22, 78, 79, 152-154.
Fisheries, 10, 74, 79, 88, 152.
Florida, 21, 24, 25.
Forests, utilised for Indians, 39, 46, 47.
Foxcroft, E. J. B., 100, 130, 132, 134, 139, (notes) 218-220.
Franciscans (missionaries), 24, 25, 51.
French, in Canada, 59, 60, 62-66, 78; in Australia, 105, 106, 140; in New Zealand, 153, 157, 158.
Fry, H. K., (notes) 218.
Fur Trade, 59, 62, 74, 79.

Georgia, 12, 16, 25.
Ghost Dance, 38, 194.
Gipps, Governor of New South Wales, 161.
Glenelg, Lord, 69, 70, 113, 158.
Grant, President, 35.
Grey, Earl, 162.
Grey, Sir George, Governor of New Zealand, 160-165, 171.

INDEX

229

INDEX

Phillip, Governor, 104, 106.
Pilgrim Fathers, 11, 20.
Pinjarra, Battle of , 113, 134.
Pitt-Rivers, G. H. L.-F., 178 (notes) 224.
Plains Indians, 61, 72.
Police, native, 124, 127, 134, 138. 139.
Porteus, S. D., (notes) 218, 219.
Port Lincoln area (South Australia), 112, 130, 131.
Port Phillip District, Victoria, 105, 111, 117, 126 seq., 130, 131.
Potlatches, 61, 62, 75.
Powhatan, 14.
Praying Indians, 9.
Price, A. Grenfell, (notes) 218-221.
Pueblo Indians, 7, 9, 24, 57.
Pulleine, R., (notes) 218.
Puritans, 11, 12, 20, 193.

Quakers, 12, 40, 193.
Qu'Appelle Health Unit, Canada, 91.
Quebec, 62, 95.
Quebec Act, 66.
Queensland, 105, 110, 111, 115, 138 seq.

Ramsden, E., (notes) 222.
Ratana Church, 169, 194, 195.
Rauparaha, 153, 154, 161.
Rua, prophet, 170.
Radin, Paul, 195, (notes) 225.
Removals, 16, 23, 33, 196.
Reservations, 17, 20, 23 seq., 27, 30 seq., 32, 38 seq., 68, 72, 75, 79, 82, 85, 92, 93, 116, 123, 124, 125, 129, 131, 132, 137, 139, 140, 142, 144, 147-149, 190, 200.
Rhoads, Commissioner, 40, 43.
Risdon Cove, Tasmania, massacre, 108, 109.
Ringatu Church, 169.
Robinson, George, (Tasmania), 109.
Rockefeller, John D., Jr., 42.
Roosevelt, President F. D., 3, 24, 40, 43, 57, 58, 186, 201, (notes) 215.
Roth, Dr. W. E., 132, 135-137, 139.

Rusden, G. W., 106, (notes) 218, 219.
Russians, on Pacific coast, 59, 73, 74.

St. Lawrence, river, 6, 59, 62, 63.
Sauer, Carl C., 102, (notes) 218.
Scalp bounties, 12, 79.
Scattergood, Assistant Commissioner (U.S.), 40, 43.
Schmeckebier, L. F., (notes) 212-214.
Scott, Ernest, (notes) 219, 220.
Sealers, 106, 108, 119, 152, 153.
Searcy, A., 115, (notes) 219.
Segregation, 23, 33, 98, 142, 143.
Selwyn, Bishop, (New Zealand), 156, 162, 167, 168.
Seminole, 21.
Seymour, F. W., 52, 54.
Shann, E. O. G., 110, (notes) 219.
Shortt, A., and Doughty, A. G., (notes) 216.
Sioux Indians, 9, 18.
Skinner, H. D., (notes) 221.
Smallpox, 6, 19-21, 25, 73, 74, 77, 78, 118, 119, 134, 196.
Smohalla (Indian prophet), 37, 38.
Social diseases, 6, 21, 74, 77, 119, 153, 196.
Soil erosion, 44, 49, 50, 55, 189.
South Australia, 105, 110-114, 117, 119, 120; policy to aborigines, 130 seq.; policy in Northern Territory, 140 seq.
Spanish Government, 24-27.
Speck, F. G., 65, 77, 89, (notes) 215-217.
Spencer, Baldwin, 131.
Squamish, reservation, 96.
Sutherland, I. L. G., 187, 188, (notes) 221-225.
Stirling, Governor, 113, 116, 134.
Sydney, 104, 107, 116.

Tadoussac, 77.
Tahiti, 150.
Taplin, G., 131, (notes) 219, 220.
Tasman, 152, 153.

231